The Social Origins
of Political Regionalism

CALIFORNIA SERIES ON SOCIAL CHOICE AND POLITICAL
ECONOMY
Edited by Brian Barry, Robert H. Bates, and Samuel L. Popkin

The Social Origins
of Political Regionalism
France, 1849–1981

WILLIAM BRUSTEIN

UNIVERSITY OF CALIFORNIA PRESS
Berkeley   Los Angeles   London

University of California Press
Berkeley and Los Angeles, California

University of California Press, Ltd.
London, England

Library of Congress Cataloging-in-Publication Data
Brustein, William.
The social origins of political regionalism.

(California series on social choice and political economy)
Bibliography: p.
Includes index.
1. Regionalism—France.   2. France—Politics and
government—19th century.   3. France—Politics and
government—20th century.   4. France—Social conditions.
5. France—Economic conditions.   I. Title.   II. Series.
JN2610.R4B73   1988   306'.2'0944
ISBN 0-520-06155-1 (alk. paper)

Printed in the United States of America

1   2   3   4   5   6   7   8   9

In Memory of Alexander Louis Brustein

Contents

Maps and Figures

Tables

Acknowledgments

As a young college student studying in France in the late spring of 1968, I was struck by the deep attachment of French students to their nation's rich political past. For instance, I remember during that spring of revolutionary turmoil how the students' debates at the Odéon conjured up images of Danton and Robespierre vying for the minds of the Convention's delegates and how those radical sociology students at Nanterre, by calling themselves "les enragés," made me recollect accounts of the original "enragés" and their attempt to radicalize the French Revolution.

The political fervor of the French students, conscious of their revolutionary predecessors, fueled my own interest in French politics in the late 1970s when I was a graduate student in sociology at the University of Washington. This time, however, the puzzle of French political regionalism sparked my interest, one that has led, finally, to the publication of this book.

I have accumulated many debts in drafting this book. I am especially grateful to Michael Hechter, who as both mentor and example inspired me to write this book. I am also grateful to Margaret Levi, Charles Tilly, Debra Friedman, John R. Hall, and Herb Costner; they gave graciously of their time to read through the manuscript and provided me with invaluable assistance in formulating every aspect of it. For their many helpful suggestions I owe a debt of appreciation to Daniel Chirot, Guenther Roth, Mary Brinton, Malka Appelbaum, Susan Kinne, and the members of the University of Washington Seminar in Macrosociology during 1979–1981. And I give special thanks to Robert L. Kaufman, Lauren Krivo, and Jerry Hertig; their methodological and statistical suggestions helped me to organize and present the data. On the technical side I appreciate the efforts of William Schmid and Greer Prince, who had the unenviable tasks of coding and analyzing data; Jim Lehning and Jamie McBeth, who spent many hours proofreading; and Elisabeth Reed, who checked my French spelling. I must also thank

Sheila Levine, my editor at the University of California Press, for her commitment to my manuscript and Michael Hanagan and Ronald Rogowski, the two readers for the Press, whose criticisms helped me to reformulate and strengthen the book's argument.

During several trips to France I benefited greatly from the comments of Maurice Agulhon, François Furet, and Gerard Cholvy. I also want to thank the staffs of the Bibliothèque nationale, the Archives nationales, and the central and regional offices of the Institut national de la statistique et des études économiques. I owe special gratitude to the staffs of the twenty-six departmental archives in which I worked for patiently and courteously assisting me in my data collection.

I have benefited from the assistance of institutions as well. My research was funded by fellowships from the Social Science Research Council, University of Utah Research Committee, and University of Utah Faculty Fellow Award.

Finally, I wish to thank my wife, Yvonne, without whose support and encouragement I would never have completed this book.

INTRODUCTION: THE PROBLEM

To the tourist, the cantons of Argentré-du-Plessis, in the western French department of Ille-et-Vilaine, and Bonnieux, in the French Mediterranean department of Vaucluse, are brief distractions on the way to more exciting attractions. For most, Argentré-du-Plessis offers little more than a crossroad to the treasures of Mont-Saint-Michel and the castles dotting the Loire Valley. Bonnieux offers little to the tourist other than marmalade and wines, and proximity to Avignon, with its Palace of the Popes and its unfinished bridge of children's song, and Aix-en-Provence, that mecca of Impressionist painters.

What first strikes the traveler entering Argentré-du-Plessis is its isolation. Argentré-du-Plessis is part of a vast woodland in which farms and villages are separated by hedgerows (*bocage*) that give the landscape the appearance of an enormous chessboard. The population is greatly dispersed and the roads are few. These features, along with the rains that can last uninterruptedly from November to May, put a damper on the canton's social activity, leaving the impression that the inhabitants of Argentré-du-Plessis are withdrawn. Though perhaps socially detrimental, the abundant rainfall yields acres upon acres of luscious grassland, which in turn nurtures the livestock, the basis of the canton's principal economic activity.

In contrast to Argentré-du-Plessis, Bonnieux lies in the shadows of Mount Luberon and is part of the foothills of France's southern Alps. On entering Bonnieux, the traveler expects to hear Spanish or Italian spoken rather than French since the area has a definite Mediterranean flavor. The compact villages of Bonnieux are mostly perched high on hills. The streets are narrow and winding, for medieval architects knew that a winding rather than undeflected street could better serve as a bulwark against the mistral—that continual winter wind that irritates the entire Mediterranean region. But for the most part, the blue sky and warm days kindle the animated and constant

social life (it seems as if people never sleep here) that charac-
terizes the villages of Bonnieux. Though the Mediterranean
weather encourages social activity, the relatively low annual rate
of precipitation makes the countryside of Bonnieux considerably less verdant than that of Argentré-du-Plessis. Nevertheless, there is enough precipitation to permit Bonnieux and its
department of Vaucluse to have become the "market garden"
of France, where the cultivation and sale of fruits and vegetables provide the principal economic activity for the area's
inhabitants.

What these brief traveler's descriptions of Argentré-du-Plessis
and Bonnieux do not tell us, however, is that both cantons hold
center stage in a political drama that has baffled students of
French political history since at least the beginning of the twentieth century. Though Argentré-du-Plessis and Bonnieux are
similar in having primarily agrarian economies, Argentré-
du-Plessis has consistently supported the political Right while
Bonnieux has just as invariably supported the political Left. In
three key national legislative elections—those of 1849, 1914,
and 1981—France's political landscape was divided into two
principal blocs, the Right and the Left. In the election of 1849,
1 percent of Argentré-du-Plessis's vote was for the Left while
62 percent of Bonnieux's vote was for the Left. In the election
of 1914, 16 percent of Argentré-du-Plessis's vote was for the
Left while 66 percent of Bonnieux's vote was for the Left.
Finally, in the election of 1981, 13 percent of Argentré-du-
Plessis's vote was for the Left while 72 percent of Bonnieux's
vote was for the Left. Moreover, the voting patterns of these
two cantons are far from unique. Indeed the cultivators of
western France, much like those of Argentré-du-Plessis, have
consistently voted Right while the cultivators of Mediterranean
France, much like those of Bonnieux, have consistently voted
Left. How can this remarkably different voting behavior be
explained?

The voting patterns of Argentré-du-Plessis and Bonnieux,
or more exactly of western and Mediterranean France, are instances of political regionalism, a pattern of political involvement that is strongly associated with a regional base.[1] In national elections the South's backing of the Democratic party in

the United States, Saskatchewan's espousal of cooperative socialism in Canada, and Kerala's and West Bengal's advocacy of the Communist party in India are notable instances of political regionalism. In addition, regions have diverged dramatically in their responses to such major social upheavals as the French Revolution of 1789–1795, the Mexican revolution of 1911–1912, and the Spanish civil war of 1936–1939.[2]

Scholars generally acknowledge that particular areas exhibit marked patterns of political behavior, but their explanations of these regional disparities are unsatisfactory. I attribute this deficiency to the mutual exclusivity of scholarly work in sociology and history: too few sociologists venture into the *terra incognita* of historical research, while too few historians are willing to abandon the *terra firma* of historical specificity to make broad comparative and theoretical formulations.

This book attempts to fill the void left by the absence of systematic theoretical and empirical treatments of the bases of political regionalism. In it I present a model of political behavior that weds rational-choice assumptions concerning individual behavior with the Marxist concept of the mode of production. I argue that the persistence of distinctive regional political behavior in France is based upon the existence of discrete regional modes of production. These regional social structures produce specific constellations of interests among cultivators. These interests, in turn, result in discrete patterns of aggregate political behavior. This mode-of-production theory of political behavior is tested empirically on archival data collected for three key French national legislative elections: those of 1849, 1914, and 1981.

France is an ideal place to study political regionalism for three reasons. First, at least as early as 1849, western France— comprising Brittany, the Loire country, and Lower Normandy—has invariably supported the Right, and Mediterranean France—consisting of Lower Languedoc, Roussillon, and Provence—has just as invariably voted Left.[3] Second, because these two regions are similar in being predominantly agrarian and economically and politically peripheral, variations in voting between them must be ascribed to other factors. Last, since relatively reliable and accessible ecological data are available for

Map 1. The Administrative Units of France

the nineteenth and twentieth centuries, it is possible to test the mode-of-production theory for several time periods.

The design of the book is simple. Part 1 concentrates on theoretical matters. The first chapter examines normative and structural explanations of French political regionalism. The second chapter attempts to elucidate a theory of political regionalism. The focus of Part 2 is an in-depth survey of the three principal regional modes of production that have evolved in France since the end of the ancien régime (1789). Part 3 consid-

Map 2. Departments of France

ers the meaning of Left and Right in France as it relates to the
interests of French cultivators. Part 4 presents a test of the hy-
potheses derived from the mode-of-production model and concludes with an assessment of the model and its general implications. Mode of production is found to be a significant predictor
of French peasant voting.

1
TOWARD A THEORY OF THE PERSISTENCE OF POLITICAL BEHAVIOR

1

1
EXPLANATIONS OF POLITICAL REGIONALISM

How can one explain the phenomenon of political regionalism? Why have the cultivators in western France consistently supported the Right while their counterparts in Mediterranean France have as steadfastly adhered to the Left? To begin, I must examine how scholars traditionally explain the persistence of political distinctiveness. It is convenient to divide the literature into normative and structural approaches. Briefly, the normative approach points to the transmission of values and norms from one generation to the next as the principal determinant of political preferences, whereas the structural approach sees durable social structures as the principal galvanizer of voting choices.[1]

NORMATIVE EXPLANATIONS

Most theorists base their explanations of the emergence of distinct patterns of political behavior in social and economic structures.[2] Some of these analysts, however, turn to values, beliefs, or collective memories when faced with the persistence of those patterns over time. For example, in his classic study of party loyalty in the American South, V. O. Key notes that patterns of party affiliation that were inherited from the struggle between the states have a remarkable capacity to persist long after the disappearance of the issues that created the patterns.[3] In a similar fashion, numerous studies of French regional political loyalties begin with a structural account of the emergence of political distinctiveness and then employ the notion of a cultural legacy to explain the persistence of this distinctiveness. For Yves-

Marie Bercé the sixteenth- and seventeenth-century antifiscal uprisings in southwestern France bequeathed to this region a political radicalism that persisted into the nineteenth century. For Paul Bois, Charles Tilly, and T. J. A. Le Goff and D. M. G. Sutherland, the legacy of the French Revolution continued to shape political attachments in western France long after the 1790s, whereas for Lynn Hunt the legacy of the French Revolution is instrumental in accounting for the continuing division between a more conservative North and a more radical South. And finally, for J. Gouault, J. Klatzmann, and D. Derivry and M. Dogan the persistence of French political regionalism stems from regional variation in levels of religiosity.[4] Many of these theorists are typically considered structuralists, and their analysis of events during the sixteenth and seventeenth centuries (in the case of Bercé) or the Revolution (in the cases of Bois, Tilly, Le Goff and Sutherland, and Hunt) is in fact structuralist. But a detailed examination of their works shows that these structuralists become normativists when they consider the persistence of political behavior after the specific events that they have studied.

The Legacy of the Antifiscal Rebellions

Yves-Marie Bercé has studied the political behavior of the southwestern French province of Aquitaine. Bercé argues that the villages of Aquitaine, which were marked by a strong communalism, spearheaded the resistance to the centralizing state policies of Sully, Richelieu, and Mazarin during the seventeenth century. Resistance to state centralization continued to characterize this region into the nineteenth century, as evidenced by its overwhelming opposition to the forty-five-centime tax in 1848 and its support of Bonapartist deputies during the 1870s.[5] For Bercé, Aquitaine is clearly the most *frondeuse* and antifiscal region, always willing to take up arms against the tax, always ready to express its disapproval of state policies aiming to undermine local communitarian institutions.[6]

Although Bercé's structural account of Aquitaine's substantial support of the sixteenth- and seventeenth-century antistate rebellions is sound, the author never tells us directly why the structures responsible for the opposition of the province to the state in the sixteenth and seventeenth centuries should still operate in the nineteenth century. We are left with the impression that nineteenth-century political preferences were shaped by a recollection of the sixteenth- and seventeenth-century anti-state rebellions.

Equally disconcerting, Bercé does not explain how state attacks on communal institutions elicited a particular voting choice. Why should an individual in Aquitaine be concerned about the state's attempt to dismantle communal institutions? Did communal institutions provide individuals in Aquitaine with resources they could not obtain elsewhere? If so, Bercé should explain the benefits that the inhabitants of nineteenth-century Aquitaine derived from strong communal institutions. Furthermore, the author needs to demonstrate that the disproportionate support for Bonapartist deputies in Aquitaine resulted from the Bonapartists' strong defense of communal institutions.

There are some obvious empirical problems with Bercé's thesis as well. He never clearly specifies whether support of the 1848 antitax movement and of Bonapartist deputies represents leftist or rightist political behavior. Indeed, the political behavior of the Southwest, as Goguel has made clear, is far from homogeneous. Some southwestern departments support the Right, others the Left, and many others have gone from Right to Left and vice versa. For example, the departments of the Landes and Gers supported the right between 1871 and 1902, but they have supported the Left since 1902. The departments of Gironde and Basses-Pyrénées supported the Left until 1885 and have supported the Right since 1885, whereas the departments of the Lot-et-Garonne, Lot, and Tarn-et-Garonne have joined the ranks of the Right since 1946.[7] But Bercé's analysis does not explain the weakness of the relation between areas that experienced intense antifiscal turmoil in the sixteenth and seventeenth centuries and those that joined in the resistance to the forty-five-centime tax and the election of Bonapartist deputies in the nineteenth century. Admittedly, much of the Southwest fits Bercé's characterization, but the West does not. Western France was the site of some of the largest antifiscal rebellions of the sixteenth and seventeenth centuries (for example, Nu-Pieds, Sabotiers, Papiers Timbrés, and Fronde). But this region did not participate in the resistance to the forty-five-centime tax and did not elect Bonapartist deputies. In other words, the maps of the sixteenth- and seventeenth-century antifiscal protests do not correspond to the maps of nineteenth-century resistance to the forty-five-centime tax and support for Bonapartist deputies.

The Legacy of the French Revolution

In launching a major empirical critique of André Siegfried's *Tableau politique de la France de l'Ouest sous la Troisième République,* Paul Bois presented a case study of the western department of Sarthe, which he took to be representative of the entire West.[8] In this work he argued that two different societies emerged in the Sarthe, one opposing the French Revolution and the other supporting it. The agriculturally rich western half of the department had experienced intense class conflict between a socially homogeneous peasantry and a prorevolutionary urban bourgeoisie. This antagonism, brought on largely by the sale of church property to the urban bourgeoisie, led to a peasant *prise de conscience* that instilled a strong peasant animosity toward the Revolution and what it represented. But in the poorer eastern half of the Sarthe, an emergent rural textile industry created firm ties between the peasantry and the revolutionary urban bourgeoisie, thus muting the class struggle and lessening the peasantry's antipathy to the Revolution. For Bois, these differing attitudes in Sarthe toward the urban bourgeoisie led to a particular political response and the beginnings of a regional crystallization of politics there. The French Revolution was thus greeted differently in the two zones. The result was a civil war, culminating in the savagery of the 1792–1795 *Chouannerie.* According to Bois, the legacy of these events continued throughout the nineteenth century and has remained the basis for a conservative-republican cleavage that overrides the effects of urbanization, education, and industrialization.[9]

Charles Tilly, who was considerably influenced by Paul Bois, studied the famous counterrevolutionary events of the Vendée.[10] Tilly attributes the cleavage between Right and Left in

southern Anjou to the effects of commercialization. The politically rightist, or counterrevolutionary, areas were those in
which a partial penetration of commercial activities had produced antagonism on the part of the peasants toward a prorevolutionary bourgeoisie. The politically leftist, or revolutionary, areas were those in which a full penetration of commercial
activities had led peasants and bourgeois to accept capitalism.
Thus areas where the peasantry opposed capitalism supported
the counterrevolution, and areas where the peasantry did not
oppose capitalism supported the revolution. Tilly suggests that
this pattern explains why the inhabitants of the less commercial
Mauges favored the Vendéen counterrevolution of 1793 and
the population of the more commercial Val-Saumois opposed
it. Like Bois, Tilly argues that the political characteristics of
southern Anjou endured and fashioned the area's political responses to the counterrevolutionary collective actions of 1815,
1820–1822, 1832, and 1853. Tilly notes: "In the more peaceful
ways of elections, parties, and plebiscites, too, the division between Mauges and Val-Saumois persisted through the nineteenth century into the twentieth."[11]

Both Bois's and Tilly's studies of the Sarthe and southern
Anjou are indispensable case studies of local responses to the
Revolution.[12] However, their conclusions are difficult to apply
to other areas of France. For instance, contrary to Bois's and
Tilly's claim that the more commercialized localities supported
the Revolution, many commercialized areas, especially in Mediterranean France, actually opposed it.[13] Above all, my principal
concern about the Bois and Tilly theses arises not from their
structural account of the beginnings of a Right-Left cleavage in
western France but rather from their insufficient explanation of
the persistence of this political division. Bois and Tilly acknowledge that those areas of the Sarthe and southern Anjou that
supported the counterrevolution have continued as strongholds of political conservatism whereas those areas that supported the Revolution have persisted as bastions of political liberalism. But is the persistence the result of durable structures,
or is it a cultural legacy? Tilly implies that the 1870s marked a
new era in the West, with the clergy losing their lands, the heirs
of the purchasers of church property becoming defenders of

that property, and the position of the nobility in French society
changing drastically.[14] Thus for Tilly it would appear that many
of those structures that had played so instrumental a role in
shaping the political complexion of the West since the French
Revolution had by 1870 begun to lose their ability to shape political allegiances. Having eliminated the effect of structures,
Tilly has no recourse but to imply that the cultural legacy of the
counterrevolution is responsible for the post-1870 persistence
of the Right-Left division in southern Anjou. The problem with
this explanation is that it strains logic by suggesting that voters
are influenced more by their recollection of a past event than by
their current material interests.

    Though not as well known as Bois's and Tilly's theses, Le Goff
and Sutherland's "The Social Origins of Counter-Revolution in
Western France" merits attention here both because it offers an
interesting interpretation of the causes of the western counterrevolution and because it addresses the issue of the persistence
of regional political behavior. The authors disagree with Bois's
and Tilly's commercialization thesis and propose instead that
revolutionary and counterrevolutionary zones were determined
principally by the land tenure patterns in existence. According to Le Goff and Sutherland, republicanism appealed to all
landowners, from small independent proprietors to landlords
of substantial urban and rural properties. These farmers had
gained the most from the fiscal and economic reforms of the
Revolution and thus had an interest in defending it. Popular
counterrevolution, on the other hand, appealed to leaseholders,
especially to tenants on large estates. The authors claim that tenants joined the counterrevolution because their demands for
land and security went unanswered by the revolutionary governments. To support their argument, Le Goff and Sutherland
observe that the highest incidence of popular revolution occurred in the leaseholding zones of eastern Côtes-du-Nord,
western Sarthe, central Vendée, the Deux-Sèvres, and southern
Maine-et-Loire, whereas the greatest backing for republicanism
occurred in the independent property zones of southeastern
Sarthe, on the plains south of Fontenay-le-Comte, and in the
Loire valley.[15]

In regard to the issue of the persistence of the Right-Left cleavage in the West, Le Goff and Sutherland adopt a normative approach. They claim that "the memory of *chouannerie* remained so vivid for so long . . . because of the survival of problems the revolutionaries and their descendants refused to confront. Decisions taken or not taken in the early 1790s survived to haunt the nineteenth century."[16]

Overall, I find quite sensible the authors' argument that the political attitudes of peasants toward the Revolution reflected their material interests. The authors' bipartite separation of cultivators into a prorevolutionary camp of owners and a counterrevolutionary camp of tenants is much too broad, however, and glosses over the great divergence of interests within each camp. For instance, the National Assembly's 1791 decision to sell church property in relatively large and expensive lots obviously pleased the large estate owners who could afford them but only angered the small owners. Le Goff and Sutherland also ignore a sizable category of peasant cultivators, the agricultural laborers.

But my principal concern with the authors' explanation is that they give an unsatisfactory account of the persistence of the Right-Left cleavage in the West. Le Goff and Sutherland's explanation that the memory of the *Chouannerie* shaped political attitudes more than a century later is tenuous because it assumes that individuals' attitudes are shaped more by the knowledge of an event that occurred long before they were born than by their current circumstances. Their argument appears to come as an afterthought and is not supported with evidence. A more convincing approach, and one that is consistent with their study of the origins of the counterrevolution, would have been to compare the evolution of land tenure patterns in western France (increasing reliance on leaseholding) to the evolution of that region's political behavior (increasing support for the Right).

In an original and lively account of how rhetoric, symbols, and the participation of certain groups and places shaped the ongoing experience of revolutionary change in France, Lynn Hunt examines the electoral geography of the French Revolution.[17] Utilizing the statistical technique of discriminant analysis on the voting records for deputies elected to the Convention and Directory between 1792 and 1798, Hunt finds that the Left consistently received support in departments that were relatively poor, distinctly unurbanized, woefully illiterate, and far from Paris; the Right was invariably strong in departments that were rich, literate, and near Paris. According to Hunt, the variability in political behavior resulted from the appeal of the rhetoric of revolution to the peripheries of the nation, to people who lived in economic, social, and cultural backwaters. In particular, the Left won elections in central and southwestern France, where the Jacobins of the towns and villages were able to develop relations and organizations favorable to the rhetoric of liberty, equality, and fraternity; the Right won elections in northern France, where royalists and/or partisans of order were able to galvanize their clients into movements against the innovating republic. Hunt notes that these regional political attachments, which first emerged during the French Revolution, have continued into the present. Their significance, she claims, "extended far beyond the First Republic. Many regions have continued to vote similarly to this day. In the 1970s, for example, when the left was not in power, the bastions of socialist (not communist) strength were still located in the far North and the Center-Southwest. The parties of the 'former majority' (Gaullists and Giscardiens) did best in the northern half of the country and in a string of departments extending down the Rhône River."[18] In much the same fashion as Bois, Tilly, and Le Goff and Sutherland, Hunt points to tradition as the prime factor behind the maintenance of these regional political attachments. She concludes that "the division between a conservative North and a much more radical South seems almost traditional."[19]

My criticisms of Hunt's work are both methodological and theoretical. Her choice of the French department as the unit of analysis is unfortunate because it is too large and consequently too heterogeneous. For example, the western French department of Finistère, which Hunt classifies as consistently right wing, contains the areas of Cornouaille and Léon—two areas that diverge significantly in socioeconomic characteristics and political behavior. Moreover, the political inclinations of elected deputies are an unreliable measure of the political behavior of a department's inhabitants, especially during the period from 1795 to 1798 when many individuals were excluded from the voting franchise. Most significantly, Hunt's explanation of the emergence and maintenance of regional political attachments is unconvincing. She never explains why peripheral or marginal regions should be more amenable to the penetration of a revolutionary rather than a counterrevolutionary political ideology. Hunt's inclination to attribute to tradition the persistence of France's Right-Left regional divisions suffers from the same weakness that undermines the explanations presented by Bois, Tilly, and Le Goff and Sutherland, that is, that past events exercise a greater influence on voters than do their current material interests.

Religiosity and Political Conservatism

Social scientists have long pondered the causal roles of class and culture in determining human behavior. Whereas for Marxists economic class interests galvanize behavior, for Weberians the stimulus is cultural beliefs. The class-versus-culture debate holds center stage as well in the study of political behavior. Do individuals' voting preferences reflect their economic position or their religious values? Many argue that the existence of distinct regional voting patterns in France can be attributed to regional variations in religiosity, as measured by a population's church attendance.[20] The implicit argument is that frequent church attendance reflects a set of social values associated with a rightist ideology whereas frequent absence from church reflects values associated with a leftist ideology. Thus Gouault, Derivry and Dogan, and Klatzmann propose that in areas where church attendance has traditionally been high, support for the political Right should be high and that in areas where church attendance has traditionally been low, support for the political Right should be low.[21]

But the advocates of the religiosity thesis never explain why one set of social values should lead to rightist voting and another set to leftist voting. Although I do not doubt the strong association between religiosity and voting, I believe this relation may have less to do with social values than with material interests. People who depend on the church for such material needs as education, employment, and charity are likely to support political programs that promote the welfare of their benefactor, the church. Since the French Right has more consistently advocated programs favorable to the Catholic church, people who rely upon the church for valued resources might favor the Right for purely materialist reasons.

Moreover, to associate voting for the Right with a high degree of religiosity and voting for the Left with a low degree of religiosity may be to link two effects of a common cause. That individuals hold conservative religious values does not *explain* why they vote for the political Right. Their social values may merely *reflect* another side of their conservative political behavior. What needs to be explained is why some individuals have conservative religious values and others do not.

Each normative explanation of the distinctive regional patterns that persist in French political behavior depends on the causal role of values and beliefs. Bercé, Bois, Tilly, Hunt, and Le Goff and Sutherland argue that a population's collective memory of a past set of events is responsible for persistent political behavior in a region, whereas Gouault, Derivry and Dogan, and Klatzmann claim that the religious beliefs of a population are responsible for its political behavior.

The stress on the determinant role of values in normative explanations elicits at least three important concerns. First, it is extremely difficult to assess the validity of these normative explanations because internalized values are inherently difficult to measure. Thus normative theories of political behavior appear to be both impossible to test directly and impossible to refute. Second, normative formulations appear to strain logic in supposing that individuals' votes reflect nonrational factors such as tradition rather than self-interest. It seems highly unlikely that a French voter in the 1980s would give greater weight to his knowledge of the past than to the immediate circumstances of his own life. Finally, compliance cannot be presumed simply from the subjection of individuals to a particular set of norms. There are many cases of deviant behavior across all societies.

To account for it on the basis of inadequate socialization and social control, as normative logic would suggest, appears to be a post hoc rationalization that cannot be readily confirmed by evidence.[22]

STRUCTURAL EXPLANATIONS

Structural explanations are more amenable to empirical verification because structures are easier to measure than internalized values. Moreover, structural explanations appear to be theoretically more plausible because they argue that present structures rather than cultural legacies mold current patterns of political behavior.

From Marx's discussion of the lack of a revolutionary class consciousness among some members of the proletariat to Paige's examination of divergent forms of agrarian revolts to Skocpol's analysis of why some states experienced social revolution whereas others did not, social structures have been cited as the chief cause of the various forms of political behavior. For instance, in his attempt to explain the political behavior of workers in export agriculture, Jeffery Paige predicts their political behavior from a combination of three factors: (1) the workers' own source of income, (2) what kind of upper class they confront, and (3) the repressiveness or reformist tendency of the government.[23] Because actors' political behaviors are seen as subject to a particular set of social relations, structural theorists believe that political behavior can be inferred from the relevant social structures and that as long as these social structures remain intact the political behavior should not change.[24] This argument is frequently employed in studies of the persistence of French political behavior as well. The following section of this chapter discusses three prime structural explanations of French political regionalism.[25]

Ecological Endowments

The field of French electoral sociology originated in 1913 with the publication of André Siegfried's *Tableau politique de la France de l'Ouest sous la Troisième République*. Siegfried studied the political behavior of fourteen western departments for several elections between 1876 and 1913. He identified three regional clusters in the West: the politically conservative Interior West (Vendée, Anjou, and parts of the Maine); Lower Brittany, divided between republicanism and royalism; and Normandy, sometimes conservative republican, at other times democratic Bonapartist. Siegfried believed that the explanation of western French voting differences was to be found at the level of the village. He hypothesized that such structural factors as the type of soil and vegetation, the degree of population concentration, the mode of land tenure, and the ratio of large, medium, and small farms combined to determine the extent of peasant dependence on the church and nobility.[26] Siegfried claimed that strong peasant dependence on the church and nobility produced conservative voting whereas weak dependence yielded republican voting. Conservative voting should exist most often in villages with a landscape of *bocage* (hedgerows), a low population concentration, a land tenure system of sharecropping, and the coexistence of large and small property because this combination produces considerable peasant dependence on social elites. Conversely, republican voting should predominate in villages with an open landscape, a high population concentration, and the presence of small independent peasant proprietors because this combination produces little peasant dependence on social elites.[27] Siegfried found that of all these factors, the average size of cultivators' holdings across villages had the strongest effect on peasant dependence, and consequently on a village's political behavior. He linked small holdings with political democracy, a mixture of small and large holdings with political conservatism, and medium-sized holdings with nonreformist republicanism.[28]

As a complete theory of French political regionalism, Siegfried's explanation has certain deficiencies. First, Siegfried focused his study on the French West, which has traditionally demonstrated no truly leftist tendencies. His sample incorporated only limited variation in his dependent variable. Second, he posited that political conservatism is most strongly associated with sharecropping. Unfortunately, this claim has limited relevance since sharecropping accounted for only 6 or 7 percent of the total land tenure throughout the nineteenth and twentieth centuries and today constitutes less than 3 percent of the total land tenure in France.[29] Third, and above all, Siegfried never adequately explained the way in which the dominance of the nobility and the church affect voting. One is left with the impression that the dependence of the peasantry on social elites automatically produces voting compliance. Siegfried assumed that tenants and sharecroppers, fearing eviction, comply with the dictates of the nobility by voting Right. But voting is by secret ballot and has been so since the middle of the nineteenth century. Unless landlords can effectively monitor peasant voting, they cannot be assured of compliance.[30] Although the capacity to monitor might have existed during the nineteenth century, governmental enforcement of tenant rights and the voting franchise make the monitoring of votes nearly impossible today. Furthermore, areas that voted for the Right in 1849 continue to demonstrate the same pattern in 1981. Such a persistent pattern is unlikely to have been caused solely by the dependence of the peasants.[31]

Social and Economic Crises

In examining the leftist political tendency of Lower Languedoc and Provence between 1848 and 1914, Leo Loubere and Tony Judt attributed its causes to the social and economic crisis besetting the French Mediterranean region after 1848.[32] According to Loubere, the economy of Lower Languedoc became dependent upon wine production during the first half of the nineteenth century. After 1848, the area's total dependence on wine led to economic depression and collapse. The once-thriving wine industry fell victim to the crop disease phylloxéra, to competition from Algerian wine, and, most important, to an insensitive northern-controlled government. Seeking a national voice, the Mediterranean wine producers turned to those political parties that challenged the power of this unfriendly government and favored the rights of wine producers.[33] But if all this is so, why has this region persisted in its leftist voting? To explain, Loubere suggests that as each political party was successively co-opted by northern French interests, the people of Lower Languedoc would always turn Left, toward a new party that would advance their demands.[34] For Judt, socialism emerged in the Mediterranean department of the Var chiefly as a consequence of the collapse of the Mediterranean French rural economy during the 1870s and 1880s. Where this economic crisis superimposed itself on rural areas characterized by a formerly complex social structure, intensive peasant interdependence, and a long tradition of collective interests, peasants supported the Socialist party because it alone provided collectivist solutions to their problems.[35]

Loubere and Judt's account of the effects of an economic recession on the political orientation of French Mediterranean cultivators raises a larger theoretical issue: does economic immiserization lead individuals to adopt instinctively a leftist political ideology? The authors' inclination to tie leftist political behavior to economic distress has substantial support in the Marxist literature on the political behavior of peasants. But can we readily assume that economic immiserization leads to the adoption of a leftist ideology? We would be unwise to assume that a rightist political ideology inherently divorces itself from the interests of the dispossessed. Neither the Right nor the Left has a monopoly on the economically disenfranchised. Consider the German Nazi party's stunning electoral success in the July 1932 Reichstag elections in the province of Schleswig-Holstein. Farquharson and Tilton have attributed Nazi success in part to the party's ability to appeal to this province's economically depressed farmers, who were confronted with land foreclosures and the collapse of their export market.[36] The same holds true for France. If a leftist political orientation is a function of economic recession, then it follows that western France would also have turned increasingly toward the parties of the French Left because it, too, was faced with recession. Yet just the opposite occurred. The emergence of the right-wing Dorgeriste movement during the depression in the western department of Loire-Atlantique demonstrates that peasants can turn also to the Right in times of economic crisis.

Similarly, if the leftist parties served as a voice for antigovernment sentiments, as Loubere argues, then these parties should have been popular in the West, where antigovernment sentiments have been and remain a force in the political life of

the region. Moreover, if support for the Left was chiefly a result of particular economic factors, as Loubere and Judt argue,
why didn't this support begin to dissipate when those economic
circumstances changed? The fate of the Mediterranean French
wine producers improved dramatically after 1914,[37] yet the region's support of leftist parties continued unabated.

In addition, Loubere's and Judt's explanations do not apply
to many departments in the Mediterranean region that also
developed strong rural socialist movements. Economic depression in the Mediterranean departments of the Var, Gard, and
Hérault was not mirrored in the departments of Pyrénées-
Orientales, Vaucluse, Ariège, and Aude, yet they also became
socialist.[38] Nor do their explanations hold for Lower Languedoc,
where the extent of the crisis caused by phylloxéra varied from
one locale to another. Thus the vineyards surrounding Nîmes
and Montpellier suffered extensive damage, while those in the
vicinity of Béziers and Narbonne experienced growth.[39] Contrary to their predictions, the better-off zones of Béziers and
Narbonne became more supportive of the socialist movement
than those of Montpellier and Nîmes.[40]

Ethnic Regionalism

Henri Espieux and Jacques Vedel have argued that the leftward political behavior of the French Mediterranean resulted
from this region's loss of autonomy.[41] The Mediterranean, like
Brittany, was late in being incorporated into the French realm.
These provinces had been granted special rights (*pays d'état*)
during the late Middle Ages and the ancien régime because of
their distance from Paris and their long history as autonomous
duchies. But beginning with the French Revolution, these regions were subject to increasing centralization and domination
by the Ile-de-France. Espieux and Vedel claim that as the inhabitants of the French Mediterranean region have voted Left
to protest against the centralizing policies of the Ile-de-France—
policies that they see as responsible for the dismantling of the
distinctive culture of the French Mediterranean.

These authors, however, do not explain why an ethnic region's loss of autonomy should lead to its attachment to a par-

ticular political behavior. If the loss of autonomy results in support of the Left, how then can Espieux and Vedel explain Brittany's support for the Right? Brittany also lost its former autonomy. The principal empirical inadequacy of the ethnic-regional-consciousness thesis is that the connection between regional culture and voting remains obscure. Election data show that the area of rightist voting includes Lower Normandy and the Pays de la Loire—two western provinces that are not Breton—as well as the culturally distinct area of the province of Brittany. In the case of the Mediterranean, the areas where Oc was once spoken (including those areas whose language is Provençal, a dialect of Oc) stretch from north of Bordeaux in the West, through Brive-la-Gaillarde (Limousin) in the North, to Isère in the East. This Oc area is not at all homogeneous in political proclivities. Thus the ethnic regionalist thesis is empirically incorrect because regions characterized by a particular ethnic makeup do not correspond to regions characterized by a particular political behavior.

Underlying these structural explanations of French political regionalism is the implicit claim that a group-level phenomenon—be it dependency on social elites, economic recession, or internal colonialism—has great consequences for voting behavior. By concentrating on macrostructures, these explanations reveal how individuals come to share circumstances. Because they ignore the extent to which individuals' motivations can shape their behavior and provide independent choice-making discretion, however, the explanations cannot account for the reactions of individuals to their circumstances. On closer inspection, an important link in structural explanations of political behavior appears to be missing. These explanations do not specify the mechanisms or processes by which a certain structure produces a certain behavior. In other words, a critical part of the theoretical chain is absent: the part that links the structure to an individual act. Why should a particular structure be the cause of a particular act? This question becomes critical in the study of voting behavior because structures do not vote but individuals do. Without this link, structural explanations have great difficulty clarifying the reasons that individuals in similar economic positions do not always behave alike. If they did be-

have alike, then the phenomenon of French political regionalism would not exist. What makes the comparison of western
and Mediterranean French political behavior so intriguing is
that in both regions cultivators have been and remain relatively
poor. Yet the cultivators of western France consistently vote
Right while the cultivators of Mediterranean France invariably
vote Left. The numerous empirical failings of the structural explanations of French political behavior may be attributed to this
simple inclination to infer behavior from structures, ignoring
the reasons that a particular structure should produce a particular behavior. Although structural explanations have certain
advantages over normative ones as theories of French political
regionalism, they will remain incomplete as long as they continue to ignore the link between structure and individual action.

In conclusion, normative theorists claim that the voting decision is subject to the constraints of a set of norms whereas structural theorists claim that the voting decision is subject to a set of
social relations. Neither theorist's explanation affords the individual much independent choice. Because there are so many
instances of individual noncompliance to norms or structures,
one must doubt these types of explanations. To claim that this
deviant behavior results from either poor socialization or "false
consciousness," as so many normativists and structuralists do, is
clearly unacceptable since the arguments for both poor socialization and "false consciousness" appear to be post hoc, and
neither can be readily refuted by evidence. Because voting is an
individual act, any theory of voting behavior must address the
motivations and choices of individuals. My argument is that the
mode-of-production theory of political regionalism effectively
overcomes the failings of normative and structural theories.

2
THE REGIONAL MODE-OF-PRODUCTION THEORY

As an alternative to current explanations of French political regionalism, I offer a theory that links structures to actors by combining a concern for the intentions and consequences of individual action with an appreciation of the role of structural factors. Accordingly, I argue that structures specify the constraints upon individual action and to a great extent also determine individual interests. These constraints are insufficient to determine individual behavior, however. Because the intentions and consequences of individual action are essential to the voting decision, I employ a theoretical approach that includes individual motivations as consequential determinants of individual voting behavior.

How should individuals act when confronted with choices? Upon what grounds will individuals select one course of action over another? I suggest that the answer to these questions lies in theories of rational choice. Beginning with the classic works of the Scottish moralists and English utilitarians, advocates of the rational-choice perspective argue that in choosing among alternatives in pursuit of their ends individuals will act rationally; they will adopt the most efficient means for achieving their goals.

How might this approach be employed to study voting behavior? At first glance, the rational-choice approach for a study of voting appears to be of questionable value. In his classic study of politics, Anthony Downs suggests that a rational individual should not be expected to vote since the costs of voting (the time and energy it takes to vote) outweigh the benefit of voting (the product of the improvement for an individual if his preferred party wins the election and the expected effect of his vote on the outcome of the election).[1] Since in most elections millions of individuals cast ballots, it is unlikely that a rational individual perceives that his one vote will change the outcome of the election. So according to Downs a rational individual should not be expected to vote. On the one hand, Downs's explanation can help us understand why in nearly every U.S. presidential election half of the eligible American electorate does not vote. On the other hand, it does little to help us understand why the other half does vote.[2]

The act of voting, then, may have more to do with what Russell Hardin terms extrarational or non-self-interested motives.[3] Whereas the rational-choice approach may tell us little about why individuals vote, it can help to explain why individuals who do vote select one party over another. I assume that individuals' political preferences reflect their interests as determined by their calculation of the benefits and costs associated with support of given political parties. Accordingly, I argue that individuals will select the political party or program that they perceive will provide them with the greatest benefits.[4] In elections, citizens will assign to each candidate or political party an overall welfare level. Citizens will then compare the welfare levels and will vote for the candidate or party whose welfare level is highest.[5]

While the rational-choice approach posits that individuals will select the course of action that they perceive will bring them the greatest benefits, it does not indicate what brings about this self-interested behavior. A complete theory of voting behavior should stipulate not only how individuals will react when presented with choices but also what these choices are and how they are made. This is where structures come in. Structures serve to specify the interests of individuals as well as the constraints under which individuals act. In the face of these constraints, rational-choice theory claims that individuals should act rationally: they should employ the most efficient means to reach their goals. In voting, that goal is to select the candidate or political program that most nearly approximates their perceptions of their self-interests.[6]

So why do the cultivators of western France continue to support the French Right while the cultivators of Mediterranean

France continue to support the French Left? My model of voting proposes that different modes of production are chiefly responsible for this political regionalism. The particular modes of production of western and Mediterranean France have produced divergent regional constellations of economic interests. As rational actors, the inhabitants of both the West and the Mediterranean vote for the party that they perceive reflects their interests. The interests of the inhabitants of western France are best represented by the political Right and those of the inhabitants of Mediterranean France are most clearly served by the programs of the political Left.

Marx used the term "mode of production" to describe a combination of productive forces (social and technical means by which production is organized and carried out) and social relations (the institutions and practices associated with the production, exchange, and distribution of goods). Unfortunately, this key concept in Marxist analysis has been put to little practical use. This situation may in part have resulted from the vague, and at times contradictory, statements that Marx made about the mode of production.

The concept has become the center of a long-running, almost theological debate among Marxists.[7] This debate has focused on such abstract issues as the correspondence between social relations and productive forces, the reproduction or transition of modes of production, and the question whether a particular historical period can constitute a mode of production.[8] Although these conceptual debates are useful, they tend to deflect the attention needed for developing the mode of production as an analytically useful concept capable of empirical application. Marx held out the possibility of using the mode of production as an explanatory concept when he wrote that "the mode of production in material life conditions the general process of social, political, and intellectual life."[9] For Marx, then, the mode of production offered a means of predicting the superstructure, or ideological nature, of a society.

Unfortunately, Marx did not furnish empirical indicators of the two components of the mode of production. Consequently, to employ the mode-of-production concept in explanatory analysis, suitable empirical indicators of productive forces and social relations must be identified. I have selected economic activity and property rights as reliable proxies for these two key dimensions of a mode of production. I use the term "economic activity" for forms of economic production in which individuals are engaged and the term "property rights" for the conditions or manner of holding property (that is, land, labor, tools, and seed).

According to Marx, the combination of economic activity and property rights forms the economic base of society and shapes its various social characteristics.[10] Such factors as patterns of settlement (population concentration and town-countryside association) and class composition (relative presence or absence of various classes) are affected by the mode of production, suggesting that the mode of production can be used to explain their various forms in different societies. For example, in many parts of the world the commercialized cultivation of crops is found in conjunction with a system of short-term cash tenancy or agricultural wage labor, nucleated villages, intense town-countryside association, and a heterogeneous social composition, whereas the subsistence cultivation of crops is found in conjunction with hereditary tenures or agricultural servant labor, dispersed homesteads, weak town-countryside association, and a homogeneous population. Why, for instance, should agricultural servant labor rather than agricultural wage labor be associated with a subsistence cultivation? I argue that the association follows because each component of the mode of production is capable of influencing the shape of other social components within the social unit. In the example above, farm servant labor is more practical in a subsistence economy because it solves the problem of a farm's cash flow by delaying money payments for work done until after the harvest and by paying much of the real wage in food, drink, and lodging.[11]

But how does the mode of production shape voting behavior? It affects voting both directly and indirectly. Individuals perceive that their interests are derived directly from their economic activity and property rights and determined indirectly from the dominant structure of the economic activity and property rights they possess. Their economic activity and property rights affect the specific positions they take on the major political issues. For example, market-oriented producers and subsistence producers perceive different personal economic consequences resulting from protective tariffs; and property owners and tenants see a different set of benefits and damages resulting from rent control. Thus market-oriented producers, subsistence producers, property owners, and tenants should support the political programs that best represent the particular interests of their group.

The dominant structure of economic activity and property rights determines the particular patterns of settlement and class composition. It is reasonable to expect more intense town-countryside association in regions with market-oriented economic activity and independent forms of land tenure than in those with subsistence economic activity and dependent forms of land tenure. Patterns of settlement and class composition have an independent effect on individuals' perceptions of their interests. First and most important, the patterns determine which individuals and groups in a community will control the allocation of vital resources. In this study, vital resources include real property, education, information, employment, security in times of crisis, and brokerage with the outside. To the extent that individuals wish to maintain uninterrupted access to vital resources, they will depend on the supplier of these resources and will have a stake in his welfare. Consequently, they will view political programs that worsen the lot of their supplier as threats to their own livelihood and will be unlikely to support such political programs. For example, a community that relies solely on organized religion for education will regard attempts to restrict church activity, such as the nationalization of church lands and the secularization of education, as a threat to its own well-being. Communities with alternative suppliers of education will not be as likely to regard threats to the church as direct threats to their welfare.[12]

Second, patterns of settlement and class composition influence the availability of information and play a determining role in individuals' awareness of interests. Isolated communities should be expected to have fewer sources of information than nonisolated communities. If individuals depend upon a particular source of information, such as newspapers, books, or associ-

ates, their perception of their interests—and thus their voting—
is likely to reflect the way this source formulates their interests.
This situation is especially likely to occur where elites have the
ability to inhibit their political opposition from organizing.

Third, patterns of settlement and class composition may lead
to dependence and to a situation in which individuals have conflicting material interests. For example, the long-term material
interests of cultivators may differ from their interests in the
light of their dependence on landlords. If cultivators dependent on landlords act upon their long-term material interests,
they may jeopardize their present livelihood. Consequently,
cultivators' perceptions of their interests may reflect the desires
of their landlords rather than their interests in the absence of a
dependent relationship. It should be emphasized that in voting,
however, this situation is conditional; the threat of losing one's
property or livelihood for casting the wrong vote rests on the
ability of the providers of resources to monitor the act of voting
effectively. Without such monitoring, resource providers are
unable to enforce voting compliance. By accounting for the capacity to monitor the voting decision, the mode-of-production
model offers an explanation for voting behavior more consistent with the conditions and performances of French peasants
since the end of the nineteenth century. Such structural models
as Siegfried's often assume that the tenant votes as the landlord
dictates out of fear of the denial of resources.[13] These assumptions do not, however, account for the individual who obtains
resources without complying with the landlord's dictates. This
possibility becomes an important factor in elections of the mid-
to-late nineteenth century and the twentieth century because
voting by secret ballot precluded effective monitoring of the
electorate by resource controllers and allowed the peasant a degree of freedom larger than that suggested by many structural
models.[14] The mode-of-production model suggests clients may
have voted the program or party of their patron not solely because they were intimidated but also because they shared their
patrons' interests by virtue of their material situation.

In short, the mode of production affects political preferences
by determining the universe of specific interests—interests on
which individuals base their action (Figure 1). Since both west-

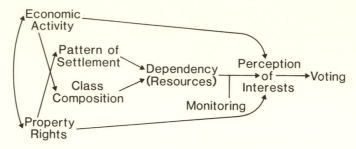

Figure 1. Regional Mode-of-Production Model

ern and Mediterranean France have been predominantly agricultural throughout the period of this study, 1849 to 1981, why should there be such marked regional variation of interests? My central proposition is that the persistence of regional patterns of political behavior is systematically related to distinctive regional modes of production. Thus, as we shall see, the cultivators of western France have supported the Right because it has consistently represented their particular interests; the cultivators of the French Mediterranean, however, have adhered to the Left because the leftist parties have best reflected their interests.

What are the particular modes of production that have produced these regional constellations of interests in France? In the following section, I will describe in detail France's three principal modes of production: the northeastern,[15] the western, and the Mediterranean. My account will examine each mode of production both before and after 1865. That year marked the completion of the railway nexus between Paris and Brest, the final link in the French national railway system of inexpensive inland transport that created a national market for agricultural and industrial goods. The emergence of this national market had consequences for each mode of production. Because 1865 marks a turning point in the evolution of my three modes of production, it serves well as my point of demarcation.

2

MODES OF PRODUCTION IN FRANCE

3
MODES OF PRODUCTION BEFORE 1865

As early as the seventeenth century there were three distinctive agricultural modes of production in France, each corresponding to a particular territory. One mode of production, the northeastern, existed in the provinces of Upper Normandy, Flanders, Picardy, Ile-de-France, Champagne, Lorraine, Burgundy, and Alsace. The northeastern mode of production was marked by commercial economic activity, cash tenancy and salaried agricultural labor, preponderance of small and medium farms, compact village settlement, intense town-countryside ties, a differentiated and hierarchical class composition, and a moderate proportion of landlord absenteeism. A second, the western, existed in the provinces of Lower Normandy, Brittany, and the Pays de la Loire. The western mode was characterized by subsistence economic activity, medium-scale share-cropping or tenancy land tenure, dispersed settlement, little town-countryside association, a bipolar class composition, and a high proportion of landlord residence. A third, the Mediterranean, existed in the provinces of Languedoc, Roussillon, and Provence. The Mediterranean mode was typified by market-oriented economic activity, small-owner cultivation or salaried agricultural labor, agglomerated settlement, intense town-countryside ties, a heterogeneous and relatively democratic class structure, and a high proportion of landlord absenteeism.

In this respect France was no different from the rest of Western Europe, for these modes of production covered most of the Continent in the eighteenth century. The northeastern mode existed as well in the German Rhineland, southeastern and midland England, and, imperfectly, in parts of the Iberian pen-

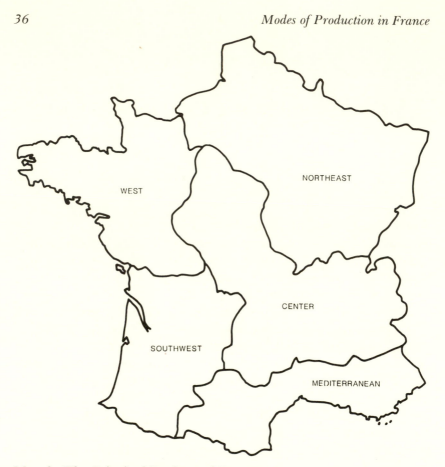

Map 3. The Principal Regions of France

insula, southern Italy, and Lombardy.[1] The western mode of
production was located principally in the strip of coastal territory stretching from Norway to northwestern Portugal, including such territories as the Hebrides, Highland Scotland,
Ireland, northwestern and southwestern England, and northwestern Spain. The Mediterranean mode was found largely in
lands stretching from north central Italy to Valencia. A similar
system existed also in southern Germany.[2]

Although Western Europe has changed tremendously since
the ancien régime, these modes of production persist to a large
degree and continue to affect social and economic organization.
Travelers to Europe still marvel over the similarities displayed

by the *treo* in Brittany, the *trev* in Cornwall, the *tref* in Wales, the *treen* in the Isle of Man, and the *townlands* in Ireland.

The uneven distribution of these modes of production in the territories of Western Europe raises the problem of their origins. Why is the western mode found principally on the Atlantic littoral and in northern Europe? Why is the Mediterranean mode oriented to the Mediterranean and why is the northeastern mode located in lands far from either sea? In answering these questions, some writers have insisted that the three types of social organization ultimately had common cultural roots.[3] Others have based explanations on the different ecological endowments of the respective territories.[4] Perry Anderson has offered a historical interpretation emphasizing both cultural and geographical causes: three distinctive areas existed in medieval Europe because of the differential impact of Roman institutions upon the barbarian social formation in its hinterland.[5] No monocausal theory appears adequate in the light of existing evidence. Cultural determinists have difficulty explaining why field systems vary within each of the Western European culture areas. Further, their expectations about the origins of such institutions as the open fields do not jibe with the English and German historical record. Ecological determinists, in contrast, cannot readily explain why areas with significant geographical variations have common institutions.[6] Thus, regardless of the merits of each approach, reasonable doubt remains. It therefore seems prudent to accept Kerridge's verdict that "very likely we shall have to reconcile ourselves to the reality that the early origins of field systems are unknowable."[7] We may say the same for the genesis of these regional modes of production more generally.

By analyzing how these modes of production have shaped the interests of cultivators in the various regions, we can gain a clearer picture of French agrarian political behavior. In this section I will describe in ideal typical terms the major French regional modes of production, discussing their economic activity, property rights, patterns of settlement, and class composition both before and after 1865. Each mode of production is an ideal type that does not entirely correspond to any actual regional social formation and tends, moreover, to accentuate the constancy of the various elements of each mode of production at the cost of neglecting the extent to which these elements have changed over time. Each regional social form represents combinations of several modes of production. Within any regional social formation, however, one mode of production predominates; its characteristic economic activity, property rights, pattern of settlement, and class composition pervade the regional social form as a whole. Although elements of all three modes of production exist in each region, these secondary elements are of lesser importance.

THE MODE OF PRODUCTION OF NORTHEASTERN FRANCE

Economic Activity

While traveling through northeastern France on the eve of the French Revolution, Arthur Young, the famous English agronomist, was struck by the vastness and richness of the seemingly never-ending open fields stretching from Flanders in the northeast to Orléans in the southeast.[8] Young's depiction of fertile open fields could easily be extended to include the French provinces of Champagne, Burgundy, Lorraine, and Alsace. Here the arable was laid out with no fences or hedges to separate one field from another and with no habitation. The open-field arable was subdivided into sections of considerable size, which in turn were subdivided into long strips (*champs ouverts et allongés*) that an animal could plough in a single day.

Grains were the principal crops of northeastern agriculture. But raising and marketing livestock were also common in some areas of Flanders and Alsace, where convertible husbandry had gained prominence since the sixteenth century.[9] In both grain and livestock, the Northeast produced far more than the other French regions, with agricultural yields before the Revolution two to four times higher than those of the West and of the Mediterranean.[10] This margin continued during the nineteenth century.

The Northeast's economic superiority stemmed from a number of factors. It possessed greater technological advantages, such as the wheeled plough, modern harness, four-, five-, and six-course rotation. The region made better use of legumes (which added valuable sources of protein to the diet while increasing soil fertility through their nitrogen-fixing properties), and it placed a greater proportion of land under cultivation. A further advantage was its application of convertible husbandry (alternation of arable and grass during periods of five years each), which augmented yields since the fields were well fertilized by manure during the years in which they served as pasture. The Northeast benefited from climatic conditions, such as summer rains, that made spring sowing possible. Finally, the proximity of major urban areas, particularly Paris and Strasbourg, created high levels of demand for its agricultural products.[11]

Property Rights

The general economic prosperity that began to emerge after 1700 had pronounced effects on property rights in the Northeast. During the Middle Ages, agriculture in that area was organized through the manorial system, a system of cooperative tillage and secure and hereditary tenure.[12] The manor was a fief that provided revenue for the landlord and his tenants and coordinated both production and distribution. This system, based on risk sharing (as evidenced by the annual rotation of strips), seems to have suited the precarious nature of agricultural production. As economic prosperity increased, independent farming and short-term cash tenancy spread dramatically across the region.

The increase in demand for agricultural products and wool raised prices and provided landlords (church, noble, or bourgeois) and a few enterprising peasants with the incentive to reattach and absorb commons and arable. Consequently, the number of large farms rose.[13] After 1760, enclosures and engrossings became common occurrences in northeastern France, greatly increasing the pasturage or arable of the landlords and enabling them to reduce production costs; thus landlords profited more than others from the rise of prices in agricultural markets, especially prices for wheat and meat. The new agricultural technology also encouraged the consolidation of property.[14] Convertible husbandry required that permanent common pastures and open fields be abandoned in favor of consolidated strips and enclosures.[15] Thus, the demands of the new agricultural system could be met only by large estates—especially those able to sacrifice cash income in the first years.[16]

Although prior to the French Revolution most peasants continued to lease holdings of less than ten hectares,[17] these tenants were also affected by the agrarian transformation. Some prospered and enlarged their holdings or even purchased their leases. Others fared less well, as landlords and richer peasants gradually appropriated the commons and replaced hereditary and secure leases with short-term leases, rack renting (a way of bolstering rents with higher prices), and higher entry fines.[18] In the districts surrounding Paris, for example, the average duration of money leases in the eighteenth century fell from nine to three years.[19] While the price of wheat in parts of northeastern France rose 40 to 50 percent, rents in those areas increased 100 percent.[20] Many tenants found that the value of their agricultural output simply did not match the ever-increasing level of their rents, and they fell from the ranks of tenants to become seasonal agricultural laborers.

Nowhere else in France before the French Revolution was the rural proletariat as large as in the Northeast.[21] The ranks of agricultural labor were further swollen by the population explosion that accompanied the Northeast's commercial expansion. Agricultural laborers often held a few acres or a garden but these plots were hardly sufficient for their subsistence. In areas outside Paris and Lille, more than three-fourths of peasant cultivators possessed less than one hectare.[22] Agricultural laborers frequently worked as seasonal day laborers (*journaliers*) on the larger tenant farms. Like small tenants, agricultural laborers depended for their livelihood on access to the common land (rough pasture, forest, and meadows) that enabled them to feed their livestock. Thus the appropriation of the commons that accompanied the commercialization of agriculture made the livelihood of laborers increasingly precarious.[23]

Though tenancy and agricultural labor were the dominant forms of land tenure in the Northeast before 1865, owner cultivation prevailed in Flanders, the valleys of the Seine and Beauce, and the *coteaux* of Burgundy, Champagne, and Alsace.[24] These districts were marked by intensive cultivation of easily marketed crops such as peas, beans, potatoes, wine, flax, dye plants, and colza.[25] With these crops peasants were able to survive on less land.

The French Revolution did little to alter the forms of land tenure in northeastern France.[26] Even before the Revolution many seigneurial obligations had already fallen into disuse. The abolition of seigneurial dues and rights and the ecclesiastical tithe (*dîme*) undoubtedly lessened peasants' burdens, but it did not radically transform property relations. And although the sales of ecclesiastical and noble émigré property did provide opportunities to purchase land, only a minority of the agricultural proletariat could afford to do so. Nor did the Revolution put an end to engrossings and enclosures or support the communal regulation of fields. Indeed, perhaps the major consequence of the Revolution for rural property was to make rich peasants richer.[27] Thus the pre-1789 pattern of land tenure, in which cash tenancy and agricultural labor dominated, remained generally intact after 1815.[28] The real revolution in the land tenure system of the Northeast would occur after 1865, and it would dramatically alter northeastern French agriculture.

Pattern of Settlement

One of the most distinctive features of the Northeast's rural pattern of settlement is its highly agglomerated population. Whether driving through or flying over northeastern France, the traveler is struck by the compact villages, or *villages urbanisés*, that dot the barren open-field landscape of the great plain. As early as the eleventh century the nucleated village was the most common settlement in the Northeast; nowhere else in France did ecology and technology combine to demand a particular pattern of settlement.[29] As in southeastern and midland England and in southwestern Germany, the manorial pattern of agriculture—based upon collective grazing rights (*vaine pâture*), the interdependence of arable and waste, communal regulation of fields, and the harnessing and pulling of the heavy-wheeled plough—clearly required extensive organization and peasant cooperation.[30] This manorial pattern combined naturally with village communities and especially with the three-field system, in which peasants owned strips in each field and needed ready access to them.[31]

The commercial transformation of the region's agriculture that got underway in the eighteenth century hardly affected the region's pattern of settlement.[32] Though individualist farming spurred some population dispersion, *solidarité villageoise* remained in force well into the nineteenth century. The bulk of the peasantry—small tenants and agricultural laborers—continued to benefit from the tightly knit village community that regulated cultivation and pasturing, especially in Lorraine, Burgundy, and Franche Comté, where the practice of *vaine pâture* died slowly. The high degree of agricultural commercialization also led to strong town-countryside ties.

Class Composition

Of the three regions, the Northeast certainly had the most differentiated and hierarchical class structure, probably the result of the extensive commercialization of the region's economic activity. A typical village of one hundred families might include two substantial tenants (*gros fermiers*), administering holdings larger than one hundred hectares; five or six medium tenants (*laboureurs*), renting farms of approximately twenty to fifty hectares; twenty small tenants (*haricotiers*), working holdings of ten hectares; and fifty farm workers (*manouvriers* and *journaliers*) possessing one hectare or less.[33] The major landowner, whether a noble, a cleric, or a rich bourgeois, usually did not reside in the village community in which he owned property.[34] Since the dominant form of land tenure was cash tenancy, the landlord did not need to worry about supplying working capital or making sure that the tenant did not cheat on his rent. The agreement between landlord and tenant simply stipulated that the landlord should receive a money rent in exchange for the usage of land. This allowed the landlord to reside in the city, where he could comfortably enjoy the luxuries of urban life.[35]

Despite moderate landlord absenteeism in the Northeast, the

proportion of property to which the noble owner had customary rights and for which the peasantry owed seigneurial dues was considerably greater than in the Mediterranean. The compensation accrued by absentee landlords for hereditary privilege became grist for the revolutionary mill in the Northeast after 1750.[36]

There are areas, however, in the Northeast, whose mode of production differed markedly from the dominant mode. Though open fields and the extensive cultivation of grains typify the Northeast, some areas rely on livestock raising and intensive cultivation of fruits, vegetables, and industrial crops. For instance, areas such as Thiérache and Hainaut in Flanders, the *pays* of Bray and Boulonnais, and the mountainous terrains of the Ardennes, Vosges, and Jura rely substantially on livestock raising. Enclosures in these areas are a common sight. In addition, intensively cultivated crops distinguish the river valleys of the Seine, Marne, Artois, and Meuse and the *coteaux* of eastern France—côtes de Champagne, côtes de Meuse, côtes de Moselle, côtes d'Or, and côtes Alsaciennes—where climate and soil combine to produce some of France's best wines and champagnes. Yet no northeastern provinces diverge more from the general pattern of open fields and extensive cultivation of grains than do Flanders and Alsace, marked for centuries by an exceptionally productive cultivation of a variety of agricultural and industrial crops.[37]

Differences in economic activity are frequently associated with differences in property rights, and so it is in northeastern France. Tenancy rules in the north whereas owner cultivation prevails in those areas of eastern France where the intensive cultivation of fruits and vegetables predominates. Many of eastern France's owner-cultivators are really owner-tenants, however, since they both own and lease parts of their holdings. Small farms prevail also in the Northeast, for they frequently accompany intensive cultivation of commercial crops and an owner-cultivation pattern of land tenure. Consequently, small farms dot the landscape of the valleys of the Seine-et-Oise and the wine-producing slopes of eastern France.[38]

On the eve of the emergence of a national market, northeastern France was marked principally by commercially active

agriculture, cash tenancy and agricultural wage labor, a preponderance of small and medium farms, a compact pattern of
village settlement, intense town-countryside ties, a differentiated and hierarchical class composition, and a moderate proportion of landlord absenteeism.

THE MODE OF PRODUCTION OF WESTERN FRANCE

Economic Activity

In contrast to the northeastern great plain, the western landscape is scored by valleys that cut the Armorican plateau in all
directions. Because of this discontinuous terrain, the land does
not lend itself (as does the Northeast) to regular open fields and
communal exploitation. Instead, cultivation takes the form of
an alternation between culture and fallow. This system is referred to by the various designations of infield-outfield (*terres
chaudes-terres froides*) or *rundale-runrig*. In this system the most
fertile land (infield) is continuously cultivated for five to ten
years, until its soil becomes exhausted. Afterward, the infield is
used for pasturing animals while the less fertile land (outfield)
is placed under cultivation. The outfield is cultivated until the
fertility of the infield is restored; this fallow usually requires
one to three years.[39] Whereas the infield-outfield system is predominant in the West, there are areas in which a hybrid form
exists. In parts of the Maine, Anjou, and Vendée, the infield-
outfield system coexists with a bipartite and sometimes tripartite division of the land, allowing for limited crop rotation.[40]
Three-field rotation involves cultivation of fast-growing crops
such as oats, barley, beans, or peas. Generally in the West, however, there is no crop rotation and no communal tillage.

Because of the diversity of the terrain and the abundance of
grass and poor soil, pastoralism (*élevage*) has been the principal
economic activity of the region: milk in Lower Normandy, pork
in Brittany, and beef in the Pays de la Loire.[41] Arable cultivation, less important than livestock raising, is predominantly
polycultural. Until the mid-nineteenth century, wheat was the
major staple; afterward, vegetables, potatoes, and apples for
cider even supplanted wheat as a major crop in many areas.[42]

The lack of an efficient transport system, the relative absence of sizable towns, and low agricultural yields meant that western agricultural production was directed not to the market but to internal consumption, meeting the subsistence needs of the family.[43] Agricultural surpluses were commonly used as feed for livestock.

Property Rights

During the ancien régime, cultivators in western France had been predominantly sharecroppers or tenants.[44] Sharecropping was found in impoverished areas, where peasants lacked reserves of capital and landlords faced shortage of laborers and uncertainty of yield.[45] The hereditary holding, or *métairie*, was of benefit to both parties: the lessee was protected against eviction, the lessor against a fall in the value of money.[46] Tenancy was a relatively minor form of land tenure before 1800 in the West, and unlike forms of land tenure in the commercial Northeast it often entailed payment in kind and, more important, a long-term lease.[47] By 1789, land owned by peasants still made up a mere one-fifth of the total in Normandy, Brittany, and Poitou (West), as opposed to one-third in Picardy, Nord, Orléans, and Burgundy (Northeast) and one-half in Languedoc (Mediterranean).[48]

The French Revolution did little to change property rights in the West. The abolition of the *tithe* (a seigneurial payment) and of feudal dues did not dramatically alter the dependency of tenants and sharecroppers on their landlords. Through liberally interpreted laws, the landlords were able to exact the same obligations from peasants as before.[49] Furthermore, the western peasantry did not purchase much of the land formerly held by the nobles and the church (*biens nationaux*) that became available during the revolutionary land redistribution.[50] Many peasants who did purchase holdings renounced their claims to ownership after 1815 under pressure from returning noble and clerical émigrés.[51]

Although sharecropping was the major form of land tenure in the West until the nineteenth century, other forms existed and in some instances were dominant in particular subregions. One such form involved the permanent agricultural laborer—the *domestique*.[52] The laborer was fed, lodged, and clothed in the home of the landowner and was most often remunerated in kind. The *domestique* was protected from changes in the cost of living and was generally assured of constant employment.[53] *Domestique* labor was preferred over wage labor on pastoral farms, which require not only care of herds but also daily milking, butter churning, and cheese making. Furthermore, farm servant labor is more practical in a subsistence economy (see above).[54] It can be argued that this system provided more security to both employer and employee than did the system of agricultural wage labor.

A distinctive form of land tenure was practiced in the departments of Finistère, Morbihan, and Côtes-du-Nord: *domaine congéable*.[55] Under this system the peasant owned all buildings, farm implements, and trees but rented the land, thus being a quasi-freeholder.[56]

Permanent agricultural labor and *domaine congéable* were restricted to particular territories, however, and in no way constituted major types of land tenure in the West. Sharecropping was, and tenancy is now, the principal form of land tenure in this region.

The typical holding in the West was medium-sized, from five to twenty hectares.[57] Despite the region's poor soil, which made partitioning uneconomical, small farms (less than five hectares) dominated in some areas, especially along the Breton littoral.[58] Small property in these quarters was largely the consequence of a richer soil, the proximity of markets, and the presence of *domaine congéable* land tenure.

Pattern of Settlement

Describing the province of Brittany, Balzac wrote, "Surrounded by lights whose beneficent warmth does not reach her, the region is like a cold coal which remains dark and obscure in a blazing hearth."[59] This depiction fits the entire region of the West, where self-sufficient subsistence economic activity, along with medium-sized tenancy and sharecropping, produced a pattern of settlement most accurately characterized by social isolation.[60] The typical western village consisted of numerous self-contained family farms in which the house was situated in the center of the field, close to the water source. The abundant rainfall in the West meant that there was no need for a common village water supply.[61] Thus the population was greatly dispersed. Contrasting the West to the East, the famous French geographer Vidal de la Blache asserted, "Le campagnard de l'Est est un villageois, celui de l'Ouest, des bocages, est un paysan."[62]

Bocage-type enclosures of hedges, dirt mounds, and ditches further isolated the western peasantry. The practice of enclosing land by *bocage* dates back to the Middle Ages. The practice emerged where cultivators found little necessity for cooperation: in western France, along the Spanish frontier, and in the Alpine lands east of the Rhône valley, where there was no common use of fallow or open fields.[63] So prevalent did enclosure become in western France that even along the wind-torn coast of Brittany, where the topography did not allow for *bocage*, stonewalls were commonly constructed.[64] In more recent times these enclosures served to protect land from the uncertainties of the environment, to protect crops from depredatory grazing, and to delineate property.[65] They were also a considerable barrier to internal communication and greatly reinforced the physical isolation of the cultivators.

Throughout this region, towns were rare; villages and hamlets were the predominant form of settlement. Even where towns existed, the interaction between town and countryside was minimal. The peasant family in western France produced generally for itself rather than for a market. In effect, commercial relations that might have brought contact with other peasants as well as with merchants, artisans, and professionals never developed.

Throughout the modern period, the western town and countryside represented two distinctive worlds, neither interested in the other.[66] This division stemmed largely from the presence of agricultural production oriented toward local consumption.[67] For instance, the French Revolution was endorsed by the western towns but not by the countryside; and since 1851, subscription to leftist causes has continued to come from the towns and not from the countryside.[68] Of the western towns, it has frequently been stated that they were misplaced; their commerce was not with the adjacent countryside but instead with the out-

side. Before 1851, the two worlds of town and countryside were
further differentiated by their social structures. Cities such as
Brest and Nantes contained a sizable literate non-Breton bourgeoisie and a large working class, whereas the countryside contained a largely illiterate peasant population.[69]

Class Composition

A mode of production characterized by polycultural subsistence
economic activity and medium-scale tenancy was not conducive
to the growth of a sizable middle class.[70] There were, then, virtually no middle and lower-middle classes in the rural West.
What middle class there was existed in the principal urban areas
of the region.

Having no economic need for the middle class, the introspec-
tive, self-reliant Western peasants viewed middle-class groups
with considerable suspicion and often treated the few artisans,
merchants, and members of the liberal professions residing in
the countryside as foreigners.[71] The class of notables, however—noble, bourgeois, and clerical landlords—made its presence felt in the West, principally as a result of its control of the
land.[72] Throughout the Middle Ages and the ancien régime, regional custom provided an additional rationale for seigneurial
rural residence. In western France, custom dictated that there
be no land ownership without a seigneur (*Nul ne peut ou ne doit
avoir terre ou autres héritages sans en avoir seigneur*).[73] Furthermore,
since a subsistence economic activity fostered land tenure based
on payment "in kind," noble landlords found it advantageous
to reside in the countryside to make certain that their tenants,
sharecroppers, and *domestiques* did not undersupply labor.[74]

The French Revolution and its aftermath augmented rather
than diminished the presence of nobles in the countryside, as
many of the region's nobles who previously had exercised political power in Paris between 1815 and 1830 returned to their hamlets and villages to supervise their estates.[75] Bois claims that in
this period noble influence over rural affairs reached its apex.[76]

The presence and wealth of the nobles in western France can
be seen in the lists of eligible voters for the period 1800 to 1848.
These lists contain the names of eligible male voters: those

twenty-five years of age and paying at least two hundred francs in property tax. Of those electors in 1806 who paid more than five thousand francs in tax, nobles composed 86 percent in Lower Normandy, 71 percent in Brittany, and 82 percent in Maine-Anjou.[77] Of those electors paying more than one thousand francs in tax during the 1840s, the following percentages were noble: Côtes-du-Nord, 41; Finistère, 33; Ille-et-Vilaine, 40; Loire-Inférieure, 30; Morbihan, 46; Manche, 32; Orne, 40; Sarthe, 26; Maine-et-Loire, 36; Deux-Sèvres, 25; and Vendée, 26.[78] All told, in 1840 the nobility of Lower Normandy, Brittany, and the valley of the Loire composed more than one-third of all electors paying more than one thousand francs in tax and two-thirds of all those paying more than three thousand francs in tax.[79] These tendencies were much greater than in other regions. For example, in my own study of the 1848 lists of eligible voters of cantons for the western departments of Finistère, Ille-et-Vilaine, and Maine-et-Loire, the mean proportion of noble electors to total electors is 15 percent; for the Mediterranean departments of Hérault and Vaucluse, the mean proportion is 7 percent (Table 1).

The class of large landowners in the West included other groups as well. Although nobles controlled the greatest proportion of large property in the Maine, Anjou, Vendée, and Brittany, large landholdings in Normandy were principally in the hands of the rich bourgeoisie.[80] Moreover, the practice in the West was for the urban bourgeoisie to purchase land and move to the countryside, emulating the life style of the noble gentleman farmer.[81] This contrasted with the practice in other regions of France, where the upper bourgeoisie, after purchasing land, resided in the major urban areas.[82]

The Catholic church also controlled sizable landholdings in the West, where Church lands were more extensive than in Mediterranean France.[83] Church power was further enhanced in many areas, such as Léon, by the traditional encouragement given children of the well-off peasantry (*Julots*) to enter the priesthood and, more important, by its supervision of local administration, schools, hospitals, and public recreation.[84]

Largely because of their resources and number, the social elites of the West exerted much authority over the countryside,

Table 1. 1848 Listes des Electeurs: Electors Belonging to Noble Families, by Canton

Western France	% Noble	Mediterranean France	% Noble
Argentré-du-Plessis	13	Adge	6
Briec	5	Aniane	0
Cancale	14	Apt	3
Candé	35	Avignon	8
Châteaubourg	13	Beaumes-de-Venise	4
Châteauneuf (I-V)	3	Bédarrides	7
Châteauneuf-sur-Sarthe	20	Bédarieux	0
Combourg	23	Béziers	4
Concarneau	17	Bollène	18
Dinard	25	Bonnieux	2
Dol-de-Bretagne	3	Cadenet	1
Douarnenez	3	Capestang	3
Doué-la-Fontaine	7	Carpentras	11
Fouesnant	10	Castries	11
Gennes	7	Cavaillon	8
Guerche-de-Bretagne	2	Caylar	5
Landivisiau	9	Claret	3
Lanmeur	17	Clermont-l'Hérault	1
Lion-d'Angers	27	Florensac	13
Morlaix	23	Frontignan	7
Montreuil-Bellay	5	Ganges	12
Pleine-Fougères	3	Gignac	2
Plouescat	12	Gordes	4
Plouigneau	17	Isle-sur-la-Sorgue	3
Plogastel-Saint-Germain	22	Lodève	0
Pouancé	10	Lunas	17
Plouzévédé	48	Lunel	11
Pont-l'Abbé	5	Malaucène	4
Pont-Croix	0	Mauguio	4
Quimper	11	Mèze	8
Retiers	22	Montagnac	8

Table 1. *(continued)*

Western France	% Noble	Mediterranean France	% Noble
Rosporden	25	Montpellier	5
Saumur	21	Mormoiron	12
Segré	21	Murviel-lès-Béziers	3
Sizun	0	Olargues	8
Saint-Malo	9	Olonzac	7
Saint-Pol-de-Léon	32	Orange	15
Saint-Servan	7	Pernes-les-Fontaines	26
Saint-Thégonnec	11	Pertuis	11
Taulé	36	Pézenas	8
Tinténiac	19	Roujan	4
Vihiers	5	Salvetat-sur-Agout	15
Vitré (Est)	24	Sault	11
Vitré (Ouest)	16	Servian	3
		Saint-Chinian	3
		Saint-Gervais-sur-Mare	3
		Saint-Martin-de-Londres	9
		Saint-Pons	7
		Sète	1
		Vaison-la-Romaine	14
		Valréas	25
Western Mean	15	*Mediterranean Mean*	7

Source: *Listes du jury,* A. D. Finistère, Ille-et-Vilaine, Maine-et-Loire, Vaucluse, and Hérault.

which the dispersion of the population and the absence of town-countryside ties further augmented.[85] The typical western community has often been referred to as a corporate society, or *hiérarchie acceptée*, where rural social relations were hierarchically structured. Le Maître has remarked that the Breton parish resembles a veritable clan where "chacun doit rester à sa place et doit tenir son rang."[86] Hierarchical structure was reflected in their folklore, religious practice, and manners of speech. For instance, a tenant frequently addressed his landlord as "not' maître," and in the countryside of Anjou cultivators employed an almost feudal expression when referring to their landlord: "Je suis de la sujétion de M. X ou Y."[87] The principal landords thus dominated every aspect of communal life. The nobles frequently shared control of the countryside with the village priest, especially in Brittany, where it was often the priest and not the largest landlord who held power.[88]

Through their control over resources, nobles maintained control over local and regional administration in the West. In no other region of France was the absence of "la force démo-cratique des petits propriétaires" so remarkable.[89] Before 1851, and especially during the ancien régime, the lack of central state rule allowed western nobles a free hand in regional administration.[90] In the case of Brittany, noble control over local and regional administration was further strengthened by the powers granted by Paris to the noble-dominated Parlement, since Brittany was a relatively autonomous *pays d'état.*

The French Revolution brought a temporary stop to the dominance of the nobility. With the 1815 restoration, however, the nobles regained their mastery over rural affairs.[91] Throughout the first half of the nineteenth century, nobles held a disproportionate amount of political power in the West. For example, between 1833 and 1844, in the department of the Manche twenty of the forty-eight cantonal *conseillers généraux* delegates were noble.[92] In the legislative election of June 1849, forty-eight of the eighty-six deputies chosen from the West to the national assembly in Paris had either noble names or names appearing to be noble.[93]

Like the Northeast, the West contains important agricultural zones that diverge markedly from the dominant regional char-acteristics; notable examples are the valleys located along the Loire River. In the valleys of Orléans, Angers, and the Touraine land is exceptionally fertile and accessible and blessed with con-siderably more sunshine than land elsewhere in western France. Farmers here specialize in cultivating fruits, vegetables, and flowers for the market. These river valleys also hold impor-tant French vineyards, including Vouvray, Saumur, and the Muscadets.[94]

Exceptions to the dominant western mode of production exist as well in Brittany and in Lower Normandy. The Rennes basin, the lime plateau of northern Brittany, and the rural surroundings of Caen, Falaise, Argentan, and Alençon contain high-yielding soils.[95] A market-oriented agriculture prevails in many districts along the Breton littoral. Here we find intensive cultivation of cabbage, peas, green beans, artichokes, and onions as well as the usual Breton practices of livestock raising and fishing.[96] The pattern of property rights along Brittany's littoral varies from the usual pattern found in the West. In this part of Lower Brittany small holdings abound.[97] Moreover, as in other areas where *domaine congéable* was once practiced, a prevalent form of land tenure here is owner cultivation.

In contrast to the general western French pattern of population dispersion, high population agglomeration is common in these pockets of rich soil and intensive cultivation: along the banks of the Loire, population concentration often runs between 170 and 200 inhabitants per square kilometer. These figures become even more significant when we consider a more typical western French region, the *Gatine tourangelle,* whose population concentration ranges between 13 and 19 inhabitants per kilometer.[98]

In zones of western France where small-scale owner cultivation prevails, social elites, particularly nobles, did not find a conducive environment; their presence is consequently less extensive here than elsewhere in the West.

Nevertheless, on the eve of the creation of a French national market western France was characterized by subsistence agriculture, medium-scale sharecropping or tenancy, high population dispersion, little town-countryside association, a bipolar class structure, and the presence of a strong social elite.

THE MODE OF PRODUCTION OF MEDITERRANEAN FRANCE

Economic Activity

Mediterranean soil erodes easily in case of neglect or unusual climatic changes. The arid summer does not favor rapid growth of trees and forests. Without trees to hold the soil, the hard rains of autumn and winter quickly erode the land. To avoid erosion, the light scratch plough (*araire*) was developed. Since this plough could be pulled rather easily, cultivation did not require extensive cooperation among producers. Nor did it require extensive use of scarce livestock: two oxen sufficed, as opposed to a team of horses. The simple construction of the *araire* also allowed peasants of only moderate wealth to possess their own ploughs and to avoid the collective obligations found in the manorial areas of northeastern France.[99] Moreover, because the conical or triangular share of the *araire* could not turn over the soil, cross-ploughing was necessary, which meant that fields were usually square in shape. These square fields differed from western family farms for there was no habitation on the Mediterranean fields.

For the most part, cultivation was carried out in a two-field rotation since the climate did not allow for transitional farming seasons (autumn and spring) and the scant rainfalls of the Mediterranean in late spring or early summer did not suit the cultivation of fast-growing crops.[100]

The Mediterranean system of farming was more flexible than that of northeastern and western France. Soil conditions in the Mediterranean favored heterogeneous cropping—wheat in rich loams, beans in less fertile areas, and vines in marginal and rocky soils. Mediterranean farmers were thus able to concentrate on the production of a single, particularly profitable, crop.[101] As early as the twelfth century, much of the agricultural production of the Mediterranean was oriented either to local urban markets, far more numerous in this region than elsewhere in France, or to long-distance trade (principally in wheat, olive oil, and wine).[102]

The propitious location of Mediterranean France between the commercially vibrant Spanish Levantine coast and Italian city-states offered agriculturalists the incentive to produce for an active market. Thus, in contrast to subsistence farming in western France, arable cultivation in the Mediterranean was practiced in a commercial setting. Throughout the Middle Ages and the ancien régime, wheat was the principal marketable crop; wine and olives were secondary. After 1800, with an increasing demand for inexpensive wine, gamay replaced wheat as the principal agricultural product.[103] Commercialization left no variety of production untouched; even such items as madder, silk, and hemp were produced for export.[104] As a consequence, cash cropping and specialization became quite advanced in Mediterranean France.

Property Rights

Unlike the tenant of the Northeast or the sharecropper of the West, the typical Mediterranean peasant was the owner of a small holding.[105] Throughout the Middle Ages and ancien régime the custom in the Northeast and West was "nulle terre sans seigneur" (no land without a seigneur); but in the Mediterranean the custom was "chacun est maître dans sa propriété" (everyone is master of his property).[106]

Why the preponderance of peasant freeholds in the Midi from such an early period? As early as the eleventh century, the institutions derived from Roman law facilitated peasant ownership by explicitly permitting the transfer or selling of land. This allodial ownership of land gave the owner the right of private property and the license to do as he wished with his holding.[107] Peasant private property may also have benefited from the imperfect feudalization of the Mediterranean.[108] Freehold lordships were extensive, as were the nonfeudal institutions of the allod and the *bail à complainte*. In addition, regional seigneurial authority was weaker and peasant obligations less exacting than elsewhere.[109] The lower nobility itself favored the development of trade, taking a direct part in commercial activities and viewing feudal obligations less as ties of personal loyalty and more as commercial agreements, as spelled out by practices of Roman law.[110] Smith suggests that the light scratch plough, by obviating the need for collective obligations and restraints, assisted in the emancipation of the Midi peasant.[111] Emancipation derived also from the practice of transhumance—the seasonal movement of animal herds—since such freedom of movement made it difficult to establish a collective system to tie the peasant serf to the land. Homans claims that in areas of precocious market economy, the buying, selling, and exchanging of lands is more common.[112] Consequently, it was easier for peasants to purchase small holdings. Moreover, intensive cultivation of commercial crops enabled peasant families to survive on smaller holdings than in the West, where extensive polycultural production resulted in medium-sized holdings, considerably more difficult to afford.

Another important support of peasant private property was the strong village communalism of the Midi.[113] As early as the thirteenth century, many Mediterranean municipalities formed independent village governments (*assemblées générales des habitants*), abolishing most forms of personal and material subjection and thus restricting evictions by lords.[114] The importance of these village governments became apparent in the seigneurial reaction of the fifteenth and sixteenth centuries (second serfdom). As a result of the large number of deaths from the fourteenth-century plagues, lords throughout Europe offered concessions to peasants to retain their labor services.[115] By the fifteenth and sixteenth centuries, however, the population had again attained its pre-plague level; seigneurs attempted to revoke earlier concessions. In numerous regions of Europe, in Eastern Europe, for instance, and to a lesser extent in western France, the lords were successful;[116] but where cultivators had access to strong village communities and urban ties, the seigneurial reaction failed.

Though owner-cultivation was the prevalent form in the Mediterranean, other forms of land tenure existed as well. Tenancy and sharecropping were practiced in mountainous areas, in zones of poor soil such as the Vendée provençale, and in the vicinity of major urban areas, specifically where city dwellers tended to speculate in land.[117] Another form of land tenure, agricultural labor, increased dramatically in the Mediterranean after 1800. Since early times it had been the practice to call on seasonal migrants from Spain, Italy, and poorer regions of the Mediterranean South to aid in the difficult tasks of *moisson* (harvesting) and *battage* (threshing).[118] Many of these seasonal immigrants remained and became integrated into Mediterranean society.

The typical Mediterranean farm was small, usually less than five hectares.[119] Landholdings in the Mediterranean had been fragmented over the years by inheritance customs such as the allodial transfer of property and the practice of *préciput*,[120] which allowed land to be parceled out.[121] Subsistence on these small holdings was made possible by crops that could be cultivated intensively, such as grapes and vegetables, and by the great variety of soil types, which allowed for crop variation.[122] In some localities of the Mediterranean, small property coexisted with large property. This was frequently the case in wine-producing areas where agricultural labor appeared.[123]

Pattern of Settlement

The pattern of habitation in the Mediterranean, as opposed to that in the West, was thus one of numerous fair-sized villages whose population was highly agglomerated (*habitat groupé*).[124] Today, as since Roman times, most of the population involved in agriculture live in large villages, towns, or small cities (*villages urbanisés*). From Andalusia to Sicily, the *village urbanisé* is populated by farmers who leave their homes in the town every day to work the surrounding fields.[125] The principal forces behind the agglomerated pattern of settlement were the intensive cultivation of crops and the preponderance of small holdings.

The agglomerated settlements of the Mediterranean served other purposes as well. By reducing the distance between producer and consumer, for example, they allowed commercial cultivators to reduce the costs of marketing and obtaining goods. They also helped to offset the disadvantage of an irregular rainfall and to provide mutual defense in the face of foreign invasions.[126]

The strength of the rural-urban connection in the Mediterranean is largely a result of the region's market-oriented economic activity. Since the Middle Ages, to a much greater extent than elsewhere, towns have determined countryside activity.[127] The town was not only a marketplace where peasants sold their surplus; it was also an administrative capital with council and magistrates, a manufacturing center, and a religious center.

Class Composition

In the Northeast and West, the typical agricultural village bore little resemblance to the urban area.[128] This was not the case in the Mediterranean. As in the cities of the region, the social structure in the typical Mediterranean village consisted of nobles, bourgeois, merchants, artisans, workers, and peasants.[129] This social structure has been referred to as *village-ville*.[130] The heterogeneous nature of the *village-ville* stemmed from its economic diversity and from its system of property rights that enabled members of all classes to own land.

Distinctions between classes in the Mediterranean have always been blurred, in large part because of the high degree of commercialization. The urban lower nobility, favorably disposed toward the development of trade, took a direct part in the commercial activities.[131] These lords were often townsmen, either nobles who had come to live in the city or bourgeois who had bought titles. An essential element of the Mediterranean social structure was the fusion of noble and bourgeois: nobles became bourgeois through business, and bourgeois became ennobled by law.[132] Before 1789, nobles and bourgeois resided in the same quarters of the village or city, shared municipal power, intermarried, and enjoyed similar leisure activities.[133] These fluid conditions were not conducive to the establishment of rigid class structures. Even distinctions between peasants and townsmen were difficult to draw, since the local markets brought the peasants into contact with urban life. In fact, some townsmen owned and cultivated small plots, whereas some peasants worked as artisans during the winter months.[134]

The typical Mediterranean village also contained a sizable stratum situated between the landlord and cultivating classes (small merchants, functionaries, professionals, and artisans). This middle stratum, or *petits notables*, tended to reside in their native villages, where they pursued careers in law, education, business, and public administration.[135] The importance of a rural structure with classes between the elites and the peasants is that these better educated and often better organized groups were able to disseminate information. It is particularly signifi-

cant that the republican movement of the 1830s and 1840s consisted almost entirely of members of these in-between classes.[136]

The presence of the *petits notables* was made even more significant by the relative absence of noble and bourgeois landholders. As far back as the Middle Ages, noble landholdings
were less extensive in Mediterranean rural areas than elsewhere in France.[137] Furthermore, landlord absenteeism was
common in the Mediterranean, where social elites chose to reside in the principal regional centers, such as Marseille, Toulon,
Avignon, Aix, Montpellier, and Toulouse, rather than on their
country estates.[138] In writing about the French Revolution in
the department of Hérault, Soboul spoke of "une faiblesse relative de la propriété privilégiée."[139] The "gentleman farmer," residing in the countryside and working or supervising his estate,
was an anomaly in the Mediterranean.[140] Instead, supervision
of the estate was often almost entirely in the hands of managers
(*régisseurs* or *maîtres-valets*).[141] Table 2, based on an 1855 agricultural survey, shows how much more prevalent *régisseurs* and
maîtres-valets were in the Mediterranean than in the West or
Northeast.

Absentee landlordism has affected the social structure of
cities of the Mediterranean. Nowhere else in France does one
find such a large class of elite *rentiers*, individuals living on their
agricultural revenues.[142] The population of Aix-en-Provence
during the eighteenth century, for example, contained 3 percent bourgeois landowners, 5 to 10 percent noble landowners,
and 5 percent church landowners.[143] Similarly, in nineteenth-
century Lower Languedoc, most landowners lived in three cities,
Montpellier, Béziers, and Nîmes,[144] just as in nineteenth-century
Vaucluse, most landowners lived in Avignon, Carpentras, and
Orange.[145]

Like the Mediterranean nobles and bourgeois landlords,
the Mediterranean clergy resided in the cities and not in the
countryside.[146] Indeed, church property was less extensive in
the Mediterranean than elsewhere.[147] Since the fifteenth century, the church in Mediterranean France had been hindered
in accumulating property by the *taille réelle* (land tax), in contrast to the *taille personnelle* (personal tax) of the Northeast and

Table 2. Landlord Absenteeism in 1855

Western Departments	Resident Managers	Total Cultivators	Ratio
Calvados	77	62830	.00122
Côtes-du-Nord	7	91982	.00008
Finistère	20	90754	.00022
Ille-et-Vilaine	17	101579	.00017
Loire-Inférieure	26	80576	.00032
Maine-et-Loire	80	69431	.00115
Manche	88	110302	.00080
Mayenne	85	35509	.00239
Morbihan	5	86410	.00006
Orne	84	57746	.00145
Sarthe	91	60983	.00149
Deux-Sèvres	41	51368	.00080
Vendée	129	63421	.00203
Mean	57	74069	.00094

Mediterranean Departments	Resident Managers	Total Cultivators	Ratio
Basses-Alpes	50	34961	.00143
Ariège	1408	58594	.02403
Aude	1827	47793	.03823
Bouches-du-Rhône	999	68992	.01448
Gard	975	71369	.01366
Haute-Garonne	7219	88552	.08152
Hérault	1094	53986	.02026
Pyrénées-Orientales	214	36471	.00587
Tarn	1257	57893	.02171
Var	532	76931	.00692
Vaucluse	140	60529	.00231
Mean	1429	59642	.02095

Table 2 (*continued*)

Northeastern Departments	Resident Managers	Total Cultivators	Ratio
Pas-de-Calais	47	174639	.00027
Somme	48	132010	.00036
Nord	48	153038	.00031
Seine-Inférieure	15	82646	.00018
Eure	28	82977	.00034
Seine-et-Oise	18	118899	.00015
Aisne	46	105577	.00044
Seine-et-Marne	96	89461	.00107
Ardennes	31	70381	.00044
Marne	60	99782	.00060
Aube	86	67053	.00128
Meuse	21	87627	.00024
Meurthe	47	83717	.00056
Moselle	59	103845	.00057
Bas-Rhin	52	148186	.00035
Haut-Rhin	39	94841	.00041
Vosges	47	95383	.00049
Haute-Marne	77	70860	.00109
Côte-d'Or	92	79165	.00116
Haute-Saône	60	84274	.00071
Doubs	38	60702	.00063
Yonne	106	88201	.00120
Saône-et-Loire	191	130844	.00145
Jura	42	83247	.00050
Seine	0	22783	.00000
Mean	56	96406	.00058

Source: *Statistique de la France,* deuxième série, Statistique agricole (Paris: Imprimerie impériale, 1860), pp. 380–93 in 1st part and 317–29 in 2d part.

West, which pressed less heavily on the clergy.[148] Not surprisingly, the sale of the *biens nationaux* (the partition of former church lands during the French Revolution) had little effect on the Midi, since there was so little to sell.

In sum, as a consequence of a market-oriented economic activity, intensively cultivated small holdings, an agglomerated population, considerable town-countryside association, and a heterogeneous class structure, intraclass interaction was intense in the Mediterranean. This intensity has been commonly referred to as *sociabilité méridionale* or *sociabilité populaire*—the propensity in Mediterranean society for political, economic, and personal business to be conducted in common, in public.[149] Thus the peasants in the Mediterranean returned nightly to the thriving community in which they resided, joining other classes of society. Popular assemblies, open to members of all classes, occurred from time to time in Mediterranean villages. During winter afternoons members of all classes assembled for pleasure in the café, which came to be referred to as a *chambrée populaire*, a place where friends could congregate and pass their time together.[150]

It was through these *chambrées populaires*, or cafés, that the republican and radical ideologies of the nineteenth century traveled from artisans and petits bourgeois to peasants.[151] This way of disseminating ideas was effective not only because of the low level of literacy among the peasants but also because many artisans, peasants, and petits bourgeois shared a distrust of interference by the rich bourgeois, the noble landlords, and the clergy in local affairs. Even so, the social elites were also able to use the cafés to their advantage at times, especially in the large urban areas. For example, the nobility of Nîmes were quite successful in mobilizing worker discontent in the 1830s through these same *chambrées populaires*.[152]

Largely because of the distinctive mode of production in the countryside, Mediterranean municipalities have sustained a vigorous democracy.[153] In the Mediterranean, communal cooperation fostered strong independent village communities. The practices of transhumance, *vaine pâture*, and *droit d'arrosage* produced peasant cooperation.[154] Coordination and supervision of commercial transactions engendered municipal cooperation.[155]

The relative weakness of feudal constraints in Mediterranean France permitted cultivators and other nonelite groups considerable freedom in supervising their affairs; thus there was less resistance from social elites to the formation of independent village governments.[156]

Since the thirteenth century, Mediterranean villages and municipalities have had independent town governments (*assemblées générales des habitants*).[157] Within these independent town governments, peasants and members of the middle classes enjoyed personal freedoms and political power unknown in other parts of France.[158]

After 1650, the communes of the Mediterranean gained nearly total control over their internal affairs. They selected their own administrators and police, devised their own municipal legislation, ran their own hospitals, and, most significant, administered their own schools.[159] Indeed, it was the municipal authority (*communauté d'habitants*) and not the church (*paroisse*) that acted as the official cadre representing the village in meetings with the French *intendants*. Elsewhere in France the religious and municipal authorities ruled jointly.

The dominance of the municipality over the church extended to other spheres of village life. In contrast to the West and Northeast, for example, the major feasts, or *fêtes de la commune*, were municipal rather than church-sponsored feasts. Because the church retained considerable influence over education and commanded considerable power through its offices and charities, conflicts between the municipal authority and church were commonplace. Yet the church was a less significant factor in community affairs in the Mediterranean than it was in the West.

Overall, nowhere else in France did the municipal authority enjoy such prestige and independence as in the Mediterranean during the ancien régime.[160] Nor did the revolutionary upheavals of 1789–1793 significantly alter the composition of the political councils of Languedoc, for these councils already included a fair representation of the social forces in the region.[161] This particular trait of rural democracy persisted into the nineteenth century. In Vaucluse, for example, although aristocrats and wealthy bourgeois possessed a monopoly of power in the large cities and in some small rural cantons, the general rule was that members of the liberal professions held positions of power.[162] Moreover, of the eligible electors of the district of Apt in Vaucluse in 1848, a disproportionate number of electors were small-scale owner-cultivators and members of the liberal professions.[163]

Mediterranean France also has its fair share of rural deviant cases such as the Vendée provençale and the Camargue (Bouches-du-Rhône), the Comtat (Vaucluse), the Garrigues (Hérault), and the mountainous zones of Ariège and the Basses-Alpes. Consider the Garrigues zone within the eastern half of the department of Hérault and the Camargue of Bouches-du-Rhône: the poor soil of this area does not easily promote a commercialized agriculture; therefore, a subsistence polyculture is generally practiced. The chief economic pursuits combine the raising of livestock with the cultivation of forest products, cereals, olives, and wine.[164] Landholdings consist of either very small domains (less than one hectare) or large domains (greater than fifty hectares). In contrast to the compact villages found elsewhere in the Mediterranean Midi, the Camargue and Garrigues have substantially dispersed populations and a preponderance of small hamlets.[165] Moreover, in these rural deviant cases of the Mediterranean, bourgeois and noble elites, along with the clergy, have succeeded in establishing control over vital resources. The Garrigues illustrates this point well. The émigré nobles returned in large numbers to eastern Hérault during the First Empire and Restoration.[166] Nowhere else in Hérault was there such a large concentration of property in the hands of nobles.[167] Through their control over resources, the nobles gained political power. Although noble mayors were few in western Hérault, where noble landholdings were minimal, they were omnipresent in eastern Hérault, where noble landholdings were great.[168] Nobles and the rich bourgeois were not the only conservative social elites residing in large numbers in eastern Hérault; the clergy was also well represented.[169] Thus, in many important respects the mode of production of these parts of eastern Hérault and southeastern Bouches-du-Rhône resembled the western mode of production.

That there are deviant cases within each region should allow for a better test of the mode-of-production model. I predict that those western and northeastern areas whose modes of production resemble that of the Mediterranean should vote more like typical Mediterranean cases whereas those Mediterranean and northeastern areas whose modes of production resemble that of the West should vote more like typical western cases. In this fashion, I hope that the exceptions will prove the rule.

Thus on the eve of the creation of a French national market, Mediterranean France was typified largely by market-oriented agriculture, small-scale owner cultivation or salaried agricultural labor, population agglomeration, intense town-countryside ties, rural class heterogeneity, and social elite absenteeism.[170]

The emergence of a national market would dramatically affect the shape of the three principal French modes of production after 1865. Yet its impact would vary regionally: in the Northeast, the national market would markedly transform the mode of production whereas in the West and in the Mediterranean, it would significantly strengthen the existing modes of production. These changes would have a major effect on each region's constellation of interests. In the next chapter, I shall describe the effects of the national market on the three modes of production and the evolution of each mode of production since 1865.

4

MODES OF PRODUCTION
SINCE 1865

The completion of a national railway system and the subsequent emergence of a national market had a marked and dramatically different impact on modes of production in the three regions. After 1865 the Northeast became industrialized, its agriculture increasingly specialized and mechanized. The West and the Mediterranean remained predominantly agricultural, the Mediterranean increasing its dependence on wine and the West continuing its dependence on subsistence polyculture. In both industry and agriculture, therefore, the West and Mediterranean fell behind the Northeast.

THE INDUSTRIALIZATION OF NORTHEASTERN
FRANCE

During the reign of Louis-Napoléon Bonaparte, former Saint-Simonians such as the Pereire brothers, with aid from the Rothschilds, pressured for the construction of a Paris-Lyon-Marseille railroad line to open up northern markets for southern wine and provide an outlet for northern industrial products.[1] By 1865 Northeastern agriculture and manufacturing, being more efficient, had begun to destroy rural industry and inefficient agriculture while the railroad began to penetrate western and Mediterranean markets.[2] Thus, whereas industrialization in the West and Mediterranean stagnated or retrogressed after 1865, it moved steadily ahead in the Northeast, as is apparent in the results of my examination of French cantons drawn from nineteenth-century population censuses (see Tables 3–5).

The discovery of coal and iron ore fields in the Northeast

after 1845 led to further advantages. These fields, made accessible to major industrial areas by railroad and by efficient and inexpensive new smelting devices, could be exploited more profitably with comparatively low production costs.[3] From 1847 to 1869 the Northeast's contribution to total iron output in France rose from 10.6 percent to 30.5 percent, and by the beginning of the twentieth century Northeastern coal production amounted to 28 million tons, 67 percent of total French production.[4]

The history of banking paralleled the movement toward concentration and centralization.[5] The trend began during the reign of Louis-Napoléon when the Banque de France campaigned for monopoly of the issue of notes and the Crédit Lyonnais shifted from Lyon to Paris, a city that already held the major banking institutions. The Parisian banks also gained nationwide control over the circulation of capital through such practices as offering lower interest rates or more flexible terms to a wider clientele. The result was the bankruptcy of small-scale provincial bankers.[6]

In the twentieth century, the economic dominance of the Northeast was further reinforced since it could fill the demands of industry for larger plants, more capital-intensive production, and more highly skilled labor and industry's increasing need for external economies and the greater purchasing power of urban industrial centers.[7] By the 1950s the Northeast, including less than half the area of France, accounted for more than 67 percent of total French production. The average income per active member of the labor force varied from 160 percent of the French average in Paris and the Northeast to less than half that level in Brittany and the far Southwest.[8] In my examination of 1975 French per capita income for the fourteen departments of western France, the eleven departments of Mediterranean France, and the twenty-six departments of the Northeast, I found that per capita incomes were 11,402 francs, 12,566 francs, and 16,347 francs respectively.[9]

A town-country explanation of this economic discrepancy is refuted in a study of regional imbalance by the Economic Commission of Europe. Marseille, Toulouse, Nantes, and St. Etienne, located west and south of the line that divides "dynamic" France from "static" France, have a gross industrial product per capita

Table 3. Population in Industry, by Canton

Northeastern France	1856–1861 (%)	1881–1886 (%)
Bassée	28	32
Haubourdin	43	35
Cysoing	36	45
Armentières	53	64
Tourcoing Nord	78	74
Roubaix	30	72
Séclin	41	46
Pont-à-Marcq	26	25
Haroué	23	22
Nancy Est	24	47
Nancy Nord	25	48
Nancy Ouest	24	40
Nomeny	20	17
Pont-à-Mousson	23	34
Saint-Nicolas	22	36
Vézelise	17	16
Auxonne	17	23
Fontaine-Française	19	25
Grancey-le-Château	18	30
Selongey	16	29
Arcis-sur-Aube	34	40
Chanvagnes	24	20
Ramerupt	29	25
Méry-sur-Seine	42	44
Mean	30	37

Sources: Nord (A.D. 473M 24, 37); Meurthe-et-Moselle (A.D. 6M 16, 23); Côte-d'Or (A.D. 10M 31–700); Aube (A.D. M 1809, 1901).

of only 85 percent (compared to the French average of 100 percent), contrasted with 160 percent for Paris and the Northeast.[10]

Despite the purported goal of post–World War II regional planning to reduce regional economic inequalities, comparison suggests no systematic relation in the departments between the per capita allocation of public investment and the level of economic development.[11] Government efforts to decentralize, such as its aid to depressed regions in 1955, the Fifth Republic's decentralization legislation, and the establishment of the *Délégation à l'Aménagement du Territoire et à l'Action Régionale* (D.A.T.A.R.), to create employment opportunities outside of the Northeast, have done little to close the gap between the Northeast and the other provinces.[12] Even now, as French regional planning becomes increasingly influenced by the European Economic Community (E.E.C.), it is likely that the Northeast's proximity to other E.E.C. countries will favor its economic growth over that of western and Mediterranean France.[13]

THE DEINDUSTRIALIZATION OF WESTERN FRANCE

The West was hardly touched by the revolutionary changes in economic organization occurring in the Northeast. In fact, western industry and commerce suffered in the nineteenth century, principally as a result of the industrial revolution.

The French Revolution and the ensuing Napoleonic wars crippled western French commerce. The maritime industry, the lifeline of western France's commerce, never reexperienced the "golden era" of the eighteenth century, when the ports of Lorient, Nantes, Brest, and St. Malo profited from colonial trade, when Breton littoral cities accounted for 36 percent of the total French production of ships (between 1762 and 1785),[14] and when Breton ships carried 50 percent of the French slave trade between Africa and the New World.[15] This boom ended with the French Revolution and the First Empire. Incessant warfare stopped the French slave trade, decreased the number of French colonies, and, consequently, ended western French maritime commerce, cutting Brittany's lifeline to the outside.[16] Breton fleets could no longer profit, as they had throughout the Middle Ages and ancien régime, from bustling trade with

Spain and Great Britain.[17] The region could not renovate its maritime trade.

Throughout the ancien régime and the early part of the nineteenth century, the rural textile industry of western France had few rivals. It flourished chiefly from the production of the fine linen of Loudéac, Uzel, Vitré, and Guérande for the internal French market and from the production of ship sails for both French and foreign commercial naval fleets.[18] This vital industry, however, was virtually destroyed in the nineteenth century. The mass production of inexpensive cotton reduced the demand for the more expensive linen (*textile de luxe*). The mechanization of the cloth industry gave the larger-scale textile producers of the Northeast a comparative advantage. The revolutionary and Napoleonic wars caused many profitable markets to close. And steam, introduced as an energy source, cut down the number of sailing ships.[19]

The maritime and textile industries showed the most significant decline, but other industries in the region followed a similar path after 1851.[20] Morlaix, a major producer of linen, flour, paper, and cotton; Loctudy, a specialist in starch; Haut-Léon, expert in tanning, hemp, and flax production; Châteaulin, an exporter of slate; and Huelgoat, renowned for its mining of lead and silver—all lost markets to the more modern and larger-scale producers in the Northeast, as well as to producers outside of France.[21]

Without an adequate regional transport system, western products could not reach urban markets.[22] Moreover, in contrast to the Northeast, the West was not blessed with major energy resources, a diversified labor pool, or a central location in relation to major cities in France and other European nations. Many of the external economies demanded by industry were therefore not available to western France.[23]

In effect, the region experienced a rural deindustrialization between 1851 and 1936. Once thriving industrial towns of the interior were transformed almost overnight into a manufacturing wasteland (Table 4).[24] The relative absence of urbanization reflected this low level of industrialization in the West. According to the 1931 census, the mean urban population of France

Table 4. Population in Industry, by Canton

Western France	1851 (%)	1886 (%)
Briec	20	14
Concarneau	33	13
Douarnenez	45	13
Fouesnant	19	9
Landivisiau	34	19
Lanmeur	30	15
Morlaix	75	33
Plouescat	11	6
Plouigneau	21	10
Plogastel-Saint-Germain	20	9
Plouzévédé	20	2
Pont-l'Abbé	36	15
Pont-Croix	18	18
Quimper	29	18
Rosporden	21	5
Sizun	10	10
Saint-Pol-de-Léon	32	10
Saint-Thégonnec	13	10
Taulé	34	10
Bierné	11	8
Cossé	17	10
Craon	14	11
Grez	16	13
Saint-Aignans	8	14
Mirebeau	10	3
Vouillé	7	5
Lusignan	10	5
Muzillac	7	5
Baud	8	8
Questembert	5	8
Saint-Jean-Brévelay	6	2

Table 4 (*continued*)

Western France	1851 (%)	1886 (%)
Rohan	5	3
Mauron	8	4
Huelgoat	9	7
Pleyben	10	15
Châteaulin	20	10
Châteauneuf	9	12
Mean	19	11

Sources: Finistère (A.D. 6M 37–41); Mayenne (A.D. 6M 34, 43); Vienne (A.D. 8M 29, 19); Morbihan (A.D. 6M 10, 22–23).

was 512 out of 1000 compared to a mean of 243 out of 1000 for the province of Brittany.[25]

There has been only one industry—tourism—in which the West has indisputably rivaled all other regions save the Mediterranean. The western littoral after 1851 became a mecca for the well-to-do, who came for the reputed medicinal values of its sea baths. Such French luminaries as Balzac, Michelet, and Hugo spent their summers in the West.

Since World War II, however, western France has become less uniformly underindustrialized and in certain respects has gained in relation to the Mediterranean seaboard. But the recent industrial surge of the West should not be overstated and should be analyzed against the backdrop of the region's former industrial backwardness.[26]

THE INDUSTRIAL STAGNATION
OF MEDITERRANEAN FRANCE

Like the West, the Mediterranean had benefited from foreign commerce before the revolutionary and Napoleonic wars.[27] Since 1050 the region's numerous ports, especially Marseille, Toulon, Sète, and Narbonne, had been among the most active in Europe in exporting raw materials, locally produced goods, and agricultural products destined for the markets of northern and southern Europe. Eventually importing also became a major regional activity: cloth from England and Normandy, linen from Holland and Champagne, silks from Germany, and spices, sugar, cotton, and drugs from the Levant.[28] The eighteenth century marked a high point for the region's commerce, as trade with the colonies stimulated the growth of local industries such as textiles, mining, metallurgy, silk, madder, chemicals, and pharmaceuticals.[29]

Although certainly affected by the closure of foreign markets, Mediterranean commerce and industry continued to expand during the first half of the nineteenth century. Lower Languedoc in particular remained a zone of flourishing local industry.[30] In the town of Nîmes, for example, almost half of the active population was involved in industry, and over a third of the total population (16,600 out of 47,215) held positions in the textile industry.[31]

Despite such success, Mediterranean industry was marked by archaic techniques and small-scale operations. During the seventeenth century, for example, iron workers were frequently paid in kind rather than in wages, and as late as 1861 fewer than one-fourth of the machines in operation in Lower Languedoc used steam power. An inadequate transport system further hindered the competitive position of the region's industry, as the center of European commerce moved from south to north after 1851.[32] The region's bourgeois were interested more in land speculation than in reinvestment for new technologies and equipment; their profit went toward wheat and wine. Many bourgeois abandoned careers in industry for *rentier* status.[33] In Montpellier, vintners, doctors, and *rentiers* replaced manufacturers and merchants as the city's notables.[34] Paradoxically, Mediterranean manufacturers made things worse by frequently supporting free-trade policies that benefited them as investors in wine but impeded the growth of their industries.[35]

The technological changes of the nineteenth century undermined Mediterranean French industry. The silk and woolen industries are especially indicative examples. Whereas in 1840 in the department of Gard there were 246 shops employing 17,400 workers, by 1896 there were only 121 shops and 10,850 workers.[36] Similarly, in the department of Hérault there were 9,637 textile workers in 1860, 6,000 textile workers in 1882, and 1,640 workers in 1906.[37] Gard and Hérault were not unusual. In neighboring Vaucluse, the city of Avignon was one of the major regional centers of silk fabrication before 1848. At the height of its activity in the July Monarchy, 10,845 individuals from a population of 30,000 either worked in or lived from the silk industry. During the July Monarchy (1830 to 1848), average yearly silk sales were approximately 10 million francs; by 1848 the amount fell to 2 million francs.[38]

The dramatic decline in textiles came about primarily because the Mediterranean's silk and woolen industries, still organized according to the putting-out system, could not compete with industries where production was more concentrated.[39] With the opening of the Suez Canal and the completion of the Paris-Lyon-Marseille line, the less expensive Japanese *soie grège* and Northeastern synthetics easily penetrated and eventually inundated the regional market. Mediterranean producers were simply not capable of lowering their prices to become competitive.[40] Similarly, the Chevalier-Cobden free-trade treaty with England in 1860 opened the Mediterranean market to less expensive English textiles.[41] The silk industry was further undermined by an infestation of the insect *la pébrine,* which destroyed a considerable portion of the *ver à soie* (silkworm).[42]

The fate that befell the textile industry was shared by other Mediterranean industries in this period (Table 5). The industrial and commercial eclipse of the French Mediterranean is perhaps best reflected in the fate of the region's primary port, Marseille. Throughout the ancien régime and nineteenth century, it was not only the busiest port in France but the number one port in Europe for maritime traffic as well.[43] Between 1870 and 1913, however, the opening of the Suez Canal, the introduction of the steamship, the economic growth of northeastern France, and the economic decline of Mediterranean France pushed Rotterdam, Hamburg, and Anvers ahead of Marseille. Even within France, Marseille's proportion of maritime traffic fell precipitously.[44]

As a result of the creation of a national market in France, northeastern French industry, which possessed initial advan-

Table 5. Population in Industry, by Canton

Mediterranean France	1851 (%)	1886 (%)
Adge	12	30
Aniane	11	17
Apt	23	20
Avignon	43	40
Beaumes-de-Venise	11	9
Bédarrides	20	33
Béziers	15	10
Bollène	12	16
Bonnieux	8	13
Cadenet	17	21
Carpentras	26	21
Castries	11	17
Cavaillon	17	25
Claret	6	8
Clermont-l'Hérault	22	23
Frontignan	8	16
Ganges	29	46
Gordes	18	13
Isle-sur-la-Sorgue	19	27
Lunas	7	18
Lunel	19	8
Malaucène	21	15
Matelles	6	8
Mauguio	8	1
Mèze	22	21
Montpellier	17	22
Mormoiron	11	19
Olargues	14	19
Orange	19	15
Pernes-les-Fontaines	11	12
Pertuis	20	17
Pézenas	20	19

Table 5 (*continued*)

Mediterranean France	1851 (%)	1886 (%)
Sault	14	18
Saint-Chinian	14	9
Saint-Gervais-sur-Mare	15	22
Saint-Martin-de-Londres	14	7
Vaison-la-Romaine	9	11
Valréas	21	25
Alzonne	23	15
Capendu	17	9
Aramon	17	9
Saint-Gilles	11	4
Saint-Mamert	7	2
Marguerittes	10	11
Lédignan	6	9
Vézénobres	6	3
Saint-Chaptes	6	4
Lussan	7	2
Alzon	11	3
Saint-André	12	1
Quissac	8	5
Sauve	16	20
Trève	7	2
Mean	15	15

Sources: Hérault (A.D. 114M 3, 18–21); Vaucluse (A.D. 6M 20, 31); Aude (A.D. 11M 15, 29–35); Gard (A.D. 6M 111, 123–26).

tages over its western and Mediterranean French counterparts, underwent a considerable expansion. In contrast, western and Mediterranean French industries declined after 1865, and these two regions continue to be relatively underindustrialized.

State policy also had a hand in pushing the West and Mediterranean to the periphery. The French Revolution did not decentralize state control, as many had hoped; rather, it increased

state power. This power served the interests of the Northeast.
When northeastern industrial centers favored higher tariffs,
the government instituted higher tariffs; when northeastern industry and agriculture demanded free trade, the government
implemented lower tariffs.[45] During the July Monarchy, for example, major Northeastern industrial groups in such cities as
Lille, Elbeuf, Roubaix, Tourcoing, and Rouen advocated higher
tariffs. The government responded by setting up tariff walls behind which these industrial groups prospered.[46] Yet when the
grain merchants of Toulouse requested that the government
impose higher tariffs on foreign grain during the Second Republic, the government instead lowered import duties on foreign grain, leading to the inundation by Russian and U.S. grain
and consequently to heavy losses for the merchants of Toulouse.[47] Such discriminatory fiscal policy continued throughout
the nineteenth and into the twentieth century, as witnessed by
the government's support for northeastern livestock and sugarbeet interests over Mediterranean wine production during the
decade preceding the 1907 "révolte du Midi."

AGRICULTURE AND THE CREATION OF A NATIONAL MARKET

The fate of agriculture was similarly uneven. By the nineteenth
century northeastern agriculture had moved from sharecropping to commercial tenancy.[48] In the course of this century,
Flanders, Picardy, Artois, Normandy, Ile-de-France, and Pays
de Beauce, areas that had been the main granary for Paris for
centuries, continued to develop a more commercial system of
agriculture, and to replace inefficient smallholdings that had
proliferated before 1865 with larger mechanized farms specializing in wheat cultivation.[49]

For the most part, the technological revolution in agriculture
had little effect on the Mediterranean and Western regions. In
the Mediterranean region, the commercial market and the two-
field system of agriculture had geared agriculture toward specialization and profit. Thus, cycles of expanding and contract-
ing production continued to characterize the agriculture in the
Mediterranean.[50] Agricultural techniques in the West were ar-

chaic, and production remained oriented toward subsistence.
Neither the technological innovations of the open-field system
in the Northeast nor the stimulus of commercial production
in the Mediterranean had parallels in the isolated regions of
the West.[51]

Thus agricultural productivity in the Northeast widened its
advantage over productivity in the West and Mediterranean.[52]
By 1900, even though the Northeast had turned to manufacturing, its agriculture still maintained a substantial lead. The
average French wheat yield in 1900 was 16.7 hectoliters per
hectare, but in the department of the Nord it reached 27 per
hectare.[53] The department of the Nord was not exceptional: between 1912 and 1914 wheat yields in Brie-Beauce were 23.5
hectoliters per hectare; in the area between the department of
Oise (Picardy) and the Belgian border, yields averaged a robust
25.9 hectoliters; at the same time in Brittany and Poitou, yields
averaged 17.4 and 15.3 hectoliters per hectare respectively.[54]
Other measures of agricultural productivity support the same
conclusion. In 1912, the gross product per hectare was 715
francs in the Northeast, 582 francs in the Mediterranean, and
513 francs in the West.[55]

One significant factor in the Northeast's superiority was its
lead in mechanizing agricultural production. Northeastern cultivators introduced the reaper, the harvester, and the tractor.[56]
Throughout the nineteenth and early twentieth centuries, cultivators in the West and Mediterranean grudgingly adopted
these improvements.[57] The prices of these machines prohibited
all but the large cultivators from acquiring them, and Mediterranean and western farms were considerably smaller than
northeastern farms.

Like industry, agriculture in the Northeast benefited substantially from a superior transport network (canals and especially
the railway) and the proximity of large urban areas, factors
largely responsible for the region's reorientation of its agriculture during the European recession of the 1870s and 1880s.
As the prices of wheat, wine, oil-seed, and textile plants plum-
meted after 1870, most French agriculturalists found their livelihood in jeopardy. But during this general recession, the prices
of two commodities, milk and meat, climbed steadily. Noticing

the burgeoning demand, northeastern cultivators turned their energies to the intensive raising of livestock. The Northeast's superior transport network and extensive urban markets enticed farmers to take advantage of new preservative technology, pasteurization, and the refrigerator car.[58] Although farmers in the Mediterranean region theoretically could also sell to large cities, they were hindered by a poor internal transport network. Furthermore, the climate and ecology of the Mediterranean were not conducive to the cultivation of the fallow plants necessary for the intensive raising of livestock. For their part, western farmers had plentiful grasslands but few major urban areas. And so economic fragility and backwardness immobilized the cultivators of the Mediterranean and the West.

In brief, economic development in France remained concentrated in areas where it had begun before 1865. The Northeast possessed an advantage over the West and the Mediterranean even before the completion of a national railway system. Since 1865 the Northeast has enlarged the gap, benefiting from the trend in industry and agriculture toward greater economies of scale and declining transport costs. The West and the Mediterranean, in contrast, have experienced economic stagnation, especially from 1851 to 1936.

THE NATIONAL MARKET AND
MODES OF PRODUCTION

The Northeastern Mode of Production since 1865

Of the three regions, the Northeast after 1865 has been the least dependent upon agriculture and the most industrialized. Agriculture nevertheless continues to occupy segments of the population in parts of Normandy, Champagne, Burgundy, and Lorraine, where economic activity has turned increasingly toward monoculture. Although agricultural specialization was well under way before 1800, the creation of a national market after 1865 allowed northeastern cultivators to emphasize those crops for which they held an advantage. As a consequence, northeastern farmers turned progressively to wheat—especially in the East—to bovine and industrial crops, and sugarbeets (*betterave à sucre*)—particularly in Flanders, Picardy, Ile-de-France, and Upper Normandy.[59] By the end of the nineteenth century, for example, five northeastern departments accounted for four-fifths of France's sugarbeet production.[60] What was extraordinary about this region's economic activity beyond its high productivity was its success in reorienting agricultural emphasis as the market dictated.

Furthermore, the post-1865 economic transformation of France significantly altered property rights in northeastern France. It increased the size of landholdings. Large holdings, some exceeding one hundred hectares, became dominant in the Ile-de-France and in parts of Normandy;[61] medium-scale farms, between ten and fifty hectares, emerged in Picardy, Artois, and Alsace. Small farms continued to proliferate in Flanders, however.[62] The reason for this wide variation in the size of farms in the Northeast lies largely in the different methods of cultivation: where extensive cultivation of wheat occurs, large farms predominate; where we find intensive cultivation of industrial crops, small farms predominate.

Although the transformation in the size of farms in the Northeast is striking, what happened to the region's agricultural laborers is far more significant. Between 1865 and 1950 agricultural laborers virtually disappeared from the northeastern countryside.[63] Not only did the mechanization of agriculture reduce the need for them, but the elimination of communal pasturing undercut the subsistence of many laborers. The higher salaries available in urban industry provided further incentive for laborers to leave agriculture.[64] By 1862, the rural exodus was already apparent. The proportion of agricultural laborers for 100 hectares in 1862 was 8.9 percent for the Northeast and 28.5 percent for Brittany. Moreover, between 1862 and 1882 the proportion of agricultural labor declined 32 percent for the Northeast.[65] No other region matched this rapid reduction in the agricultural labor force.[66]

There were changes as well in patterns of settlement and class composition in the Northeast after 1865. Rural population pressure, which had led to a great division of land and population concentration during the eighteenth and early nineteenth centuries, had declined substantially by 1900. The decrease in density of the rural population, however, did not herald the collapse of the settlement pattern of nucleated villages, for cultivators kept the open fields free of construction. More important, perhaps, was the displacement of substantial numbers of agricultural laborers from the countryside that hastened the movement toward greater population homogeneity. The typical northeastern village became the residence of prosperous medium-scale farmers, although large-scale farmers in the Ile-de-France and small owner-occupiers in sections of Flanders and Alsace remained on their farms.

The Western Mode of Production since 1865

In the West, in contrast, the creation of a national market reinforced the key components of the region's mode of production: as industry and commerce declined, the rural population became more dependent on the traditional pursuit of agriculture. Land became more abundant as sizable proportions of the rural population emigrated,[67] as new techniques eliminated fallow, and as wastelands were brought under cultivation.[68] The depressed condition of wheat cultivation spurred a movement toward raising livestock, which required relatively little work and therefore no day laborers and a minimal investment in machinery and food, since cattle could survive on grass.[69] For example, Demangeon notes that in western France between 1911 and 1936 the proportion of cultivated surface devoted to grains dropped from 41.2 percent to 30.2 percent while the proportion of land employed for raising livestock climbed from 45.8 percent to 56.3 percent.[70] In general, however, the precariousness of western agriculture led cultivators to polyculture, for it alone could meet their needs for subsistence.[71]

Increasingly during the nineteenth century, tenancy replaced other forms of land tenure. In the *bocage* area of the Pays de la Loire between 1800 and 1851, tenancy displaced sharecropping as the elimination of the fallow, the use of *plantes fourragères*, and the implementation of the *fours à choix* enabled farmers with twenty to fifty hectares to buy into tenancy.[72] In Brittany the number of day laborers declined nearly 20 percent as their small plots were absorbed into medium-sized farms.[73] Large farms underwent a similar transformation in the opposite direction: medium-sized family farms progressively replaced the largest holdings. The medium-sized farm was less sensitive to changes in the market and technology; the family itself could supply the labor needed.[74] But sharecropping did not disappear totally from the western landscape. As late as 1900, 15 to 33 percent of the total cultivated surface in the western departments of Mayenne and Vendée remained in sharecropping.[75]

The deindustrialization of the western countryside and the strengthening of subsistence polyculture further reduced the contact between town and countryside and lowered the population density. In addition, the practice of demarcating property by *bocage* spread in the post-1865 period, in response to the consolidation of small parcels by medium-scale property holders.[76] The characteristic isolation of the region was thus doubly reinforced.

Deindustrialization also caused artisans and other members of the middle class to leave the countryside. The relative absence of social classes aside from elites and peasantry augmented the power of the noble landlords, who already held considerable authority, especially after 1830 when they returned home from national political office in Paris. Indeed, during the late nineteenth and early twentieth centuries, the nobles lost little of their authority over local and regional government. In 1870, from the five departments of Brittany, 72 of the 136 *conseillers généraux* were noble.[77] In 1885, 23 of the 45 deputies elected from Brittany to the National Assembly were noble.[78] In 1909, 216 of 1500 Breton mayors were noble.[79] In 1956, 15 of the 46 *conseillers généraux* from the department of Loire-Inférieure were noble.[80] And finally, no other region in present-day France matches the West in the proportion of mayors who are noble.[81] The significance of these proportions becomes apparent when we consider that between 1849 and 1981 the noble population constituted less than 2 percent of the total population in France.[82]

Central to the continuing authority of landlords in the West was their control over organizations of peasants. Numerous agricultural *unions, sociétés, syndicats,* and *comices* emerged after 1851, ostensibly to protect the interests of western French agri-

Departments in which 3–9 percent of mayors had names with a particule

Departments in which over 10 percent of mayors had names with a particule

Source: Based on Fauvet and Mendras: *Les Paysans et la politique* (1958), p. 35.

Map 4. Noble Mayors in the 1950s

culture.[83] They were formed by large noble landowners such as Gerard de Caffarelli and François de Vogue. These organizations were responsible for political demonstrations, distribution of seeds, introduction of new animal breeds, and advice on fertilizers.[84] They left no segment of commercial activity untouched. Besides providing technical advice, they promoted the system of hierarchical social relations called *la paix sociale*.[85] La Tour du Pin, recognized as the theoretician of this strategy, saw the organizations as a counterforce to radical and socialist peasant cooperatives.[86] These peasant organizations dominated by elites have continued into the twentieth century; in many important aspects Vichy agrarian corporatism was modeled on them.[87]

Like the influence of the secular social elites, that of the clergy in the western countryside increased considerably during the nineteenth century. During this period the French church launched a massive campaign to reassert its role in the countryside and combat growing anticlericalism during the Third Republic. The church organized mass ordinations of priests and established numerous teaching and charitable congregations, such as the Frères de l'instruction chrétienne and the Petites Soeurs des pauvres.[88] Although the rate of ordinations declined after 1830 in France as a whole, it actually increased in the West.[89] In the Vendée, for example, there was one priest for every 776 inhabitants in 1907 and one priest for every 622 inhabitants in 1965.[90]

The Mediterranean Mode of Production since 1865

The Mediterranean mode of production was also deeply affected by changes during the late-nineteenth and twentieth centuries. By the mid-nineteenth century, the new national market and lower transport costs had pushed the region's agriculture toward monoculture, the production of wine. Mediterranean wheat production could no longer withstand the competition of lower-priced Northeastern, Russian, and American wheat that less expensive transportation and the removal of protective tariffs made possible.[91] At the same time, the completed national railroad line between the North and South opened northeastern markets to Mediterranean wine. Eschew-

Table 6. Areas in Gard Planted in Vines, in Hectares

Arrondissement	Before Phylloxera	1880
Nîmes	58,866	3,786
Uzès	21,322	1,238
Alès	16,278	1,296
Le Vigan	7,945	923

Source: L. A. Loubere, *Radicalism in Mediterranean France, 1848–1914*
(Albany: State University of New York, 1974), pp. 98–99.

ing wheat and olive cultures, cultivators turned increasingly to
wine,[92] and the fate of Mediterranean society became progressively tied to the future of wine. In studying the development
of wine monoculture, Loubere speaks of the region as *une sorte
de vigne sans fin* (one continuous vineyard) moving into cereal
and olive areas.[93] The trend continued, with 1875 marking the
largest wine harvest in French history—83,000,000 hectoliters.
The department of Hérault alone accounted for 15,000,000
hectoliters, 18 percent of total French wine production.[94]

An economy relying on a single crop is, to say the least, frag-
ile. The Mediterranean was no exception. Unfortunately for
the Mediterranean vintners, the "golden era" of wine ended
abruptly after 1875. The carrier of doom was a plant louse,
phylloxéra, which attacks and kills the roots of vines. In the region of Languedoc, most severely hit by phylloxéra, the surface
area planted with vines fell drastically by 1880, as shown in
Table 6.[95] Gard was among the first departments to be affected
by the plant louse; other Mediterranean departments suffered
a similar fate within the next twenty years.

As wine began to regain its prominence after 1900, the vintners of the Mediterranean encountered a new threat. By 1906,
Algerian wine inundated the French market. In the production
and marketing of table wine, Algerian vintners had the advantage of lower salaries, a more propitious climate, and the absence of tariffs.[96] Mediterranean cultivators faced a situation of
overproduction and underconsumption. Since 1900, the for-
tune of Mediterranean wine cultivation has continued to alter-

nate between depression and prosperity. Mediterranean vintners in the 1980s confront foreign competition from Italy, Spain, Portugal, Greece, and America. Mediterranean agriculturalists have failed to reorient the regional specialization. At present, the proportion of arable agricultural surface devoted to wine surpasses that of the mid-nineteenth century (Table 7).[97]

Other elements of the region's mode of production were strengthened after 1865. Because the cultivation of wine is intensive, it allowed peasants to survive on small holdings and even to own property. Indeed, the ownership of small property increased throughout Lower Languedoc, Roussillon, and Provence after 1865. According to J. H. Smith, the increasing commercial intrusion of the wine market into the Mediterranean between 1850 and 1870 led to a sudden accession of property among small holders. Smith notes, moreover, that in the village of Cruzy over 50 percent of the propertyholders appearing for the first time in records between 1867 and 1876 had acquired one hectare or more.[98]

The recurring crises in wine production forced many peasants into bankruptcies and sales of land, however. The proletarianization of the industry led to the emergence of large wine estates, employing agricultural labor. By 1950 one-third to one-half of the farms in the departments of Var, Bouches-du-Rhône, Hérault, and Pyrénées-Orientales were estates larger than 100 hectares.[99] Agricultural labor grew additionally from a flood of peasants who had quit the mountainous areas and Spanish and Italian immigrants who had come seeking employment on the large estates. The major recipients of these *mains-d'oeuvre* were the departments of Lower Languedoc. Consequently, after 1865 agricultural labor became a principal form of land tenure in the Mediterranean, exceeded only by owner cultivation. Accompanying the growth of small-scale owner cultivation and of agricultural labor was a rise in the proportion of landlord absenteeism. Seeking profits, urban investors speculated in wine and then ploughed their profits into land.[100]

Intensive cultivation also reinforced the population's social intercourse. The frequent market fluctuations and competition from large estates engendered solidarity among small owners.[101] Also, the proletarianization of wine production caused an

Table 7. Arable Surface in Wine, by Canton

Mediterranean France	1862 (%)	1970 (%)
Adge	67	77
Aniane	18	45
Apt	23	16
Beaumes-de-Venise	32	76
Bédarrides	41	35
Bédarieux	36	50
Bollène	27	38
Bonnieux	13	55
Cadenet	17	40
Capestang	83	86
Carpentras	17	34
Castries	32	67
Cavaillon	6	27
Caylar	1	1
Clermont-l'Hérault	50	76
Florensac	75	87
Frontignan	60	86
Ganges	24	34
Gignac	46	59
Gordes	21	34
Isle-sur-la-Sorgue	12	30
Lodève	19	35
Lunas	11	10
Malaucène	16	38
Mauguio	44	53
Mèze	66	68
Montagnac	62	85
Mormoiron	9	66
Murviel-lès-Béziers	74	96
Olonzac	47	79
Orange	22	40
Pernes-les-Fontaines	11	18

Table 7 (*continued*)

Mediterranean France	1862 (%)	1970 (%)
Pertuis	5	46
Pézenas	74	92
Roujan	73	94
Servian	74	92
Sète	36	73
Saint-Chinian	67	92
Saint-Gervais-sur-Mare	5	55
Saint-Martin-de-Londres	16	11
Valréas	24	41
Mean	36	55

Sources: A.N. F 2703, 2711; 1970–1971 Recensement général de l'agriculture (Ministry of Agriculture).

increase in the numbers of agricultural laborers and enhanced interaction and organization among peasants.[102] Even in the mountainous territories of the Mediterranean, inhabitants who had previously left to work on wine estates in the more fertile valleys returned and spread the radical ideologies circulating among the organized agricultural proletariat.[103] The association between town and countryside improved also as a result of the growing specialization of economic activity. Thus the movement toward agricultural specialization solidified the communication network among Mediterranean peasants and between countryside and city.

Mediterranean rural class structure also underwent a transformation. Deindustrialization, although not as extensive as in the West, led to the exodus of petits bourgeois and artisans from the countryside. This exodus, however, also included many of the principal notables and therefore reinforced the influence of the liberal professions.[104] Furthermore, the increase in landlord absenteeism diminished the influence of the social elites.

The post-1865 agricultural crises besetting Mediterranean

France sparked a movement toward agricultural worker organizations. In contrast to western organizations, which were not based on class but hierarchically structured and controlled by nobles, the Mediterranean associations were organized by peasants and largely infused with radical ideology. Mediterranean cultivators could therefore rely for resources on their fellow cultivators rather than on the social elites. As Judt notes, "the strong traditions of communal loyalty and common action transferred themselves from pre-industrial protest to post-industrial politics." [105] In this fashion, the post-1865 changes strengthened the democratic bases of Mediterranean social relations.

All told, the creation of a national market had varying effects on the modes of production. The most dramatic changes occurred in the Northeast, where small-scale farmers lost out to medium- and large-scale farmers, and agricultural laborers were made redundant by machines. In the West and the Mediterranean, the creation of a national market reinforced many essential elements of regional modes of production. In the West, polycultural subsistence was intensified. Tenancy supplanted sharecropping and day labor. Medium-sized family farms replaced small and large holdings. Links between town and countryside and between peasants and middle class decreased. *Bocage*-type enclosures proliferated. And social elite authority expanded. In Mediterranean France, economic activity turned progressively to market-oriented monoculture. Small-scale owner cultivation and agricultural labor grew at the expense of sharecropping, tenancy, and day labor. Landlord absenteeism rose. The communication network existing between peasants and between town and countryside received a boost. And the authority of rural social elites declined.

Before concluding this section on classifying French regions by modes of production, I should mention that the literature contains alternative regional classificatory schemes, including Bloch's field systems, Goubert's large agricultural regions, Furet and Ozouf's literacy levels, Le Bras and Todd's family structure, Barral's social relations, Fox's land versus water orientation, and Le Roy Ladurie's inheritance patterns.[106] The concept of the mode of production seems preferable to these schemes because it insists upon the essential holism of a social organization—a holism sacrificed when field systems, literacy, family structure, inheritance patterns, and other dimensions of a social formation are treated as autonomous, unconnected by an underlying social structural logic. The best rationale for using the mode of production is that it indicates the presence of a single social structural logic at the base of social forms.

Many of these attempts to classify French regions are compatible with the mode of production, however. In their study of French literacy, for example, Furet and Ozouf employed the proportion of males signing their marriage contract in 1866 as a measure of male literacy. Their results indicate a clear regional divergence that corresponds with France's three principal modes of production. The departments of the Northeast score consistently above the 80 percent level of literacy; the departments of Mediterranean France score invariably between 50 and 80 percent; the departments of the West with a few exceptions score between 30 and 70 percent. We may attribute the correspondence between mode of production and literacy in part to the link between economic activity and literacy and in part to the link between pattern of settlement and literacy. We would expect to find higher literacy in zones marked by a market-based economy and high population concentration than in zones marked by a subsistence-based economy and high population dispersion. We may draw a similar link between mode of production and social relations. Barral has regionalized France by systems of social relations. According to Barral, strong family ties prevail in the West; global social ties predominate in the North and Midi Mediterranean; village ties predominate in the East. Again, economic activity and pattern of settlement may explain these differences. Western France's subsistence economy and high population dispersion place a greater importance on the family whereas the market-based economies and highly grouped habitats of the North and Mediterranean shift emphasis from the family to the needs of individuals.

In this section, I have attempted to trace the evolution of France's three principal modes of production since the ancien régime because the mode of production is the structure that has been responsible for divergent constellations of material interests. But how do these interests shape the voting of French cultivators? Where there is a correspondence between individuals' interests and the program of a particular political movement, it is expected that individuals, as rational actors, should vote for the party that best represents their interests. In the next chapter, I shall examine the constellations of interests for individuals tied to different modes of production and discuss the interests of cultivators as derived from each element of the mode of production. Following that I shall attempt to show that one ideal-typical constellation of interests corresponds to the program of the Right while another ideal-typical constellation of interests corresponds to the program of the Left. This distinction will allow me to examine how modes of production influence regional voting behavior.

3
MODES OF PRODUCTION, INTERESTS, AND VOTING

5

THE MODE OF PRODUCTION AND
THE PERCEPTION OF INTERESTS

The contrasting regional perspectives of French cultivators on major social and economic issues—issues that directly influence their material interests—may be attributed to regional variations in economic activity, property rights, pattern of settlement and class composition. These issues are state subsidization, defense of small farms, land redistribution, progressive taxation, capitalistic practices, church-state separation, and rural democracy.[1]

ECONOMIC ACTIVITY AND THE PERCEPTION OF
INTERESTS

Economic activity can be characterized by the extent of its direction toward a market. At one extreme, subsistence cultivators are by definition autarkic producers. Their principal economic purpose is to produce and store foodstuffs for the satisfaction of their families' needs; they achieve this goal with their own resources and therefore have limited contact with the outside. They are usually suspicious of strangers and interference in their own affairs, an attitude characterized by George Foster and Edward Banfield as the "image of limited good" and "amoral familism." The principle they live by is to "maximize the material short-run advantage of the nuclear family; assume that others will do likewise."[2] They are generally not interested in market events or in the state's economic policy if these do not touch their material situation. Moreover, since subsistence farmers control their production and distribution, they do not de-

velop the antagonism toward other classes that arises from the
need to compete within a market.

By contrast, market-oriented cultivators specialize in the production of goods for sale rather than for family consumption.
Their economic needs are met through involvement in a market. Whereas subsistence cultivators are normally polycultur-
alists, producing a variety of crops, market-oriented farmers
tend to rely on a single product for their livelihood. Since they
depend on exchange with the outside, they are vulnerable both
to fluctuations in the international commodity market and to
manipulations by middlemen.[3] Market events, state economic
policy, and the role of big business are their primary concerns.
Market-oriented cultivators should favor the state's intervention in the market if the state pursued policies consistent with
their interests, such as securing their access to new markets or
subsidizing their product in times of crisis. Furthermore, they
should support restrictions on monopolies and middlemen that
would enhance their share of the market.

Hence subsistence farmers are likely to oppose state intervention in economic affairs whereas market-oriented farmers
are likely to favor state protection of domestic markets. Subsistence farmers are likely to be less troubled by monopolistic
practices than the market-oriented farmers, who will regard
this issue with considerable interest.[4]

PROPERTY RIGHTS AND THE PERCEPTION OF INTERESTS

The methods used to distribute and cultivate land have a pronounced effect on how cultivators perceive their interests. The
principal forms of land tenure in France since the Revolution
have been tenancy and owner cultivation, whereas sharecropping has declined and agricultural wage labor is secondary. By
1963, 50.1 percent of agricultural land was cultivated by owners, 44.7 percent by tenants, 3.8 percent by sharecroppers, and
1.4 percent by laborers.[5]

Tenant farmers do not own the land they work but lease it
for a period designated by contract, during which they pay rent
to the landlord. But tenants do own their tools and livestock. It

is in the interests of tenants to oppose land redistribution, especially if their lease holdings are relatively large. Tenant farmers perceive themselves as "fighting their way up the social scale by acquiring these tenancies."[6] For many tenants, renting is an intermediate step in acquiring ownership of land. Tenancy is a form of risk sharing. Tenants enjoy many of the benefits of landowning but avoid many of the costs; renting provides them with more land than their resources would otherwise make possible. Since the Revolution, advocates of land redistribution have called for partitioning large noble and bourgeois estates. But in partitioning large estates, land redistribution would terminate the rental risk-sharing arrangement. In addition, tenants would find themselves competing with other buyers for land and would likely be unable to purchase a holding as large as that to which they had access before land redistribution; as a rule, tenancies are larger than holdings of owner-cultivators.[7]

Tenant farmers are also likely to oppose progressive taxation, which sets the amount of tax in proportion to the size of one's holding. Since tenancies are larger than holdings of owner-cultivators, they are also more heavily taxed. Passed on to all tenants in the form of higher rent, the tax would also encumber those tenants who plan to buy their leases. In any case it is not in the interests of most tenant cultivators to support progressive taxation. The larger sizes of tenant holdings might also make tenant farmers oppose the interests of wage laborers since, as frequent employers, they are interested in keeping wages low.

To be sure, not all tenants are likely to oppose land redistribution or progressive taxation. Those tenants whose holdings are small may favor partitioning the large estates, especially if they believe they will be able to augment their well-being by purchasing land. Similarly, small tenants should tend to support progressive taxation if their share of the tax burden is small.

Sharecropping, a major form of land tenure before 1851, is an arrangement in which one party supplies the land, tools, and seed and the other party supplies the labor; the parties agree to distribute the proceeds.[8] Like tenant farmers, sharecroppers enjoy many of the benefits of landowning and avoid many of the costs; in other respects sharecropping entails more risk sharing than tenancy. Whereas tenants bear the full burden of blights, crop failures, and bad weather, sharecroppers share these risks with their landlords.[9] Like tenant farms, moreover, shareholdings are usually much larger than owner-cultivator holdings. We would expect sharecroppers' interests to parallel those of tenant farmers, especially on the issues of property redistribution, progressive taxation, and wage labor. Like small-holding tenants, however, small-holding sharecroppers may find land redistribution and progressive taxation in their material interest.

In the owner-cultivator system in France, in contrast, most cultivators have small holdings, primarily as a result of the financial barriers to the purchase of large holdings.[10] It costs less to rent fifty acres than to purchase them. Unlike tenants, small-scale owner-cultivators are likely to favor land redistribution. Breaking up the large estates would increase their meager holdings, weaken their principal adversaries (the large estate owners), and therefore enhance their well-being. Owner-cultivators should also favor progressive taxation, since it places a heavier burden on larger properties. And, finally, since owner-cultivators have no need for additional laborers, they have no incentive to oppose the interests of wage laborers. By contrast, where large-scale owner cultivation dominates, especially in areas of commercially labor-extensive agriculture, large owner-cultivators are likely to oppose land redistribution, progressive taxation, and higher wages for agricultural labor.

Agricultural wage labor prevails in commercial areas of France. Agricultural laborers own no land; they are hired for varying periods and are remunerated by wages. Agricultural wage laborers are engaged in nonisolated work, usually on large farms; they invariably suffer seasonal or prolonged unemployment.[11] A notable exception is the permanent agricultural laborer, such as the *domestique,* who resides and works in the same village and is often paid partly in kind. The permanent agricultural laborer is usually engaged in isolated work and suffers less frequent unemployment.[12]

Salaried agricultural laborers are concerned principally with increasing their wages. Since the employer (the farm owner) is interested in maximizing profits and minimizing costs, employers and laborers have conflicting interests. We would expect laborers to support land redistribution, because land ownership could provide an escape from seasonal unemployment, from dependence on wage labor, and from a position at the bottom of the social ladder. They would be likely to favor progressive taxation, for they would probably have few taxable resources. By contrast, since permanent agricultural laborers have greater security in full-time employment, we would expect them to be less responsive to calls for land redistribution and progressive taxation. Since they are frequently remunerated in kind, they are unlikely to be as concerned with wage levels.

To conclude, medium to large tenant farmers, sharecroppers, and owner-cultivators may oppose land redistribution, progressive taxation, and wage increases, whereas small owner-cultivators and salaried agricultural laborers may favor land redistribution and progressive taxation. Small tenants and sharecroppers may also favor land redistribution and progressive taxation. Salaried agricultural laborers are likely to favor wage increases.

PATTERNS OF SETTLEMENT AND THE PERCEPTION OF INTERESTS

I have argued that economic activity and property rights directly affect the interests of cultivators. By producing specific patterns of settlement and class composition they also indirectly influence the interests of cultivators. These two factors are largely responsible for determining which individuals and groups in a community will control the allocation of vital resources. If cultivators require resources, they will depend on the suppliers of those resources. Since dependence varies with the number of alternative suppliers, the more suppliers, the less dependence cultivators have on a single source. The greater their dependence on one source, the greater their interest in the welfare of that supplier.

Some rural communities are dispersed whereas others are grouped. A great physical distance between cultivators makes social interaction more difficult; dispersion is therefore not conducive to the emergence of organizations among cultivators. In

such cases, allocation of resources usually falls to the traditional
elites that maintain hierarchical organizations, namely, church
and landlord. A relatively concentrated population, by contrast, facilitates social interaction and thus lowers the costs of
organization. Under such conditions traditional elites cannot
monopolize resources, and as a result cultivators are less likely
to depend on one source.

Any discussion of patterns of settlement should similarly rec-
ognize the association between town and countryside. Some
rural communities are closely tied to towns; others are completely isolated. Where town-countryside association is low, cultivators have a limited number of suppliers from whom to pro-
cure resources, and they depend increasingly on traditional
elites.[13] Where town-countryside association is high, cultivators
have access to alternative suppliers and therefore depend less
for resources on traditional elites.[14]

Whether because of dispersion or town proximity, the more
cultivators depend on traditional elites, the more likely they are
to be intimidated by the elites, to receive information from
them, and to support their welfare. Thus, other things being
equal, the cultivator who depends on the church and landlord
for resources has a strong incentive to oppose church-state separation, progressive taxation, land redistribution, curtailment
of capitalistic practices, and rural democracy, whereas the cultivator who does not depend on the church and landlord for resources has no such incentive.

CLASS COMPOSITION AND THE PERCEPTION OF
INTERESTS

The recipient of resources is interested in securing the uninterrupted flow of those resources. Rural communities may be
characterized by the presence or absence of resource-controlling elites. As long as the church or landlord continues to furnish resources, and as long as comparable resources are not
available elsewhere, it is in the interests of the recipient to support the welfare of these groups. Their relation resembles, in
large part, a patron-client relation. The patron (resource con-
troller) provides a valuable asset to the client (resource recipi-

ent); in return the patron demands a service from the client. That service may be a vote. It is frequently assumed that the client will comply because to do otherwise would result in the denial of resources.[15] As I have pointed out earlier, this assumption ignores the issue of monitoring. Without effective monitoring, providers of resources are unable to enforce voting compliance. Therefore clients comply chiefly because their perception of their material interests so dictates. First of all, clients want to secure the uninterrupted flow of their resources. If the landlord and church control the dissemination of information, cultivators are more likely to identify their interests with those of these elites. Moreover, dependence of the cultivators on the church and landlord increases the opportunity for intimidation by the elites. In contrast, when the landlord or church is absent and other groups provide vital resources, cultivators are unlikely to have much interest in the welfare of the landlord or the church. Thus, other things being equal, the cultivator who depends on the church and landlord for resources should oppose church-state separation, progressive taxation, land redistribution, curtailment of capitalistic practices, and rural democracy, whereas the cultivator who does not depend on the church and landlord for resources should not.

In the preceding discussion of the relation between the mode of production and interests I have separated the mode of production into its components and have examined each component's effect on the perception of interests. However, as I hope I have made clear, the knowledge that certain cultivators are tenants does not explain their outlook on progressive taxation. Cultivators' views may be influenced also by the size of their holdings or by their economic activity, whether market or subsistence oriented. Their views depend also on the extent to which their surroundings are characterized by population dispersion, town-countryside association, and the presence of social elites. The more a region is marked by these elements—subsistence economic activity; medium- to large-scale tenancy, sharecropping, or owner cultivation; a dispersed population; low town-countryside association; and the presence of social elites—the greater should be the tendency for cultivators in that region to oppose state subsidization, defense of small farms, church-state

Table 8. The Interests of Cultivators Related to Mode of Production

	State Subsidization	Defense of Small Property	Land Redistribution	Progressive Taxation	Curtailment of Capitalistic Practices	Church-State Separation	Rural Democracy
Favored by	Market-oriented economic activity	Small owner-cultivators Agricultural wage labor Population concentration Strong town-countryside ties Social elite absence	Small owner-cultivators Agricultural wage labor Population concentration Strong town-countryside ties Social elite absence	Small owner-cultivators Agricultural wage labor Population concentration Strong town-countryside ties Social elite absence	Market-oriented economic activity Small owner-cultivators Population concentration Strong town-countryside ties Social elite	Population concentration Strong town-countryside ties Social elite absence	Small owner-cultivators Agricultural wage labor Population concentration Strong town-countryside ties Social elite absence

Opposed by	Subsistence economic activity					
	Medium-to-large tenants	Medium-to-large tenants	Medium-to-large tenants	Medium-to-large tenants	Medium-to-large tenants	Medium-to-large tenants
	Medium-to-large share-croppers	Medium-to-large share-croppers	Medium-to-large share-croppers	Medium-to-large share-croppers	Population dispersion	Medium-to-large share-croppers
	Medium-to-large owner-cultivators	Medium-to-large owner-cultivators	Medium-to-large owner-cultivators	Medium-to-large owner-cultivators	Weak town-countryside ties	Medium-to-large owner-cultivators
	Population dispersion	Population dispersion	Population dispersion	Population dispersion	Social elite presence	Population dispersion
	Weak town-countryside ties	Weak town-countryside ties	Weak town-countryside ties	Weak town-countryside ties		Weak town-countryside ties
	Social elite presence	Social elite presence	Social elite presence	Social elite presence		Social elite presence

separation, progressive taxation, land redistribution, curtailment of monopolistic practices, and rural democracy. By contrast, the more a region is typified by these elements—market-
oriented economic activity; small-scale owner-cultivation land
tenure or salaried agricultural labor; a grouped population; intense town-countryside association; and the absence of elites—
the greater should be the tendency for cultivators in that region
to favor state subsidization, defense of small farms, church-state
separation, progressive taxation, land redistribution, curtailment of monopolistic practices, and rural democracy (Table 8).

To this point I have discussed the relation between the mode
of production and the perception of interests. But what is the
connection between a particular constellation of interests and a
particular political preference? In the next chapter I shall attempt to show that support for the Right corresponds to one set
of interests, support for the Left to a different set.

6

POLITICS AND THE INTERESTS
OF CULTIVATORS

RIGHT AND LEFT IN FRENCH POLITICS

One hundred forty years ago Alexis de Tocqueville struck on a distinctive French trait. His countrymen, according to Tocqueville, had a predilection for political debate and theorizing. His depiction of the French political landscape is as true today as it was in the 1840s.

Since the French Revolution, French political movements and parties have fallen into two competing groupings—those that would conserve and respect traditional structures, the Right; and those that would change the existing structures, the Left. During the French Revolution, the conflict was between Aristocrats and Patriots, Feuillants and Jacobins, Girondins and Montagnards; during the Restoration it was between Ultras and Liberals; in the July Monarchy it was between Resistance and Movement; during the Second Republic it was between Parti de l'Ordre and Nouvelle Montagne; from 1857 to 1885, between Monarchists and Republicans; and since 1885, between Right and Left. It might be argued that a tripartite division of *blanc, bleu,* and *rouge*—Right, Center, and Left—would be more appropriate, to take into account such movements of the political center as the Republican-Constitutionalists of 1849, the Opportunists of 1885, and the Radicals of 1928. And yet in the elections of 1849, 1873, 1885, 1902, 1914, 1924, 1936, 1974, and 1981, French politics crystallized into two distinctive camps: the Right and Left.[1] Thus, at key moments in French political history, the center always dissolved and its disparate elements joined with either the Right or Left.

The French Right and Left have always consisted of coalitions of political movements and parties, and party constituencies have not remained the same. Some groups, such as the Orleanists, Bonapartists, Jacobins, Carlists, Poujadists, and Dorgeristes, have disappeared, often to resurface within newer movements; others, such as Republicans and Radicals, have moved from Left to Right.

Since 1789, the French Right has incorporated three general political strains: one supporting the monarchical restoration and counterrevolution (Legitimism), a second supporting a combination of social and political order and economic liberalism (Orleanism), and a third supporting a virulent nationalism and the concept of a strong leader (Bonapartism and Gaullism).[2] In particular, the Right includes those political groupings that joined the Party of Order in 1849, the Conservative bloc of 1885, the anti-Dreyfusards of 1900, the opposition to the policies of Waldeck-Rousseau and Combes in 1904, the movement for the three-year military conscription in 1914, the *bloc national* in 1919, the opposition to the *Cartel de gauche* in 1924 and to the Popular Front in 1936, and the Center-Right majority in 1981.[3]

The Left has been at least as diverse as the Right. There are those who seek social change through conciliatory means (Democrats) and those who seek social change through revolutionary transformation (Marxists). But all these groups support the French Revolution and see the need to expand upon its contribution. More specifically, the Left embraces political elements that supported the Jacobins in 1792; the Party of Movement in 1849; the coalition of Republicans, Radicals, and Radical-Socialists in 1885; the Dreyfusards in 1900; the anticlericals of 1904 to 1910; the coalition for two-year military service and fiscal reform in 1914; the *Cartel de gauche* in 1924; the Popular Front in 1936; and the Left Opposition in 1981.[4]

To be sure, we cannot assume that the member parties of each bloc share a general purpose or specific goals. Each party pursues goals it expects will bring the most benefits and frequently cooperates with other parties that share specific aims. In 1849, for example, the Legitimists and Orleanists held divergent views of the French Revolution, French economic policy, restoration of the Bourbon monarchy, and the Protestant church,[5] but when it came to the May-June elections, they buried their disagreements and formed an anti-Left coalition. The same is true of the various leftist movements and parties (for example, Socialists and Communists during the twentieth century).

Numerous issues have divided the French Right and Left since 1789; despite shifting alliances many of these issues have directly affected the material interests of French cultivators. Several issues lost their significance as time passed. In the election of 1848, for example, the Right supported an initiative that would have allowed farmers to enclose their lands and thereby prohibit the access by peasants to common pasturing grounds. The Left opposed this initiative. Soon after, the commons disappeared, and the enclosure issue was no longer important.

Other issues, however, have persisted and continue to divide the French Right and Left, thereby giving the French political landscape touchstones of enduring political identity. The Right (from the Feuillants of 1791 through the Party of Order of 1849 to the present Right) has opposed land redistribution, progressive taxation, rural democracy, and state intervention into local affairs; it has supported clericalism, specifically church control of education. The Left (from the Jacobins of 1792 through the Movement of 1849 to the present coalition of Socialists and Communists) has supported land redistribution, small land-holdings, progressive income taxation, state subsidies to small farmers, rural democracy, the curtailment of capitalistic practices, the nationalization of large capitalist enterprises, and state-church separation, specifically free and obligatory education.[6] The contrasting positions of the Right and Left on these issues deserve examination in more detail.

State Subsidization

Although pro- and antistate forces exist within both the French Right and Left, it is the Left that has most emphatically promoted state aid to small farmers.[7] The Right has more often sought support from the large landholders and has not favored state-sponsored financial aid to agriculture. By contrast, as early as the election of 1849, the Left proposed that the state create credit institutions for small cultivators.[8] To paraphrase Félix Pyat's 1849 statement of Democratic-Socialist principles, the state should be responsible for providing cheap credit to ensure that land ownership becomes a reality for all peasants.[9]

Not until the economic crises of the 1870s and 1880s did the question of state subsidies to agriculture become central to the leftist program, as it is today. In the early 1950s the French government pursued agricultural policies that promoted the modernization of French agriculture and in particular benefited the large farms of the North. Because these programs created much disruption, small farmers organized a resistance in July 1953 (most notably, "the day of the barricades").[10] The Left came to the aid of the small farmers by demanding active state intervention on their behalf.[11] The Socialist party (S.F.I.O.) called for a government guarantee of stable prices and credit in case of an agricultural crisis.[12]

The Communists have echoed the Socialist summons for state aid to agriculture,[13] and both Socialists and Communists have continued to support state aid to small farmers during the conservative Fifth Republic. The Left-sponsored Mouvement de defénse des exploitations familiales (M.O.D.E.F.) has asked the state to furnish loans and credit at low interest rates for small producers.[14] Mitterand's 1981 Socialist program included the nationalization of banking and credit institutions.[15] In contrast, the Right, in particular the Rassemblement pour la République (R.P.R.), in 1981 called for a reduction in public subsidies to cut taxes.[16] During the 1980s the French Communist party has come to the aid of small cultivators of wine, fruits, and vegetables by opposing the proposed enlargement of the European Common Market—an enlargement that would include such wine, fruit, and vegetable producers as Greece, Spain, and Portugal.[17]

Defense of Small Property

It may seem paradoxical that a leftist policy supports private property, but it has been and continues to be the case in France. French Marxists have frequently advocated one policy for industry, nationalization of the means of production, and another policy for agriculture, championship of small private property.[18] Since the French Revolution, when the Montagnards implemented the *Code rural,* the French Left has unceasingly supported the rights of small peasant cultivators and opposed the large noble and capitalist estate owners.[19] Over one hundred years ago, Ledru Rollin eloquently stated the French Left's position on property. "Property is liberty. We will therefore respect property, but on condition that it will be infinitely multiplied. We do not want it for some; we want it for all."[20]

In contrast, the Right has advocated the interests of large propertyholders. Thus, the rightist majority during the Fifth Republic favored the movement in French agriculture toward capitalist large-scale production.[21] Under de Gaulle, the state promoted the capitalization of agriculture, thereby rescinding the gains won by small cultivators during the Fourth Republic. The new agricultural policy abrogated the indexing of agricultural and manufacturing prices, lowered the tax refund from 15 percent to 10 percent, and increased the tax on fertilizer.[22] Responding to the Fifth Republic's advocacy of capitalist large-scale agricultural production, the Left initiated the M.O.D.E.F. to organize small holders as a political force.[23] And since 1973 the Left has supported the establishment of *offices par produits* (produce offices) and *offices fonciers* (land offices). The produce offices are responsible for regulating markets and imports to guarantee a minimum income for small farmers; the land offices are charged with controlling land speculation and allowing landowning peasants to acquire more land.[24]

Land Redistribution

That a small proportion of the French population controls a large proportion of land has been the core of the struggle between Left and Right since 1789. In 1848, 5,580,000 small cultivators in France possessed an average of 2.65 hectares each, and 34,700 landowners possessed an average of 273 hectares each.[25] In 1892, 61 percent of all French cultivators held property of five hectares or less, constituting 13.7 percent of the total arable land; 2.5 percent of all cultivators held property of more than forty hectares, constituting 46 percent of the total arable land.[26] In 1955, 56 percent of all cultivators operated farms of less than ten hectares, constituting 16.3 percent of the total arable land; 4 percent of all cultivators owned farms of more than fifty hectares, constituting 26 percent of the total arable land.[27] The Left has favored and the Right has opposed breaking up large noble, church, and bourgeois estates. With the prompting of the Montagnards, the Revolutionary Assemblies of 1791–1793 began selling these large estates.[28] Besides augmenting the holdings of the relatively well-to-do, these land sales and the partitioning of common lands allowed many peasants to become landowners. And throughout the nineteenth century and into the twentieth, the Left has advocated land redistribution by proclaiming "There is land to redistribute" and "Land to those who work it."[29]

Although land redistribution occasions less debate in the twentieth century, the Left continues to promote the expropriation of large estates in major statements on agriculture.[30] For example, the Communist party's agrarian program of the 1950s called for a total confiscation of land, animals, and buildings from the largest estates.[31] The party's statement leaves no doubt that the small owner-cultivator was the intended recipient of this largesse: "Et un grand nombre de petits propriétaires-exploitants verront arrondir leurs domaines de quelques hectares au moment de la distribution de terres."[32]

Progressive Taxation

The Left and Right have been at odds over the issue of taxation. The Left favors a progressive taxation intended to force the rich to carry the tax burden. The Right opposes any tax system that would force the wealthy to pay more. Throughout the nineteenth century and into the twentieth, a progressive income tax stood out as a major point of controversy between Left and Right.[33] In 1848 the conservative Party of Order proclaimed its opposition to any progressive income tax.[34] The leftist Democratic-Socialist program of 1848 placed the tax issue at the top of its demands: to improve the conditions of peasants, it proposed the abolition of taxes on alcohol and the reimbursement of the forty-five-centime tax (chief concern of the Midi vintners); it proposed a tax on luxury items and capital and, most important, a progressive income tax.[35] Unfortunately for the Left, the Right won the 1849 election. A progressive income tax failed to materialize.

A progressive income tax reemerged as a divisive issue during the 1890s. In the 1892 Socialist program, the party proposed an agricultural retirement pension that would be financed by a special tax on the income of large property,[36] but twenty years elapsed before the debate reached the national level. In 1909, in the hope of instituting fiscal reform, the national legislature sponsored a progressive income tax bill. The Left and Right lined up on opposite sides of the issue.[37] The national debate reached a high point in the election of 1914 when taxation served, with the controversies surrounding church-state relations and three-year military service, as the principal demarcation between the Left and the Right.[38] For eight years the fight raged, until finally a progressive income tax became law in 1917. Since then the Left has argued for extending the progressive income tax as well as taxing personal wealth, and the Right has mobilized its resources against more progressive taxation. Whereas other divisive issues have stirred political emotions in elections and then have waned, the controversy surrounding taxation has lost none of its fervor. In the 1981 political campaign, the French Right and Left placed taxation of wealth and profits at the center of the national debate. Jacques Chirac, the leader of the conservative Rassemblement pour la République, campaigned in favor of a massive tax reduction and abolition of the *taxe professionnelle* (business tax).[39] As for the Left, if there was one political issue on which communists and socialists could agree, it was support for a new tax on wealth and a higher tax on bank and business profits.[40]

Capitalistic Practices

Class conflict, which may seem more relevant to a discussion of the politics of industrial workers, has considerable relevance for agricultural producers as well. Since the 1740s, attempts to make agriculture more productive and competitive have emphasized the concentration of land into large holdings. These efforts have met with intense opposition among the peasantry, organized for the most part by the Left.

As early as 1789, large landholders tried to eliminate the *biens communaux* (commons), first through purchasing and then by enclosing these lands. The *biens communaux* served as a common pasturing ground for small herds owned by peasants; loss of these lands would have caused the peasants hardship.[41] The Left made defense of the commons an important issue in the elections of 1848–1849.[42] With the movement toward large-scale capitalist wine production after 1851, the Left became involved in defending and promoting the rights of agricultural laborers and small-scale owner-cultivators. It took part in the earliest organization of agricultural worker syndicalism in the Midi,[43] and it placed in its 1914 platform the establishment of disability insurance for agricultural laborers.[44] In 1907, the Left launched an attack on the large wine merchants and estates, accusing them of responsibility for the slump in wine prices and appealing to the small Midi vintners who perceived the oligopolies and middlemen as their chief rivals.[45] In every electoral campaign between 1892 and 1919 the Left made the protection of small farms from monopolistic practices a cornerstone of its agrarian program.[46] The Popular Front of 1936 campaigned similarly against middlemen and capitalist merchants who, it argued, were responsible for the fluctuating prices of agricultural produce. During the 1960s M.O.D.E.F. took an active role in fighting unfair monopolistic practices.[47]

Church and State

Probably no issue since the French Revolution has divided the Right and Left more than church-state relations.[48] The Left has worked unequivocally to purge the church's influence from civil matters and to reduce the church's economic resources, while the Right has struggled just as unrelentingly to protect the privileged position and authority of the Catholic church. Both Left and Right believed a strong church could profoundly shape the individual's preferences.

During the French Revolution, the lines were drawn between Left and Right by the Civil Constitution of the Clergy, which the government wrote to force the clergy to support the Revolution. The revolutionary government further alienated the clergy by confiscating church property. The Right supported the clergy's resistance to these measures. After the Revolution many church-related issues continued to separate Right from Left. The Right favored restoring to the Catholic church all its former privileges, rights, wealth (in particular, church property confiscated during the Revolution), granting state funds for religious institutions, and recognizing the Catholic church as the state church of France.[49]

During the nineteenth century, one issue stood above all others: the role of the church in education. The church had a monopoly over education until 1833. Catholic religious services were presented in schools, and such primary education as existed was in the hands of religious orders. In 1833 the Orleanists instituted the Guizot educational act,[50] which removed exclusive control of primary education from the Catholic church. This act also ensured that religious instruction would no longer be imposed on children against the wishes of their parents, that each commune would have a school and a qualified teacher, and that this teacher would be furnished with lodging and a yearly salary of two hundred francs.[51] The church reacted, demanding the right to establish its own schools (*écoles libres*) organized on purely Catholic lines. The church refused, moreover, to accept any negotiation with the state, claiming that education fell within the church's domain. The Right mobilized its forces against the secularizing policies of the July Monarchy. The Left pushed for additional reforms, and in its 1849 electoral campaign called for obligatory and free education and for an improvement in teachers' economic conditions.[52]

In 1850, with passage of the Falloux law, the state moved closer to the Right's position on education. This law formally abolished the state's monopoly over education and gave the Catholic church a considerable measure of freedom over secondary education. The controversy over education remained relatively subdued until the 1880s, when the Republicans had gained control of the state; under the sponsorship of Jules Ferry, the government enacted laws that made primary education free, secular, and compulsory.[53] The election of 1885 was principally a struggle over the government's policy on education: the Left backed the Republicans' secularization of primary education; the Right launched a massive antigovernment campaign, enlisting the Catholic church.[54] Religious sermons included warnings to the peasantry that a leftist victory would result in the loss of personal property. The priest of Saint-Germain de Tallevende in the department of Calvados proclaimed from the pulpit, "Voulez-vous le bonheur de la France, votre malheureuse France, conserver vos propriétés, votez tous pour la liste conservatrice."[55]

The struggle over church-state relations intensified during the period 1900 to 1910 and centered on two pieces of legislation. In 1901, the state enacted a law on associations prohibiting members of unauthorized religious orders from teaching; police were ordered to close any schools that violated the law. In addition, this law assigned church property to lay associations.[56] The second of the two edicts dealt with the separation of church and state: the state would remain neutral in religious matters, enforcing only freedom of conscience. The Catholic church had always held that Catholicism was the state religion of France; now the state recognized no official religion.

After 1910 the church-state controversy subsided. However, the passions of Left and Right could be aroused by questions concerning Catholic schools: should the state financially aid Catholic primary education; should parents have a choice between public or Catholic education for their children?[57] During the Fourth Republic, one divisive question was the 1948 Poinso-Chapuis decree, sponsored by the pro-Catholic Mouvement républicain populaire, which provided a measure of state aid to Catholic schools. The Left opposed the law; the Right favored it. Two other laws caused considerable debate during the Fourth Republic, the Marie law and the Barange law; they provided state scholarships for qualified pupils at church schools and furnished financial aid to church schools. And finally, the Debre law, enacted by the Fifth Republic, caused a storm of controversy. The Debre law promised financial aid to Catholic schools in exchange for state control.

Rural Hierarchy versus Rural Democracy

Because advocates of the Right have stood for tradition and advocates of the Left for change, they hold divergent notions on how society should be structured. For advocates of the Right, society is like a good patriarchal family; it should be hierarchical, with the elites in control.[58] Berger, in writing about the French Right's outlook on rural hierarchy, states:

> The properly ordered rural society is based on a hierarchy of harmonious interests. The basic unit is the family, the natural social group, the parish. Social harmony results not from the equality of individual members of rural society, but from the relationships between families that arise in joint work. Each man has particular social responsibilities associated with his place in society, and the organic solidarity of society is based on the mutual recognition of complementary social functions.[59]

Political groupings of the Right, from the Ultras of 1815 through the Party of Order of 1849, the Conservatives of 1885, and the anti-Popular Front movement of 1936 to the Gaullists of the Fifth Republic, have emphasized the importance of social order.[60] For the Right, France's political instability is a consequence of the Left's attempts to undermine the social order. Especially in rural areas, the Right has made considerable effort to maintain a social hierarchy, as in numerous noble-sponsored agricultural syndicates formed after 1851.[61] Even after World War II the Right was instrumental in creating such agricultural associations as the Confédération nationale de la mutualité de la coopération et du crédit agricole, Fédération nationale des syndicats d'exploitants agricoles, and the Assemblée permanente des présidents de chambres d'agriculture.[62] There is probably no better example of the Right's vision of the properly ordered society than that embodied in the corporatism of the 1930s and 1940s. Although corporatism under Vichy was not supported by all political factions of the French Right, it nonetheless embodied the Right's essential notions of social hierarchy,[63] with a central premise that the entire rural population should be in one hierarchically arranged nonclass organization.[64]

The Left has been diametrically opposed to this paternalistic structuring of society. For the Left, the French Revolution delivered the first blow to the traditional elitist-controlled society. Ever since the Revolution the Left has pushed for a more democratic social structure. During the nineteenth century the Left, consisting of the Republicans, Radicals, and Radical Socialists, made "la République démocrate et sociale" a cornerstone of its program.[65] The Marxist Left has, however, argued for a virtually classless society. Although the non-Marxist and Marxist Left have differing notions of social democracy, they are firmly united in opposition to the Right's vision of rural hierarchy.

CONCLUSION

Although some of these issues no longer dominate the French political landscape, others continue to divide the Right and Left. In particular, the Right opposes while the Left supports state subsidies for small farmers, the defense of small property, land redistribution, progressive taxation, curtailment of capitalistic practices, church-state separation, and rural democracy (Table 9).

The particular positions that the Right and Left take on these issues should help explain why some cultivators vote Right and others vote Left. Cultivators inhabiting regions marked by subsistence economic activity; medium- to large-scale tenancy, sharecropping, or owner cultivation; a dispersed population; low town-countryside association; and the presence of social elites should, as rational actors, share the Right's views on the major issues. That is, they should oppose state subsidies, defense of small farms, land redistribution, progressive taxation, church-state separation, and rural democracy; and they should favor capitalistic practices. Thus they are likely to vote Right. In contrast, cultivators inhabiting regions typified by market-oriented economic activity, cultivation of land by small-scale owners or by salaried agricultural labor, a grouped population, intense town-countryside association, and the absence of elites should, as rational actors, share the Left's views on the major issues. That is, they should favor state subsidies, defense of

Table 9. Material Interests and Political Orientation

	State Subsidization	Defense of Small Property	Land Redistribution	Progressive Taxation	Curtailment of Capitalistic Practices	Church-State Separation	Rural Democracy
Favored by	Left	Left	Left	Left	Left	Left	Left
Opposed by	Right	Right	Right	Right	Right	Right	Right

small farms, land redistribution, progressive taxation, church-state separation, and rural democracy; and they should oppose capitalistic practices. Thus they are likely to vote Left.[66]

This argument may seem counterintuitive. For instance, why should owners of the means of production vote Left and non-owners like sharecroppers and tenant farmers vote Right? In writing about the French peasants' support of the conservative Louis-Napoléon Bonaparte, Karl Marx argued that "the small-holding peasants form a vast mass, the members of which live in similar conditions but without entering into manifold relations with one another. Their mode of production isolates them from one another instead of bringing them into mutual intercourse."[67] Since then other scholars have used similar arguments. Citing evidence from diverse countries, Arthur Stinchcombe and Jeffery Paige argue that the small-holding system is associated with political conservatism whereas family-sized tenancy and sharecropping are linked more to political radicalism. According to Stinchcombe, "the proceeds between cropper and landlord, the immense social distance separating them, the technical ability of the peasant, and the leadership of wealthier tenants combine to produce political sensitivity and effective leadership. The family-sized tenancy produces not only intense class conflict but also overt revolutionary action."[68] Juan Linz also found a positive correlation between rightist voting and owner cultivation.[69] In contrast to these contemporary arguments, Eric Wolf, in *Peasant Wars of the Twentieth Century*, argues that the small-scale owner-cultivator is most likely to support revolutionary collective action because he is more sensitive than nonowners to changes in the world economy and has more economic organizational resources than the landless sharecroppers and plantation laborers.[70] The consensus, except for Wolf, is that owner-cultivators tend to support right-wing parties and tenants left-wing parties—the opposite of what I argue.

Although the findings of these scholars may be applicable elsewhere, they do not seem tenable for France because none of them treats the importance of either *the size of the holding* or *the beneficial risk-sharing arrangement* provided by leasing and sharecropping. The interests of small and large owners would probably differ on the issues of land redistribution and progressive taxation; with small owners in favor and large owners opposed. Under the risk-sharing arrangement commonly found in medium- to large-scale tenancy and sharecropping, leaseholders have access to more land than they could control with equal resources in an open market and are therefore likely to oppose legislation to redistribute land. Accordingly, Paige errs in assuming that all sharecropping systems are marked by insecurity of tenure, rent racking, and intractable zero-sum conflict.[71] His depiction may apply to such commercial labor-intensive agriculture as wet-rice or grape cultivation, where holdings tend to be minuscule and leases insecure, but it does not correspond to a largely subsistence-oriented agriculture or to labor-extensive cultivation of such crops as corn or wheat, where holdings tend to be substantial and leases secure.[72]

What does the preceding examination of regional modes of production, the interests of cultivators, and the meaning of Right and Left tell us about political behavior in northeastern, western, and Mediterranean France? The Left's program, and in particular its call for breaking up noble and ecclesiastical estates and for progressive taxation, should have met with a receptive audience in the Northeast before 1851, since in this period the majority of northeastern cultivators were agricultural wage laborers and impoverished small tenants—cultivators who should have benefited from these reforms. When northeastern property rights changed during the first half of the nineteenth century, however, causing the virtual disappearance of agricultural labor and the replacement of small-tenant holdings by medium- to large-scale farms, northeastern cultivators should gradually have abandoned their support of the Left. The Left should have obtained sizable support from Mediterranean cultivators throughout the nineteenth and twentieth centuries and, in particular, increasing support after 1865. Growth in the leftist proclivities of Mediterranean cultivators after 1865 should be attributed to the strengthening of the region's dominant mode of production, especially to the proliferation of small-scale market-oriented owner-cultivator farms. By contrast, the Left's program should not have been well received in the West because of the prevalence of medium-scale subsistence tenancy. Western tenants did not favor the Left's advocacy of breaking up the large estates. That the emergence of a national market did little to alter the West's dominant mode of production should explain why the region's cultivators held steadfastly to their politically conservative inclinations after 1865.

The mode-of-production analysis therefore hypothesizes different voting patterns in the West and in the South of France. It is time now to test these propositions against the behavior of the French electorate in the nineteenth and twentieth centuries.

4
HYPOTHESES, FINDINGS, AND IMPLICATIONS

7

A TEST OF THE MODE-OF-PRODUCTION MODEL

In his classic studies of villages in the West and the Mediterranean Laurence Wylie showed that the two areas differ even in their ideas of heroism. He observed that the cultivators of Chanzeaux (West) hold to the myth of the people rising up to protect their religion, king, and nobles from the attacks of a hostile government.[1] The cultivators of the Vaucluse (Mediterranean) look up to the martyred young revolutionary Viala, who sacrificed his life to prevent the Catholics and royalist troops from crossing the Durance River.[2] These stories symbolize the persistence of distinctive patterns of political behavior in the West and Mediterranean. Throughout the nineteenth and twentieth centuries, the West has remained identified with the political Right while the Mediterranean has been identified with the political Left.

The mode-of-production model of political behavior argues that persistent voting for the Right in western France and voting for the Left in Mediterranean France are the consequences of divergent constellations of interests. These contrasting interests are the products of distinctive modes of production.

On closer inspection, the mode-of-production theory as developed here entails a number of specific propositions. To examine the theory more fully, I will test the following propositions:

(1) The various mode-of-production factors are strongly interrelated and thereby constitute a totality. In particular, a market-oriented economy corresponds to small-scale owner cultivation or agricultural wage labor, population concentration, and the absence of social elites whereas a sub-

sistence-oriented economy is associated with medium- to large-scale tenancy, population dispersion, and the presence of social elites.

(2) One of these constellations of social factors or modes of production predominates in western France and the other in Mediterranean France. More specifically, the Mediterranean region should exhibit market-oriented economic activity, small-scale owner cultivation or agricultural wage labor, a concentrated pattern of settlement, strong town-countryside ties, and the absence of social elites. The western region, in contrast, should exhibit subsistence-oriented economic activity, medium-scale tenancy, dispersed population, weak town-countryside ties, and the presence of social elites. The Northeast region should more closely resemble the Mediterranean before 1851 but should more nearly approximate the West after 1851.

(3) Each mode of production has changed in specified ways: the West has been marked increasingly by subsistence medium-scale tenancy with population dispersion; the Mediterranean has been characterized increasingly by market-oriented small-scale owner cultivation or agricultural wage labor with population concentration. The Northeast has shifted from commercial small-scale tenancy and agricultural wage labor to commercial medium- to large-scale tenancy or owner cultivation.

(4) Voting for the Right corresponds to a mode of production characterized by a subsistence oriented economy, medium- to large-scale tenancy or sharecropping, population dispersion, and the presence of social elites. Voting for the Left corresponds to a mode of production characterized by a market-oriented economy, small-scale owner cultivation or salaried agricultural labor, population agglomeration, and the absence of social elites.

(5) The mode-of-production model of political behavior is a more satisfactory predictor of French political behavior than other explanatory constructs.

(6) Market-oriented small-scale owner-cultivators and agricultural wage laborers in a social structure with a concentrated

population and an absence of social elites vote for the Left because its program most closely corresponds to their interests. Conversely, subsistence-oriented medium- to large-scale tenants and sharecroppers in a social structure marked by a dispersed population and the presence of social elites vote for the Right because its program most closely approximates their interests.

Before proceeding to test my propositions and examine the empirical results, I shall discuss a number of issues concerning the data and methodology used for this test.

SELECTION OF ELECTIONS

To study regional political phenomena, it is necessary to analyze elections from periods in French electoral history when the central issues separating the Left and Right were clearly demarcated. To explore the persistence of voting patterns I selected three such elections that coincided with intervals of approximately sixty years. Moreover, I decided to analyze national legislative elections rather than either local or presidential elections because national party platforms are more likely than local ones to reflect key issues and because in legislative elections personalities are emphasized less than in presidential ones. A lack of reliable data makes it impossible to test the mode-of-production model of political regionalism during the French Revolution. This lack is unfortunate because preliminary investigation indicates that the mode-of-production model may help explain such issues as the Northeast's fervent backing of antiseigneurialism and the West's support of counterrevolution between 1792 and 1795.[3]

The three national legislative elections I shall analyze are those of 1849, 1914, and 1981. Each one took place at a period in French political history when various parties of the Right and Left coalesced into two separate blocs.[4] The 1849 election occurred at a significant juncture in French history. It served as one of the earliest examples of universal male suffrage and it fell within the chaotic tenure of the French Second Republic, marked by the successive collapses of the July Monarchy in the

February Revolution of 1848 and the Eighteenth Brumaire of Louis-Napoléon Bonaparte in December 1851. This election, furthermore, came at a time when the Right (Party of Order) and the Left (New Mountain) argued over the path of the Second Republic.[5]

The 1914 election took place on the eve of World War I. As in 1849, the Right and the Left coalesced into competing blocs. Above all, this election was distinguished by acrimonious debates between the Left and the Right over the three-year military service law, the institution of a personal income tax, and the role of the Catholic church in education.[6]

The 1981 election marked the victory of François Mitterand's socialist-dominated Left bloc. After several years of disharmonious relations, the Socialists and Communists joined forces and ousted the Right, which had held power since the inception of the Fifth Republic. Involving the most recent data, this election therefore affords an ideal test of the current validity of the mode-of-production model.[7]

For each election the proportion of all votes for the Left provides a straightforward measure of leftist voting tendencies. In 1849 the political Left is represented by the Democratic Socialist list. I identified candidates who belonged to the list through a study of the local press of 1849. Because the Left and Right were represented by several candidates (in each department, one candidate per assembly seat), I selected that candidate from the leftist list who received the most votes. In most cases, there was little variation among votes received by candidates within each list.

The political Left is represented by the leftist bloc in 1914 (that is, the various socialist parties, the Unified Radicals, the nonbinding Radicals, and the nonbinding Democratic Republicans). In 1981, it is represented by the Left Opposition (that is, the Democratic Movement, the Left Radical Movement, the Unified Socialist party, the French Socialist party, the French Communist party, and the Workers' Struggle party). Electoral data for the 1914 and 1981 elections are gathered from the first ballot, when each party presents a candidate and individuals are more likely to vote their political preferences. By the second ballot, when some parties remove their own candidates and support other parties' candidates, individuals begin to assess which candidate is most likely to win. For both the 1914 and 1981 elections the proportion of leftist voting is computed for each case by adding sums of votes for each political party; each sum is divided by the party's rank on a designated scale of Leftness, from the most leftist to the least leftist.

SELECTION OF CASES

To examine French political behavior thoroughly requires a base unit that meets the rigorous criteria of systematic analysis. The unit should be small enough to reduce internal variation of key variables but large enough to constitute a whole. The French canton fulfills these criteria. Larger administrative units such as the department and arrondissement are too heterogeneous. The smaller commune (village) is a relatively homogeneous collectivity but is frequently only a subdivision of the productive unit. For example, many large landholdings extend beyond the commune's boundaries, thereby complicating the placement of farms into one village or another. Thus I have selected the canton as the most propitious unit of analysis, for it comes nearest to being a homogeneous productive unit.

My study includes Mediterranean and western cantons as well as cantons from France's other principal region, the Northeast. I decided to include northeastern cantons to provide a fuller range of variation in mode of production and voting and thereby to increase the generalizability and reliability of my theory. The criterion for inclusion of a canton in this study is that a minimum of 30 percent of its population engaged in agriculture in 1975 (the date for which I have been able to collect the most recent population data). Moreover, because they have a greater degree of urbanization, I included those northeastern cantons where 25 percent or more of the population is engaged in agriculture. It can be assumed that these cantons were even more agricultural during the nineteenth and early twentieth centuries.

There are, however, many cantons that meet all the criteria for inclusion yet cannot be included in this analysis because data were incomplete. These problems exist especially in the

Northeast; to compensate, I have collected data from three northeastern departments that I believe are representative of the region: the Somme, the Meuse, and the Seine-et-Marne.

A fairly comprehensive analysis of French voting is possible for the 1849 and 1981 elections but not for the 1914 election. The unfortunate destruction of the 1892 and 1929 agricultural censuses for much of France renders an analysis of the 1914 election by canton impossible. I have succeeded, however, in locating copies of these two agricultural censuses for a number of cantons from the Western departments of Vendée, Morbihan, and Ille-et-Vilaine and from the Mediterranean departments of Vaucluse, Hérault, Aude, and Pyrénées-Orientales—all highly representative of the diversity within both regions.

All told, for the 1849, 1914, and 1981 elections, I have complete data on 327, 58, and 413 cantons, respectively. Among the 327 cantons for the 1849 study are 69 Mediterranean, 181 western, and 77 northeastern cantons. Among the 58 cantons for the 1914 study are 31 Mediterranean and 27 western cantons. Among the 413 cantons for the 1981 study are 112 Mediterranean, 273 western, and 28 northeastern cantons. For the 1849 election, I made an exception to the criterion for selecting cases. To maintain as large a sample as possible of northeastern cantons without biasing the analysis, I included an additional 49 cantons that were predominantly rural in 1849. I excluded them from the 1981 analysis, however, because their agricultural population had fallen below the 25 percent level.

SELECTION OF INDEPENDENT VARIABLES

To test my propositions, I selected suitable measures for the major concepts that comprise the mode-of-production theory and alternative constructs; these concepts are summarized in Table 10 and explained more fully below. Choosing valid measures is frequently a herculean task, certainly so for the mode-of-production concepts of economic activity and class composition. *Economic activity* indicates the forms of economic production in which individuals are engaged and the extent to which those forms are market oriented. One might think that average crop yield would be a satisfactory measure; however, the great variation in crops within and between regions makes any comparison meaningless. A better indicator of economic activity would be the value of the product per hectare; unfortunately, this measure exists only at the overly heterogeneous level of the French department. Therefore, as the best proxy I selected the mean price of a hectare of agricultural land. To the extent that the value of agricultural land measures the land's yield or productivity, as the land's value increases so should the regional economy's ability to generate a surplus and, hence, the more the region should be characterized by a market orientation.[8]

For *property rights,* I am interested in the conditions or manner by which individuals hold property and, in particular, the various forms of land tenure and farm size. The agricultural censuses provide four different measures: (1) the proportion of all cultivators who are owner-cultivators; (2) the proportion of all cultivators who are tenants; (3) the proportion of all cultivators who are sharecroppers; and (4) the proportion of all cultivators who are agricultural laborers.[9] The proportion of sharecroppers is combined with the proportion of tenants in this study, both because sharecropping becomes a relatively insignificant mode of land tenure by 1849 and because the mode-of-production model assumes that sharecroppers' and tenants' interests are virtually the same on the major issues separating the Left and Right. The censuses do not provide information on the actual acreage associated with each form of land tenure, making it impossible to ascertain directly the size of each owner-cultivated or tenant holding. The agricultural censuses do, however, furnish independent measures for farm size. For the purposes of this study, the proportion of farms of less than ten hectares and the proportion of farms of between ten and fifty hectares have been employed as measures of small and medium farm size, respectively, for the 1849 and 1914 elections. For the 1981 election, the proportion of farms of less than twenty hectares and the proportion of farms of between twenty and fifty hectares have been used as measures of small and medium farm size, respectively. These changes were made for the 1981 election because twentieth-century agricultural mechanization has altered the meaning of small- and medium-sized farms.

Unfortunately, the dates of French population and agri-

Table 10. Operationalization and Sources of Independent and
Dependent Variables

Variable	Operationalization	Source
Economic Activity	Mean price of a hectare of agricultural land	1862 and 1892 Agricultural Censuses; 1980 *Le Prix des terres agricoles*; 1981 *Petites Régions agricoles*
Property rights	Proportion of cultivators who are owner-cultivators	1862, 1892, and 1979–80 Agricultural Censuses; 1975 Population Census
	Proportion of cultivators who are tenants	
	Proportion of cultivators who are sharecroppers	
	Proportion of cultivators who are agricultural laborers	
	Proportion of farms of less than 10 hectares	
	Proportion of farms of less than 20 hectares	
	Proportion of farms of between 10 and 50 hectares	
	Proportion of farms of between 20 and 50 hectares	
	Proportion of farms of more than 50 hectares	
Pattern of Settlement	Proportion of total population that is agglomerated	1881, 1886, 1911, 1921 and 1975 Population Censuses
Class Composition	Proportion of electors paying more than 1000 francs in taxes yearly	1843–1848 Listes des electeurs
	Proportion of electors who are noble	

Table 10 (*continued*)

Variable	Operationalization	Source
	Ratio of priests to population	1881, 1886, 1891, 1896 and 1975 Population Censuses
Wine Production	Proportion of total cultivated surface under grape cultivation	1862, 1892–1929, 1979–80 Agricultural Censuses
Region	Dummy variable	Geographic location of cantons
Religiosity	Proportion of the adult population that attends Sunday mass on a regular basis	F. A. Isambert and J. P. Terrenoire, *Pratique religieuse des catholiques en France* (Paris: Presses de la Fondation des sciences politiques, 1980)
Tradition	Proportion of leftist voting in 1849	A.N. (C. Series)
Voting	Proportion of votes that were for the Left	A.N. (C. Series); 1981 departmental voting results in local press (see Bibliography of Archival Sources)

cultural censuses do not correspond to the dates of national legislative elections; the discrepancy is especially large for the 1849 and 1914 elections. In selecting censuses, I have chosen the most reliable from those that approximate the dates of the designated elections. Agricultural measures are taken from the 1862, 1892, 1929, and 1979–1980 national agricultural censuses and from the 1980 issue of *Le Prix des terres agricoles* and the 1981 issue of *Petites Régions agricoles.*

Pattern of settlement refers to the extent of population concentration. The various population censuses provide the proportion of total population that is agglomerated in the *chef-lieu;* agglomeration refers to the extent to which dwellings are clustered together. For inhabitants of a village to be counted among the agglomerated population, their dwellings cannot be more than two hundred meters from the nearest dwelling; there must be at least fifty inhabitants in the settlement. As a measure of population concentration, population agglomeration is superior to population density alone, since population density is strongly affected by an area's topography. For example, to the extent that a region's topography precludes settlement in the mountainous areas, its population density will be low; yet in the remaining habitable areas, the inhabitants may be agglomerated. Consequently, population density is a less adequate measure of a unit's population concentration. The first reliable measure of population agglomeration becomes available in 1881. The measures of pattern of settlement are taken from the 1881, 1886, 1911, 1921, and 1975 population censuses.[10]

The aspect of *class composition* with which I am most concerned is the presence or absence of elites. I have been unable to locate measures for church and nonchurch elites for each election largely because of problems with the data. I have therefore employed two indicators of nonchurch elites for 1849 and one indicator of church elites for each of the subsequent periods. The 1843–1848 *Listes du jury* suggest the makeup of nonchurch elites by delineating the proportion of electors paying more than one thousand francs in taxes yearly and the proportion of electors of noble extraction.[11] French social historians have generally assumed that electors paying more than one thousand francs in taxes on their assets belong to the highest circle of social elites. For the 1914 election, population censuses of the 1880s and 1890s furnish the ratio of priests to population, and the 1975 population census furnishes the ratio of priests to population for the 1981 election. These indicators are certainly sufficient to measure church presence.

It was also necessary to construct a composite measure for mode of production, since I have argued that these variables constitute one system. To measure mode of production, an index has been created by transforming each of the mode-of-production variables into standardized scores and adding together the values for all of these standardized scores for each canton. Each mode-of-production variable has been standardized to have a mean of zero and a variance of one. The mode-of-production index has been created by adding the standardized scores for each variable. The proportions of tenants, of medium-sized farms, of priests, of noble electors, and of electors paying more than one thousand francs in taxes are all negatively related to the ideal Mediterranean mode of production according to the model. Thus, to add them to the index each has been multiplied by a minus one. In this way all cases can be accurately arranged with respect to the ideal Mediterranean mode of production. The index is ordered so that a positive score indicates the ideal Mediterranean mode and a negative score the ideal western mode.

It was also necessary to locate measures for the alternative explanatory constructs that are to be tested against mode of production. I would like to have used a suitable measure for each model presented in chapter 1. Since that is not possible, from the available data I have selected proxies that reflect several of these explanations. In particular, there are suitable proxies for two of the structural theses of variation in French political behavior: that based on wine production and that based on region. My measure of *wine production* is the proportion of total cultivated surface under grape cultivation. This measure is available for 1862, 1892–1929, and 1979–1980. To measure the effects of *region*, a dummy variable is created for each region by separating the cantons into their respective departments in the West, Mediterranean, or Northeast. For 1849 and 1981 dummy variables contrasting the effects of the Mediterranean, West, and Northeast are employed, whereas for 1914 a dummy variable that contrasts the effect of West versus Mediterranean is utilized.

There are also excellent proxies for two of the normative theses of variation in French political behavior: the tradition and the religiosity theses. My measure for *tradition* is a canton's proportion of leftist voting in the earliest election. My measure for *religiosity* is the proportion of the adult population that attends Sunday mass on a regular basis (*messalisants*). To my knowledge this is the most reliable measure of French religiosity. Unfortunately, data on religiosity are available only for very recent periods. Therefore, this test is limited to the 1981 election.[12]

METHODS

An examination of this study's propositions requires a number
of statistical techniques. To test the interrelation of the various
mode-of-production factors, zero-order correlations are calculated for all pairs of mode-of-production indicators. To test the
proposition that one mode of production predominates in western France and another in Mediterranean France, a Pearson
correlation is calculated for the two variables—region and mode
of production. If my prediction is correct, the correlation of
mode of production and the Mediterranean region should be
positive and significant, and the correlation of mode of production and the western region should be negative and significant.[13]

To test the proposition that each mode of production has
changed in specified ways between 1849 and 1981, I compared
the means and standard deviation of each mode-of-production
variable within each region in 1849 and 1981. If the means of
the variables have increased and their standard deviations have
decreased between 1849 and 1981, this would suggest that the
region has become more closely identified with a particular
mode of production.

To test the proposition that rightist voting corresponds to one
ideal mode of production and leftist voting to another, it is necessary to develop a testable model. Figure 1 in chapter 2 was a
conceptual representation of the regional mode-of-production
model. This model demonstrated how the mode of production determines voting. Yet this model is not in a testable form
because such intermediary variables as dependency, monitoring, and the perception of interests cannot be measured with
the available data. Figure 2 represents this model in a simplified
and testable fashion. A preliminary examination of the direction and magnitude of the relation between mode of production and leftist voting is done by using zero-order correlations.
To examine the explanatory value of the mode-of-production
index for voting, a bivariate analysis is undertaken in which the
proportion of leftist voting is regressed directly on the index of
the mode-of-production indicators.

To test the proposition that mode of production is a predictor of voting superior to other explanatory constructs, a mul-

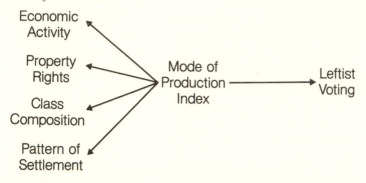

Figure 2. Regional Mode-of-Production Model (Testable)

tiple regression analysis has been employed. For each election, leftist voting is regressed separately on measures of each alternative explanation along with the mode of production. Last, leftist voting is regressed simultaneously on measures of all the alternative explanations and the mode of production.

Some may question my use of correlation coefficients as appropriate tests given the absence of a random sample and the presence of collinearity between the independent variables. However, since it is the population of cantons that I am examining rather than a sample of a canton's population, the relations are actual rather than suggestive: consequently I can ignore the significance levels other than as a gauge of strength.[14] Furthermore, I have inspected the data and found that the correlation coefficients are not being produced or affected by extreme values. With regard to collinearity a difficulty can arise from the inability to specify the separate effects of the different independent estimates and low t-scores. Standard techniques within regression, however, allow us to cope with problems of collinearity and in particular to determine if the collinearity is creating problems in estimating the effects of each variable.[15] I apply such techniques in running my regressions and find collinearity is not so severe as to create difficulties in estimating the effects of each variable.

A pitfall encountered by social scientists in longitudinal studies of political behavior is reliance on aggregate-level data to infer individual-level relationships. In a seminal paper published in 1950 Robinson claimed that whenever an investigator uncritically assumes an identity between aggregate and individual coefficients, he commits an ecological fallacy.[16] Investigators cannot assume that because a particular set of geographical units with a particular pattern of social and demographic characteristics behaves in a particular way, individuals in these geographical regions who possess most or all of the characteristics will all behave in the same fashion.[17] An association at one level may disappear at another, or the association may even be reversed. Therefore, since my data are at a cantonal level, I must caution the reader, in technical terms, that rather than predicting the behavior of individual cultivators I am actually predicting proportions for aggregates of cultivators. For instance, rather than claiming that a cultivator with certain characteristics will behave in a certain way, I am claiming that an aggregate, or group of cultivators whose characteristics can be summarized, will exhibit an average of behaviors.

Although I cannot unambiguously infer individual behavior from group data, I need not refrain from suggesting interpretations about individuals from my group data. By interpreting the aggregate data so that they make sense of individual behavior, I will present conditions that reduce concern about the ecological fallacy. To this end I will provide evidence from the literature on French social protests showing a consistency between the individual and aggregate levels of analysis. Added up, individual actions are consistent with action at the aggregate level.

EMPIRICAL RESULTS AND DISCUSSION

In this section propositions of the mode-of-production theory are tested, and results are presented in Tables 11 thru 29. Following each set of tests is a brief discussion of the findings.

Proposition 1.   The various mode-of-production factors are interrelated and thereby constitute a totality. In particular, a market-oriented economy corresponds to small-scale owner-cultivation land tenure, population agglomeration, and the absence of social elites whereas a subsistence-oriented economy is associated with medium-scale tenancy, population dispersion, and the presence of social elites.

Tables 11 to 13 present the results of the intercorrelations of mode-of-production factors for the three periods.[18] A zero-order correlation is given for all pairs of mode-of-production indicators. These results show considerable support for the proposition. As can be seen in Table 11, 25 of the 35 postulated relations for 1849 are significant. Eight of the 10 nonsignificant relations involve either noble jury or jury paying tax. Especially strong are the correlations of population agglomeration with land value and agricultural labor, small farms with medium farms, and tenants with owner-cultivators and agricultural labor.

With respect to the 1914 results, 17 of the 27 hypothesized relations are significant, and 21 of the 27 relations are in the predicted direction. Agricultural labor and the ratio of priests to population are almost totally nonsignificant correlations. The strongest correlations for the 1914 election are found among population agglomeration and the property rights measures, except agricultural labor. Of the intercorrelations for 1981, 25 of the 27 are significant and 26 of the 27 are in the predicted direction. The two nonsignificant relations involve the ratio of priests to population. Again, as with the 1914 results, the strongest intercorrelations exist among the property rights measures. By contrast, those relations involving the ratio of priests to population are generally weak.

The intercorrelations of the various mode-of-production factors for the 1849, 1914, and 1981 elections show that the results generally support the hypothesis. There is, however, considerable variation in the strengths of the relations between the earliest elections and the most recent one. More specifically, the relations of the class composition measures with other mode-of-production indicators are consistently weak. Agricultural labor seems to be weakly correlated to other factors in 1914, a result we might attribute to the questionable validity of this measure for the 1914 period. With the exception of agricultural labor, the property rights measures show a strong relation among themselves as well as with other mode-of-production factors for the three periods.

Proposition 2. One constellation of social factors, or mode of production, predominates in western France and the other in

Table 11. Zero-order Correlations of Mode-of-Production Factors for the 1849 Election, Mediterranean, Western, and Northeastern Regions

	Land Value	Owner-Cultivators	Tenants-Share-croppers	Agricultural Labor	Small Farms	Medium Farms	Population Agglom-eration	Jury Noble	Jury Taxed
Land value									
Owner-cultivators	.0995*								
Tenants-sharecroppers	-.3513*	-.5410*							
Agricultural labor	.3248*	-.2870*	-.5620*						
Small farms	.3290*	.1686*	-.1732*	.0477					
Medium farms	-.3187*	-.1769*	.3191*	-.2005*	-.8752*				
Population agglomeration	.5376*	.0099	-.4413*	.4761*	.1889*	-.2463*			
Jury noble	-.0837	-.0232	.2411*	-.2310*	.0002	.0630	-.2826*		
Jury taxed	-.0069	-.2226*	.0511	.1366*	-.0313	.0066	.1618*	.2260*	

Note: All correlations based on 327 cases.
*Significant at p less than .05

Table 12. Zero-order Correlations of Mode-of-Production Factors for the 1914 Election, Mediterranean and Western Regions

	Land Value	Owner-Cultivators	Tenants-Share-croppers	Agricultural Labor	Small Farms	Medium Farms	Population Agglomeration	Priests
Land value								
Owner-cultivators	.1818							
Tenants-sharecroppers	−.4276*	−.7750*						
Agricultural labor	.1328	−.5000*	.0937					
Small farms	.2870*	.5364*	−.5620*	−.2174*				
Medium farms	−.2588*	−.6236*	.6519*	.2483*	−.9284*			
Population agglomeration	.4841*	.6184*	−.7463*	.0016	.4995*	−.5577*		
Priests	−.2651*	.3304*	−.1057	−.1879	.1118	.0025	−.0688	

Note: All correlations based on 58 cases.
*Significant at p less than .05

Table 13. Zero-order Correlations of Mode-of-Production Factors for the 1981 Election, Mediterranean, Western, and Northeastern Regions

	Land Value	Owner-Cultivators	Tenants-Share-croppers	Agricultural Labor	Small Farms	Medium Farms	Population Agglomeration	Priests
Land value								
Owner-cultivators	-.1172*							
Tenants-sharecroppers	-.2800*	-.5609*						
Agricultural labor	.4316*	-.3855*	-.5463*					
Small farms	.5191*	.3576*	-.4691*	.1568*				
Medium farms	-.4751*	-.3445*	.5272*	-.2349*	-.8034*			
Population agglomeration	.3173*	.0263*	-.3983*	.4139*	.2644*	-.3370*		
Priests	-.1447*	-.0034	.0902*	-.0951*	-.0297	.1208*	-.1066*	

Note: All correlations based on 413 cases.
*Significant at p less than .05

Table 14. Correlation of Mode of Production and Region, 1849, 1914, 1981

	Mode of Production		
Region	*1849*	*1914*	*1981*
Mediterranean	.4809*	.7139*	.6366*
West	−.6326*	−.7139*	−.6249*
Northeast	.2787*		.0613
Number of cases	327	58	413

*Significant at *p* less than .001

Mediterranean France. More specifically, the Mediterranean region should exhibit market-oriented economic activity, small-scale owner-cultivator land tenure, agglomerated population, and the absence of church and nonchurch elites. The western region, on the other hand, should exhibit subsistence-oriented economic activity, medium-scale tenancy, dispersed population, and the presence of church and nonchurch elites. If my hypothesis is correct, we should expect that the correlation of mode of production and the Mediterranean region is positive and significant and that the correlation of mode of production and the western region is negative and significant.

Table 14 gives the results of the Pearson correlations between mode of production and region for the 1849, 1914, and 1981 periods. As evidenced by these results, the direction of the relation between mode of production and region is significant and in the predicted direction for each election. With respect to the third region, the Northeast, the relation between the two variables is strongly positive and significant for 1849 but weakly positive and nonsignificant for 1981. This result suggests that the northeastern mode of production has indeed moved away from such Mediterranean features as small-scale farms and agricultural labor since 1851. All told, the data strongly support the proposition that the West is characterized by one constellation of social factors and the Mediterranean by another.

Proposition 3.   The western and Mediterranean modes of production have intensified whereas the northeastern mode has
undergone a major shift since 1851. The West is marked increasingly by a subsistence medium-scale tenancy with population dispersion. The Mediterranean is typified increasingly by
market-oriented small-scale owner cultivation or agricultural
wage labor with population agglomeration. The Northeast has
shifted from commercial small-scale tenancy and agricultural
wage labor to commercial medium- to large-scale tenancy or
owner cultivation.

To assess this proposition I have compared the means and
standard deviations of the mode-of-production variables in
1849 and 1981 within each region. If this proposition is correct
for the West and Mediterranean, the means should be higher
for 1981 than for 1849 and the standard deviations should be
lower for 1981 than for 1849. Tables 15 to 17 present the results. As can be seen, the West has experienced an increase in
the proportion of medium and large farms between 1849 and
1981. However, its population agglomeration has grown rather
than declined; its proportion of tenancy has diminished slightly,
although intraregional variation in the proportion of tenancy
has fallen; its land value has increased, although at a slower rate
than in the Mediterranean (adjusting for inflation). According
to the findings, the Mediterranean has followed the expected
changes more closely. Although the proportions of population
agglomeration and of small farms have dropped slightly between 1849 and 1981, the region's land value and its proportion
of owner cultivation have increased substantially. The findings
for the Northeast show that it has indeed undergone the predicted changes. The Northeast has experienced the disappearance of agricultural labor and small farms and the emergence
of medium- and large-scale owner cultivation and tenancy between 1849 and 1981.[19]

While the findings do not overwhelmingly support the proposition that the West and Mediterranean have changed in specified ways, they do nonetheless demonstrate that the West and
Mediterranean continue to be marked by distinctive modes of
production. The West remains a region of medium- to large-

Table 15. Means and Standard Deviations for
Mode-of-Production Factors for the 1849 and 1981 Elections,
Western Region

	1849		1981	
	Mean	*Standard Deviation*	*Mean*	*Standard Deviation*
Land value[a]	2569.7	863.6	17656.2	7009.5
Owner-cultivation	21.5	14.2	47.4	6.0
Tenants-sharecroppers	46.5	20.7	40.2	5.3
Agricultural labor	32.4	16.6	12.4	6.5
Small farms	62.2	20.3	32.1	8.9
Medium farms	34.6	19.1	37.2	10.0
Large farms	3.2	1.7	30.7	9.6
Population agglomeration	30.2	12.1	43.7	10.2

Note: All means and standard deviations based on 178 cases.
  [a] With the exception of the numbers for land value, means and standard deviations are given in percentages.

scale tenancy whereas the Mediterranean is still a region of small-scale owner cultivation. Moreover, in comparison to the Mediterranean and northeastern populations, that of the West remains less agglomerated and its economic activity less market-oriented. For the Northeast, in contrast, the findings show that it has gone from a region of market-oriented small farms and agricultural labor to one of market-oriented medium- to large-scale tenancy and owner cultivation.

Proposition 4.   Rightist voting corresponds to a mode of production characterized by a subsistence-oriented economy, medium-scale tenancy or sharecropping, population dispersion, and the presence of social elites. Leftist voting corresponds to a

Table 16. Means and Standard Deviations for
Mode-of-Production Factors for the 1849 and 1981 Elections,
Mediterranean Region

| | 1849 | | 1981 | |
	Mean	Standard Deviation	Mean	Standard Deviation
Land value[a]	3984.0	1775.0	33908.8	17171.0
Owner-cultivation	37.6	21.3	57.1	8.1
Tenants-sharecroppers	14.7	13.6	24.9	7.4
Agricultural labor	44.0	22.9	18.2	11.1
Small farms	72.5	21.8	69.2	23.2
Medium farms	21.7	13.8	22.3	16.3
Large farms	5.8	4.6	8.5	4.3
Population agglomeration	63.5	25.4	61.0	27.2

Note: All means and standard deviations based on 68 cases.
    [a] With the exception of the numbers for land value, means and standard
deviations are given in percentages.

mode of production typified by a market-oriented economy,
small-scale owner cultivation or salaried agricultural wage labor,
population agglomeration, and the absence of social elites.

To test this proposition I have correlated the proportion of
leftist voting with each indicator of the mode of production.
Table 18 presents these correlations for the three periods. The
correlations demonstrate strong support for the proposition for
all three years with few exceptions. All are in the predicted direction. Assessing the zero-order correlations between the mode of
production factors and leftist voting, we find substantial support
for the hypothesis. In particular, for 1849 all the mode-of-
production factors except population agglomeration and small
farms are significant predictors of leftist voting. For 1914 all but
agricultural labor and the ratio of priests to population are sig-

Table 17. Means and Standard Deviations for
Mode-of-Production Factors for the 1849 and 1981 Elections,
Northeastern Region

	1849		1981	
	Mean	*Standard Deviation*	*Mean*	*Standard Deviation*
Land value[a]	3554.1	928.8	25116.0	6013.3
Owner-cultivation	18.8	14.1	42.8	5.8
Tenants-sharecroppers	34.0	12.8	38.5	3.6
Agricultural labor	48.3	13.5	18.7	6.7
Small farms	67.7	10.6	26.8	11.4
Medium farms	29.6	10.9	30.0	9.3
Large farms	2.7	0.9	43.2	11.6
Population agglomeration	82.5	16.4	83.3	12.3

Note: All means and standard deviations based on 25 cases.

[a] With the exception of the numbers for land value, means and standard deviations are given in percentages.

nificant predictors. It is not surprising that agricultural labor in 1914 is a less than satisfactory predictor of leftist voting since the problem of validity mentioned above makes its adequacy suspect. The effect of the ratio of priests to population in 1914 is similar in magnitude to its effect in 1981, although it is non-significant (probably because of the small sample size in 1914). One would expect the religious measure to be an extremely strong predictor of leftist voting in 1914 since the church-state issue was at its zenith. That the ratio of priests to population is not a good predictor of leftist voting in 1914 and yet becomes a good predictor in 1981 is probably the result of poor measurement associated with the 1914 sample size; the 1981 results demonstrate considerable support for the hypothesis.

This test may provide a clue to the relative strengths of the

Table 18. Zero-order Correlations of Leftist Voting
for the 1849, 1914, and 1981 Elections,
Mediterranean, Western, and Northeastern Regions

	1849	1914	1981
Land value	.1586*	.6122**	.1350*
Owner-cultivators	.2790**	.4236**	.4716**
Tenants-sharecroppers	−.3081**	−.6091**	−.6410**
Agricultural labor	.1114*	−.1006*	.2364**
Small farms	.0822	.3980**	.3954**
Medium farms	−.1187*	−.4770**	−.4257**
Population agglomeration	.0137	.7142**	.3257**
Jury noble	−.1019*		
Jury taxed	−.1342*		
Priests		−.1427	−.1837**
Number of cases	327	58	413

*Significant at p less than .05
**Significant at p less than .001

mode-of-production factors as predictors of leftist voting. Because economic activity and property rights constitute the economic base of the mode of production and thus shape voting,
both directly and indirectly, through the pattern of settlement
and class composition, these factors should furnish the greatest
explanatory power. The results show that with the exception of
agricultural labor, the measures of property rights consistently
emerge as the best predictors of leftist voting. Although significant for the three elections, the measure of economic activity
(land value) does not maintain as consistently high explanatory
power, a result that may be attributed largely to the problems
associated with land value's validity as a measure of economic
activity. In sum, this test suggests that among the mode-of-
production factors, those of property rights are the best predictors of leftist voting.

The results of the previous set of tests support the predicted associations between leftist voting and the various elements of the mode of production. Since I have claimed that the mode of production is a constellation of social factors, however, it is necessary to examine the explanatory power of this constellation for voting. To test this explanatory value, the proportion of leftist voting is directly regressed on the index of the mode of production described above. Table 19 gives the results of the bivariate analyses of leftist voting and mode of production for the 1849, 1914, and 1981 elections. In all three tests of the effect of the mode of production on leftist voting, the relation is positive and significant at the .001 level, as predicted.[20] The results of the bivariate analyses indicate that the model's fit improves from the earliest election to the most recent ones. More specifically, the proportion of explained variance rises from a meager .068 for 1849, to a quite respectable .483 for 1914 and .364 for 1981. Yet differences in sample size across the three elections make this comparison somewhat suspect. For example, the higher proportion of explained variance for the 1914 election may be attributed largely to the small number of cases in 1914. To compare the model's fit systematically, from one election to another, it makes more sense to compare the 1849 and 1981 proportions of explained variance. Accordingly I have performed an additional test, including only those 271 cantons on which I have complete data for both the 1849 and 1981 elections. As seen in Table 20, the results of this analysis show that the proportion of explained variance increases from .089 for 1849 to .404 for 1981. This can certainly be interpreted as strong evidence that the model's fit improves over time.[21]

Proposition 5.   The mode-of-production model is a more satisfactory predictor of French political behavior than other explanations.

Until this point, I have examined the mode-of-production model in relative isolation from other explanations. Implicit in this study is the assumption that the mode-of-production theory of political regionalism is superior to the other theories. To evaluate this claim we turn now to a comparison of our theory

Table 19. Regression of Proportion of Leftist Voting on Mode of Production, by Year

Independent Variables	1849		1914		1981	
	Unstandardized	Standardized	Unstandardized	Standardized	Unstandardized	Standardized
Mode of production	1.032* (.207)**	.266	2.462* (.334)**	.702	.509* (.033)**	.605
Constant	29.810		26.290		26.248	
R²	.068		.483		.364	
Number of cases	327		58		413	

*Significant at p less than .001
**Standard error for unstandardized coefficient

Table 20. Regression of Proportion of Leftist Voting
on Mode of Production, by Year

	1849		1981	
Independent Variables	Un-standardized	Standardized	Un-standardized	Standardized
Mode of produc-tion index	1.196*	.303	.491*	.637
	(.229)**		(.036)**	
Constant	30.990		26.453	
R²	.089		.404	
Number of cases	271		271	

*Significant at *p* less than .001
**Standard error for unstandardized coefficient

with competing explanations. The following tests cannot be interpreted as *definitive* proof of the value of these competing theories, but the results will be highly suggestive.

Even the most cursory comparison of western and Mediterranean France shows that wine production is virtually nonexistent in the West but ubiquitous in the Mediterranean. This raises
the possibility that the divergent political behavior of the two
regions is somehow tied to wine. Might we assume that wine-
producing areas are more likely to manifest left-wing politics than non-wine-producing regions? Admittedly, the wine-
producing Mediterranean is more supportive of the Left than
the livestock-raising West, but this by itself does not prove a relation between leftist voting and grape growing. In contrast, it
is generally acknowledged that vintners in the Bordeaux and
Burgundy regions do not share the leftist proclivities of their
counterparts in the Mediterranean. By the same token, the
Limousin region of central France, which votes consistently
Left, produces little if any wine. And in the West the major
wine-producing department of Maine-et-Loire has been a bas-
tion of political conservatism since 1849.

Yet it is important to test the strength of wine production as a
predictor of leftist voting in France as an alternative to my the-

ory. The zero-order correlation between wine production and leftist voting is positive and significant for 1849, 1914, and 1981.

	1849	*1914*	*1981*
Wine production	.233*	.686*	.516*
Mode of production	.262*	.702*	.586*
Number of cases	327	58	413

* Significant at *p* less than .001

As with the mode of production, the association of wine production with leftist voting improves from the earliest to the most recent elections. To determine whether this relation remains after controlling for the mode of production, leftist voting is regressed on both wine production and mode of production. As the standardized coefficients in Table 21 show, the mode of production is a stronger predictor of leftist voting for all three elections, although the differences are rather small for 1849 and 1914.[22]

Given that wine production correlates positively with leftist voting, how might we explain this relation? Loubere suggests that the collectivist and fluctuating nature of Mediterranean wine production fostered a propensity for radical politics among vintners. He is certainly on the right track, but his explanation remains incomplete. I would argue that the mode-of-production theory affords a more thorough understanding of the strong relation between wine production and voting. In France, most wine-producing cantons vote Left *not* because they produce wine per se but rather because they possess a market-oriented economy based on small-scale owner cultivation or agricultural wage labor and a highly agglomerated settlement pattern and, thus, their interests are best represented by the Left. In other words, wine-producing cantons vote Left because their mode of production closely approximates the Mediterranean ideal type. If we could locate wine-producing cantons with medium- to large-scale sharecropping or tenant farming and a highly dispersed settlement pattern, we would probably find them voting Right.

In this way the wine production argument complements

Table 21. Regression of Proportion of Leftist Voting on Wine Production and Mode of Production, by Year

Independent Variables	1849		1914		1981	
	Unstandardized	Standardized	Unstandardized	Standardized	Unstandardized	Standardized
Mode of production	.771*	.196	1.490*	.425	.410*	.478
	(.196)**		(.516)**		(.056)**	
Wine production	.154	.143	.293*	.354	.034*	.136
	(.143)**		(.122)**		(.016)**	
Constant	28.813		25.175		26.196	
R^2	.079		.524		.347	
Number of cases	327		58		413	

*Significant at p less than .001
**Standard error for unstandardized coefficient

rather than competes with the mode-of-production theory. The data support the claim that wine production and mode of production are closely related. The following example presents the correlations between wine production and mode of production for 1849, 1914, and 1981.

	1849	1914	1981
Wine production	.458*	.783*	.796*
Number of cases	327	58	413

* Significant at p less than .001

In all three years the relation between these two factors is positive and quite substantial, demonstrating that wine-producing cantons tend to be characterized by market-oriented small-scale owner cultivation or agricultural wage labor, population agglomeration, and the absence of social elites.

It has been suggested that the extremely strong relation between mode of production and region that I found in an earlier study may indicate that region rather than mode of production is responsible for leftist voting in the Mediterranean and rightist voting in the West.[23] Though the advocates of this perspective claim that region affects voting behavior, they cannot explain exactly what it is about region that influences people's voting choice. Nevertheless, I have evaluated the relative predictive strengths of mode of production and region by regressing leftist voting on dummy variables that represent regional location and mode of production. If after controlling for region I find the mode of production is still a significant predictor of voting, then I can assume that mode of production has an effect on voting independent of other regional influences.

Table 22 presents the results of this test. As can be seen, after controlling for region, I found the relation between mode of production and leftist voting to remain quite strong and significant for each of the three elections. Hence, when the effects of region are removed, mode of production is still an empirically significant predictor of voting.

As discussed earlier, numerous scholars have also attributed variation in political behavior to the degree of a population's religiosity. The more religiously faithful individuals are, the greater

Table 22. Regression of Proportion of Leftist Voting on Region and Mode of Production, by Year

Independent Variables	1849		1914		1981	
	Unstandardized	Standardized	Unstandardized	Standardized	Unstandardized	Standardized
Mediterranean	10.906* (3.040)**	.238	12.560* (3.202)**	.444	3.921* (.040)**	.417
West	-7.742* (2.669)**	-.176			-.316 (.652)**	-.036
Mode of production	.778* (.257)**	.200	1.432* (.397)**	.408	.266* (.040)**	.316
Constant	29.354		22.255		25.498	
R^2	.171		.603		.480	
Number of cases	327		58		413	

Note: The two region variables are dummy variables that identify locations in the Mediterranean and West, respectively.
*Significant at p less than .001
**Standard error for unstandardized coefficient

the likelihood that they will be politically conservative. As proof of this proposition, adherents of the religiosity theory point to the strong relation between regions of conservative voting and those of frequent church attendance, on the one hand, and between regions of leftist voting and those of infrequent church attendance, on the other. This association, however, does not automatically demonstrate a causal relation. I hold that the relation between rightist and leftist voting and degree of religiosity is in fact that between two effects of a common cause. The same structural factors that cause divergence in political behavior are responsible for divergence in religious behavior. In the following test I hope to establish that the mode of production and religiosity are highly correlated and that the mode of production is a better predictor of leftist voting than religiosity.

Table 23 presents the results of the zero-order correlation between religiosity and leftist voting for 1981. The results demonstrate that religiosity and leftist voting do bear a strong negative relation to one another ($r = .-544$). That is, those cantons with high church attendance vote Right whereas those cantons with low church attendance vote Left. I am interested here, however, in whether this relation holds after I have controlled for mode of production. The results of this analysis (Table 24) show that mode of production and religiosity are both significant predictors of leftist voting, although the standardized coefficient shows that the effect of mode of production on voting

Table 23. Correlations among Mode of Production, Religiosity, and Proportion of Leftist Voting for 1981

	Mode of production	Religiosity	Leftist voting
Mode of production			
Religiosity		−.317*	
Leftist voting		.605*	−.544*
Number of cases		413	

*Significant at p less than .001

Table 24. Regression of Proportion of Leftist Voting on Religiosity and Mode of Production for 1981

Independent Variable	Unstandardized	Standardized
Religiosity	−.072* (.007)**	−.392
Mode of production	.404* (.031)**	.480
Constant	29.314	
R²	.501	
Number of cases	413	

*Significant at p less than .001
**Standard error for unstandardized coefficient

is somewhat stronger. The two variables together explain substantially more of the variance in leftist voting than either does alone. Whereas I had argued that religious behavior is akin to political behavior in that both are shaped largely by the economic structure or mode of production, I find instead that, at least for France, religiosity has an effect on political behavior that is independent of economic structure. It thus appears from these results that voting preferences of individuals are influenced by both their economic interests and cultural attitudes.

To examine the relation between voting and religiosity and between voting and mode of production, I have performed the same multiple regression analysis within my principal regions, the West and Mediterranean (Table 25). To discern whether one explanation affords a greater explanatory value for a particular region, I compared the unstandardized coefficients of religiosity and mode of production in both regions. For each unit increase in religiosity, leftist voting falls by twice as much in the West as in the Mediterranean. All told, for the 273 western cantons, when leftist voting is regressed on mode of production and religiosity, religiosity is clearly the stronger predictor. By contrast, for the 102 Mediterranean cantons, when leftist voting is regressed on mode of production and religiosity, mode of production is clearly the stronger predictor. This suggests that

Table 25. Regression of Proportion of Leftist Voting on Religiosity and Mode of Production for 1981, by Region

	Mediterranean		West	
Independent Variables	Un-standardized	Standardized	Un-standardized	Standardized
Religiosity	−.038**	−.218	−.079**	−.559
	(.012)***		(.007)	
Mode of production	.430**	.678	−.065*	−.068
	(.044)***		(.050)***	
Constant	31.923		28.460	
R²	.53		.30	
Number of cases	102		273	

*Significant at *p* less than .05
**Significant at *p* less than .001
***Standard error for unstandardized coefficient

religious beliefs play a more important role in shaping voting behavior in the West, *pace* Marx, and economic interests play a more consequential role in shaping voting behavior in the Mediterranean, *pace* Weber.[24]

But it would be hasty to conclude that mode of production is a weak determinant of voting in western France, since the model argues that mode of production affects voting both directly and indirectly. Thus far I have examined only its direct effects on voting. According to the model, however, the mode of production should affect voting indirectly by determining which individuals or groups in a community will control the allocation of vital resources. To the extent that individuals wish to maintain access to these resources, they will depend on the suppliers and will thus probably support the political programs of these suppliers (see Figure 1 in chapter 2). I argued above that in western France the mode of production has created an environment in which the Catholic church serves as the principal provider of resources (that is, of employment, charity, education, land, and social activities). Cultivators who are interested in obtaining ac-

Table 26. Decomposition of the Total Effects on Voting
in Western and Mediterranean France

Effects of Religiosity	*Western*	*Mediterranean*
Direct Effects	−1.839	−.238
	(−.545)	(−.290)
Effects of Mode of Production		
Direct Effects of Mode of Production	−.065	.405
	(−.075)	(.706)
Indirect Effects of Mode of Production via Religiosity	3.160	.369
	(.269)	(.024)
Total Effects of Mode of Production	3.105	.774
	(.194)	(.73)
Spurious Effects of Religiosity		
	.112	.626
	(.035)	(−.370)

Note: In addition to the unstandardized metric coefficients, this table
presents the standardized path coefficients in parentheses.

cess to these resources are likely to attend church regularly and
to support political programs favorable to the Catholic church.
If this argument is correct for western France, we should expect to find that religiosity is an intervening variable between
mode of production and voting. Table 26 and Figure 3 present
the path coefficients of mode of production and religiosity on
leftist voting. The results confirm my hypothesis and demonstrate that mode of production affects voting in western France
through the intervening variable of religiosity. By contrast, in
Mediterranean France even the weak relationship between religiosity and leftist voting and the strong relationship between
mode of production and leftist voting are consistent with the
mode-of-production theory: by virtue of their mode of produc-

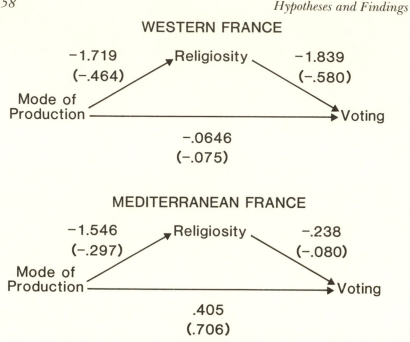

Note: The path coefficients in parentheses are the standardized coefficients.

Figure 3. Effects of Mode of Production and Religiosity on Voting: Causal Model

tion, cultivators in Mediterranean France have not been dependent on the Catholic church for resources and should thus have little interest in attending church or in supporting its political programs.

In short, the religiosity thesis, essentially as an intervening variable, may in certain cases complement rather than compete with mode of production as an explanation of French voting behavior.

The final alternative theory I treat has without doubt the firmest grip on scholars who analyze voting behavior. Party loyalty is always the answer when structural explanations fail; it implies that individuals hold an attachment to particular parties as a consequence of an earlier association or of parental or group socialization. To test the strength of tradition as a predictor of left-

Table 27. Correlations among 1981 Mode of Production, 1849 Leftist Voting, and 1981 Leftist Voting

	1981 Mode of Production	*1849 Leftist Voting*	*1981 Leftist Voting*
1981 Mode of Production			
1849 Leftist Voting	.286*		
1981 Leftist Voting	.637*	.466*	
Number of cases	271		

*Significant at *p* less than .001

ist voting I correlated the proportion of individuals voting Left in 1849 with the proportion voting Left in 1981 (Table 27).[25] My supposition here is that a canton's present voting behavior should mirror its former voting behavior if tradition, or party loyalty, is truly a significant factor. The zero-order correlation between 1849 leftist voting and 1981 leftist voting is .466, which is highly significant but less than the .637 correlation between mode of production and 1981 leftist voting. To compare more accurately the effects of tradition and mode of production on voting I regressed 1981 leftist voting on both 1849 leftist voting and 1981 mode of production. As evidenced by the results in Table 28, both variables have significant effects on voting. The effect of mode of production on voting is stronger than that of 1849 leftist voting, however, and suggests two important findings. First, mode of production would appear to be a better predictor of voting than tradition. In other words, material interests rather than nonmaterial associations play a larger role in shaping political preferences among French cultivators. Second, although the relation between 1849 leftist voting and 1981 leftist voting is significant, it is not as strong as we might have expected. This may imply that although the political Right remains strong in the West and the political Left in the Mediterranean, there has been meaningful intraregional change in voting behavior. Some cantons appear to have moved leftward and

Table 28. Regression of Proportion of Leftist Voting on 1849
Leftist Voting and 1981 Mode of Production for 1981

Independent Variable	Unstandardized	Standardized
1849 Leftist Voting	.062*	.309
	(.009)**	
1981 Mode of Production	.423*	.549
	(.035)**	
Constant	24.534	
R^2	.490	
Number of cases	271	

*Significant at *p* less than .001
**Standard error for unstandardized coefficients

others appear to have moved rightward since 1849. That 1981
leftist voting is related more strongly to mode of production
than to tradition might suggest that much of the intraregional
change in voting may be attributed to changes in the modes of
production.

In a final test of mode of production as a satisfactory predictor of leftist voting after controlling for the effects of variables
measuring alternative explanations, I entered the alternative
constructs along with mode of production into a single multiple
regression of voting. The results are presented in Table 29. For
each election, after controlling for the effects of the other variables—region, religiosity, and tradition—I find that mode of
production is still a significant predictor of leftist voting.

Proposition 6.   Market-oriented small-scale owner-cultivators
and agricultural wage laborers in a social structure with a concentrated population and an absence of elites vote for the Left
because its program more closely approximates their interests.
Conversely, subsistence-oriented medium- to large-scale tenants and sharecroppers in a social structure marked by a dis-

Table 29. Regression of Proportion of Leftist Voting on Region, Religiosity, 1849 Leftist Voting, and Mode of Production, by Year

	1849		1914		1981	
Independent Variables	Unstandardized	Standardized	Unstandardized	Standardized	Unstandardized	Standardized
Mediterranean	10.906* (3.040)**	.238	12.560* (3.202)**	.444	3.105* (.650)**	.337
West	−7.742* (2.669)**	−.176			.727 (.552)**	.087
Religiosity					−.060* (.007)**	−.344
1849 Leftist voting					.031* (.009)**	.153
Mode of production	.778* (.257)**	.200	1.432* (.397)**	.408	.244* (.041)**	.318
Constant	29.354		22.255		26.668	
R²	.171		.603		.623	
Number of cases	327		58		269	

Note: The two region variables are dummy variables that identify locations in the Mediterranean and West, respectively.
*Significant at p less than .05
**Standard error for unstandardized coefficient

persed population and the presence of elites vote for the Right because its program more closely approximates their interests.

The preceding data analysis demonstrates that agricultural systems with a large proportion of market-oriented small-scale cultivators or salaried agricultural laborers, an agglomerated settlement pattern, and an absence of resource-controlling elites tend to vote Left whereas agricultural systems with a sizable proportion of subsistence-oriented medium-scale tenants or sharecroppers, a dispersed settlement pattern, and the presence of resource-controlling elites tend to vote Right. Yet the existence of these correlations does not prove that people acted for the reasons I have proposed. More specifically, the data suggest but do not confirm that certain groups in the countryside supported the Left because it advocated land redistribution, progressive taxation, and the curtailment of monopolistic practices. With equal inconclusiveness they suggest that other groups supported the Right because it opposed church-state separation and land redistribution. To confirm these data would require asking peasants to say why they were voting for either the Left or the Right.

A systematic examination of the expressed political preferences of individual French cultivators since 1849—nearly 140 years—would require an effort beyond my reach. In lieu of conducting such a survey, I will review the literature on French social protests to determine what peasants participated in right-wing and left-wing collective actions and what their motivations for participation may have been. For instance, if it can be demonstrated that market-oriented small-scale owner-cultivators and agricultural wage laborers participated in social protests espousing progressive taxation, credit to small farmers, and restraint of middlemen and monopolies and that subsistence-oriented medium-scale tenants and sharecroppers participated in social protests advocating the defense of church and noble privilege, then I can argue with some certainty that particular kinds of peasants would likely have voted Left or Right for the reasons I have suggested. This should both support my claim that individual actions, added up, are consistent with action at the aggregate level and, as a consequence, lessen any fear of the ecological fallacy. An examination of the secondary literature on French social protest should reap an additional benefit: it will demonstrate that the regional mode-of-production model of political behavior reframes and synthesizes the complex and variegated literature on French social protest.

The Vendée is one of the loveliest departments of western France, with its pristine beaches of pure white sand and tall pine forests. But the Vendée evokes a different meaning to students of French social protests, for the department lent its name to one of France's well-known counterrevolutionary protests in the 1790s. In his richly detailed study of the Vendéen counter-revolution, Charles Tilly furnishes a view of two contrasting societies: the politically conservative Mauges that provided a disproportionately large number of recruits to the counter-revolution and the republican Val-Saumois that provided few or none. Tilly notes that during August 1792 numerous anti-republican social protests occurred in the Mauges. Estimates of the number of protesters, often led by mayors and local nobles, ranged from five to ten thousand. They protested the central government's conscriptions and attacked symbols of the re-public; many insurgents were heard to shout, "Vive le roi, vive la noblesse!" In contrast, military conscription proceeded with-out incident in Val-Saumois.[26]

How can we explain the enthusiastic support for counter-revolution in the Mauges and the virtual absence of support in Val-Saumois? Tilly bases his explanation on a detailed study of the agricultural systems of the Mauges and Val-Saumois in two representative villages. La Pommeraye in the Mauges was a rural community geared largely toward subsistence production, with 68.1 percent of its population engaged in agriculture. Further-more, out of a total of 508 adult males, 231 rented large farms from (mostly noble) landlords and 77 rented small farms.[27] In short, subsistence cultivation by tenants characterized the village of La Pommeraye. In contrast, Grézillé in the Val-Saumois was more market-oriented, specializing in wine production. In this market-oriented community, 74.8 percent of the population worked in agriculture. Out of a total of 155 males, only 11 rented large farms and 18 rented small farms. Most males, Tilly ob-serves, owned and cultivated small plots. Thus, Grézillé typified market-oriented small-scale owner cultivation. Neither La Pommeraye nor Grézillé were exceptions; subsistence tenancy was common throughout the Mauges, and cash-crop smallholding was prevalent throughout Val-Saumois.[28] The social composition of the Mauges and Val-Saumois argues that the Vendéen counterrevolution disproportionately recruited tenants from a subsistence economy rather than owner-cultivators from a cash-crop economy.

That tenants rather than owner-cultivators constituted the backbone of the West's counterrevolutionary movement finds additional support in T. J. A. Le Goff and D. M. G. Sutherland's study of the social origins of counterrevolution in western France.[29] In examining the occupational distribution of the counterrevolutionary Chouans, Le Goff and Sutherland found that the tenants on large estates were on the counterrevolutionary side whereas landowners of all sorts ranging from small independent proprietors to substantial urban and rural landlords were on the republican side.[30]

The French peasantry appeared again in the events surrounding Louis-Napoléon Bonaparte's seizure of power in December 1851. Although Karl Marx, in *The Eighteenth Brumaire of Louis Bonaparte*, considered peasants to be the backbone of support for Bonaparte, it is quite clear that his depiction of a reactionary peasantry does not apply to all French peasants.[31] Studies of the social protests in response to the coup d'état demonstrate that a sizable proportion of market-oriented small owner-cultivators and agricultural wage laborers actively resisted the coup.

The resistance to the coup d'état (widely referred to as the 1851 Insurrection) was organized primarily by the Democratic-Socialists. Between 1848 and 1851 the Democratic-Socialists had come to power in many rural districts. They campaigned on such issues as abolishing the wine tax and shifting the general burden of taxation from the poor to the rich; guaranteeing full employment and higher wages; providing low-interest loans through state banks; and fulfilling popular demands for rights of usage to common lands.[32] We would expect individuals who resisted the coup to have come from the ranks of those with the most to lose from dismantling the Democratic-Socialist organization, since a principal goal of Louis-Napoléon Bonaparte's coup d'état was to eliminate the Democratic-Socialist movement.[33]

Ted Margadant's analysis of the occupational background of a sample of individuals arrested in 1851 throughout France shows that 44 percent were employed in agriculture, 48 percent in crafts and commerce, and 6 percent in liberal professions. Peasants were especially subject to prosecution in Mediterranean France, where 53 percent of those in Margadant's sample were cultivators.[34] The proportion climbs to 67 percent in the vicinity of Béziers, where the resistance received overwhelming support from the wine-producing agricultural wage laborers.[35] Detailed accounts by Loubere, Smith, Agulhon, and Margadant indicate that these Mediterranean French insurgents were typically small-scale owner-cultivators and agricultural wage laborers engaged in cash-crop production.[36]

Leaders of the resistance were frequently owner-cultivators. According to Margadant, owner-cultivators accounted for nearly half the village leadership in rebel zones of southeastern France.[37] In particular, Margadant notes that in the vicinity of Béziers six out of nine peasant leaders were owner-cultivators while in the central Drôme six of the twelve high-ranking leaders were owner-cultivators.[38] Louis Comte is an example of an owner-cultivator who provided important leadership to his village of Puy-Saint-Martin during the resistance. Addressing a sympathetic crowd of one hundred to one hundred fifty peasant cultivators, Comte declared, "My friends, we must not steal, pillage or burn, but we must preserve the *Democratic* and *Social Republic*."[39]

Salaried agricultural laborers contributed substantially to the resistance as well. In Béziers, Largentière, Apt, Manosque, and Forcalquier, where peasants composed the majority of those prosecuted for participation in the 1851 Insurrection, agricultural wage laborers were overrepresented.[40]

Statements made by many of those who participated in the tumultuous events leading to the 1851 Insurrection provide additional evidence that owner-cultivators and salaried agricultural laborers supported the Democratic-Socialists. A peasant from the department of the Gard testified that he joined the republican movement because "I was often told that if we had the real Republic, we would pay less taxes, only the rich would pay them. Wages would be higher, and we'd have money at 3 percent at the mortgage bank."[41] A second peasant, who cultivated vines, claimed that he joined a leftist secret society and participated in the 1851 Insurrection because those who recruited him assured him that in a Democratic-Socialist republic he could sell his wine at 50 or 60 centimes a liter rather than at the current price of 25 centimes a liter.[42] And a third peasant, an agricultural laborer in the vicinity of Béziers, declared that he joined a leftist secret society because "I was recruited by Laurent Hermen (shoemaker from a neighboring village), who told me that our position was very difficult, it only depended on us to make it better, and to reach this aim I must enter a secret society whose purpose was to unite the lower classes in the election. It was necessary to bring to power the leaders of the Red Party (Republicans), with their government. We would earn large daily wages and be perfectly well off. So I agreed."[43]

Whereas popular support for the 1851 Insurrection against Louis-Napoléon was considerable among peasants in the rural areas of Mediterranean France, it was virtually nonexistent in the agricultural zones of western and Northeastern France. In Finistère, for example, the government did not have to dismantle a single Democratic-Socialist organization, for none existed. Moreover, there were few disturbances during the brief life of the Second Republic and not a single arrest at the time of the coup d'état.[44] Similarly, in Loir-et-Cher there were no demonstrations against the coup. Nonetheless, 137 Democratic-Socialist militants were arrested. They were generally from the liberal professions.[45]

In his illuminating study of politics in Loir-et-Cher, Dupeux notes that Louis-Napoléon's seizure of power received general approval throughout the department's rural districts. But some variation did exist. The postcoup referendum calling for approval of Napoléon's seizure of power obtained an 88 percent "yes" vote in the canton of Mondoubleau. On the other hand, the "no" vote reached 22 percent in the canton of Marchenoir. By delving further into Dupeux's study we learn that in the canton of Mondoubleau 80 percent to 90 percent of all farms were tenancies and that holdings were generally medium-scale whereas in the canton of Marchenoir there was, by contrast, a sizable proportion of small-scale owner cultivation.[46]

The literature on the 1851 Insurrection shows clearly that in agricultural areas leftist support came primarily from market-oriented owner-cultivators and salaried agricultural laborers. Apparently, these particular groups had the most to lose from the elimination of the Democratic-Socialist movement. The evidence suggests that the Democratic-Socialist program of low-cost credit, progressive taxation, emasculation of noble and clerical power, and curtailment of monopolistic practices corresponded closely with the perceived self-interests of small-scale owner-cultivators and salaried agricultural laborers engaged in commercialized economic activity.

The first two decades of the twentieth century ushered in two noteworthy social protests, one concerning the separation of church and state, the other concerning the making of table wines. Each protest mobilized a large number of peasants and each was rooted in a particular French region.

During the 1880s the French state had launched a campaign to separate church and state. Governmental legislation limiting the power of the Catholic church over education provoked opposition throughout France. The opposition grew consistently; by 1905 it crystallized in a series of large-scale social protests. No French province was as convulsed by these protests as Brittany. Three pieces of legislation appeared to have ignited the crisis in 1905: the law of 1 July 1901 on religious congregations; the decree of 29 September 1902 on the use of the Breton language in churches; and the legislation of 12 December 1905 on the separation of church and state.[47] To implement the new regulations the police had to close schools and expel the nuns who taught in them. In the department of Finistère alone, sixty-four schools were closed by force. Throughout Brittany, the police encountered angry crowds who shouted insults and threw objects. At Saint-Méen, Ploudamel, and Le Folgoet, battles erupted between police and protesters. The largest incident occurred at Quimper, where twelve thousand protesters attacked a counterdemonstration comprising republicans and socialist workers from the city of Brest.[48] Berger's account of these protests does not specify the social composition of the demonstrators. However, my examination of Finistère's population and agricultural censuses indicates that the villages of Saint-Méen, Ploudamel, and Le Folgoet, as well as the area surrounding the city of Quimper, contain a disproportionate number of tenants and *domestiques* (agricultural servants). A thorough examination of the social composition of these demonstrations should show that subsistence-oriented tenant farmers and *domestiques* were well represented.

A very different social protest erupted in Mediterranean France at about the same time, originating in the *vin ordinaire* industry. In 1901 Mediterranean vintners grew increasingly concerned about the importation of Algerian wine and the northern French production of adulterated wines from beet sugar.[49] Mediterranean vintners mobilized pressure on the national government to halt these practices. To make matters worse, the French table wine industry experienced a series of slumps caused mainly by overproduction between 1901 and 1907. In response to falling prices, large wine producers reduced the wages of vineyard workers and attempted to gain total control of the wine market.[50] Wine merchants also began to demand an increased share of small producers' profits from the sale of wine. Opposing these practices of large wine producers and wine merchants, agricultural wage laborers and small owner-cultivators formed "Committees for the Defense of Winegrowing."[51] These committees demanded that the large landowners respect the customary hourly wages for vine workers and that small producers have the right to sell natural wines on the market at a reasonable profit to themselves (rather than to merchants or other middlemen).[52] The French Socialist party offered its full support for the demands of these committees.[53]

Intransigeance by large wine producers, merchants, and the national government sparked numerous strikes and large-scale demonstrations between 1903 and 1907.[54] In Roussillon and Lower Languedoc 123 villages experienced strikes between 1904 and 1905. From an agricultural work force of 33,154, a total of 32,701 agricultural workers participated in these strikes.[55] In 1904, Barral comments, 43,067 agricultural workers struck, resulting in over 200,000 work days lost.[56] The collective action reached its climax in 1907 with the "Révolte du Midi," a series of large-scale demonstrations by agricultural wage laborers and small-scale owner-cultivators against the government, large landowners, and wine merchants. The magnitude of these demonstrations, which were marked by considerable violence and property damage, can best be appreciated by the numbers of participants: 100,000 in Béziers, 172,000 in Perpignan, 200,000 in Carcassonne, 150,000 in Nîmes, and 500,000 in Montpellier.[57] In response to the "Révolte du Midi" Premier Georges Clemenceau flooded the region with troops and arrested many of the leaders. In one case soldiers from Languedoc refused to obey orders and mutinied.[58]

Thus we have another example of social protest where the goals of the protesters corresponded closely to the programs of a particular political party. In the case of the 1903–1907 agricultural strikes and demonstrations, wine-producing agricultural wage laborers and small owner-cultivators demanded government assistance, higher wages, and restraint of monopolies and middlemen—demands that were central tenets of the Left's program.

Two other social protests deserve attention here, for both furnish additional evidence that right-wing collective action attracted subsistence-oriented medium-scale tenants and that left-wing collective action appealed to market-oriented small-scale owner-cultivators and agricultural wage laborers. During the 1930s a right-wing peasant movement sprang up in western France. Referred to as the Dorgeriste movement, the Défense paysanne, or the Chemises vertes, this movement shared many features with European fascist movements of the 1920s and 1930s. The Dorgeriste movement appears to have arisen in reaction to the agricultural crises of the 1930s. Its program consisted of denunciations of government bureaucrats, hatred for Communism, and vague references to fascist ideology.[59] In keeping with the style of fascist movements, the members of the Dorgeristes wore green shirts. By Hazo's account, the movement found its greatest backing in the areas of Chateaubriant, Redon, and Presqu'île Guérandaise (parts of the departments of Loire-Inférieure and Ille-et-Vilaine).[60] These areas are, not surprisingly, strongholds of medium-scale tenant farming. In one demonstration in the city of Quimper a crowd of fifteen to twenty thousand people gathered to listen to speakers from the Dorgeristes and another predominantly right-wing peasant group, the Landerneau movement.[61]

A more recent social protest, by winegrowers in 1953, revived memories of the 1907 "Révolte du Midi." The protest was in response to the government's implementation of the *Code du vin*. The *Code du vin* required the government to lower the quota price of wine alcohol regularly purchased by the *Service des alcools* from 30,000 to 22,000 francs the hectoliter. Angry vintners formed a *Comité de salut viticole* and demanded that the price be readjusted to 30,000 francs. The government refused the Committee's demand; the next day winegrowers barricaded roads throughout the French Mediterranean.[62] In his study of the 1953 winegrowers' protest, Warner observed that small wine producers were the principal participants.[63] Again in 1953, as in 1851 and 1907, the French Left's program embodied the demands of these protestors; in particular, the S.F.I.O. (Socialist party) called for a guarantee of price stabilization and accessible credit.[64]

This sample of the secondary literature on French agrarian social protests furnishes evidence that owner-cultivators and laborers participated in left-wing protests whereas tenants participated in right-wing protests, in patterns consistent with patterns of leftist and rightist voting and consistent with the Left and Right's positions on the issues of state subsidies, defense of small farms, progressive taxation, land redistribution, curtailment of capitalistic practices, church-state separation, and rural democracy.

Finally, this examination of the secondary literature may provide a means to integrate the invaluable case studies of French rural political behavior into one holistic synthesis. Situating the peasants who have been the focus of the numerous local studies along a continuum between the ideal Mediterranean mode-of-production model at one end and the ideal western model at the other brings coherence to the rich mosaic of studies about these French peasants. The model helps explain, for instance, why Tilly's and Bois's tenant farmers of the Vendée and Sarthe supported the counterrevolution and why Loubere's and Smith's wine producers and Agulhon's and Judt's smallholders favored the socialists.

CONCLUSION

The preceding tests have demonstrated the value that the mode-of-production model has in explaining the persistence of French political regionalism. Several propositions—all deriving from the mode-of-production theory—have been analyzed. The results indicate that the data generally support the model. The various mode-of-production factors constitute a totality. One constellation of social factors corresponds to the western region and the other to the Mediterranean region. All three modes of production have generally changed in specified ways. Leftist voting is, as predicted, negatively related to subsistence-oriented economic activity, medium-scale tenancy and sharecropping, population dispersion, and the presence of social elites; it is positively related to market-oriented economic activity, small-scale owner cultivation, agricultural wage labor, population agglomeration, and the absence of social elites. The index of the mode of production is a significant predictor of leftist voting for 1849, 1914, and 1981. And finally, when tested against the competing explanations of region, religiosity, and tradition, mode of production remains a strong predictor of French political behavior.

But how are we to make sense of the relation between a region's mode of production and its voting behavior? By themselves, structures cannot explain anything. The rational-choice assumption that voters select the political party or program they think will provide them the greatest benefits offers a means to explain this relation between the two aggregate levels. Only by taking into account the impact of regional modes of production upon (rational) individuals can we understand the aggregate effects of these structures. That is why I find rational choice useful: it links structures to actors and produces determinate (and sometimes counterintuitive) outcomes. The following two examples should make this point clearer. First, in his examination of the French peasantry, Marx argued that Louis-Napoléon's support came largely from small-holding peasants, in whom social conditions nurtured a "false consciousness" that caused them to support the politically conservative Louis-Napoléon. But the data show that cantons marked by a large population of smallholders voted Left and not Right. How then are we to explain this occurrence? As rational actors the small-holding peasants supported the Left because the Left's programs corresponded to their material interests. Similarly, it was not because they nurtured a "false consciousness" that landless tenants and sharecroppers supported the Right but rather because its programs more closely approximated their material interests.

Second, in contrast to Siegfried's explanation, a rational-choice theory offers a more realistic explanation of the political conservatism of western French cultivators. Siegfried argued that support for the Right persisted in western France because elites enforced compliance from their dependent cultivators by threatening them with the removal of resources. Although his explanation may be valid for the nineteenth century, it is less compelling for the twentieth century, when the capacity of land-lords to monitor voting has declined by virtue of governmental enforcement of the rights of tenants and the voting franchise. Moreover, the data demonstrate that cantons marked by high numbers of tenants and sharecroppers continued to vote for the Right and not the Left during the twentieth century. Rational-choice theory helps to make sense of this finding by proposing that western cultivators should have supported the Right because as subsistence-oriented medium-scale tenants or share-croppers they found that the programs of the Right reflected their material interests (even in the absence of landlord intimi-dation). By linking structures to individuals, rational-choice the-ory offers an explanation for these aggregate relations.

Too often historians and sociologists have shied away from macrolevel theories and their empirical verification. This chap-ter has demonstrated that a macrolevel theory of voting persis-tence can be tested empirically and, more important, that the mode-of-production theory is a valid explanation of French po-litical regionalism. For the time being, however, we must pro-ceed cautiously in assessing the quantitative findings of this re-search. Because of problems in measurement and the use of group-level data to infer the behavior of individuals, the conclusions drawn from these tests will remain more suggestive than definitive. But the fact remains that the mode-of-production model has considerable promise as an explanation of the persistence of French political regionalism. Greater acceptance of the value of this theory will come as it can be shown to have relevance for cases of political regionalism elsewhere. It is to the wider implications of the mode-of-production model that I now turn.

8

IMPLICATIONS

In the previous chapter the mode-of-production model was shown to hold considerable promise as an explanation of the persistence of French political regionalism. But the promise of this model extends beyond the French case. In fact, the mode-of-production model should provide important explanatory keys to the existence of political regionalism elsewhere.

RURAL VOTING PATTERNS

France is not the only country for which a mode-of-production model of voting may have relevance. Consider Italy for instance. In Italy, at least as early as the election of 1904, the North (comprising the provinces of Piedmont, Lombardy, and Venezia) has supported the Center-Right; the North-Center (comprising the provinces of Liguria, Emilia, Tuscany, and Umbria) has supported the Left; the interior South (comprising the provinces of Campania, Apulia, Lucania, Calabria, and Sicily) has supported the Right.[1] These three political tendencies correspond in many respects to those of France's three principal regions and may derive in large part from the different regional modes of production in Italy. Northern Italian agriculture shares many features with northeastern French agriculture; it is largely dominated by intensive capitalistic farming, mechanization, medium-scale owner cultivation or tenant land tenure. North-central agriculture has much in common with French Mediterranean agriculture, including the cultivation of grains, vines, and olives in a market-oriented setting. The principal forms of land tenure in the north-central region are *mezzadria* (small-scale sharecropping) and small-scale owner cultivation. Mezzadria sharecropping differs from the system found in

174

western France insofar as the mezzadria system involves market-oriented small-scale units rather than subsistence-oriented medium-scale ones. Agriculture in the interior South mirrors in some significant respects that found in western France. In the interior South small-scale subsistence farming (*latifondo contadino*) predominates. Farmers produce for the needs of their families; contact among villages and towns is infrequent; and cultivators are dependent on their landlords.[2] These similarities between Italy and France suggest that future research may demonstrate a connection between the voting patterns and modes of production of Italian farmers, because their modes of production have created particular constellations of interests corresponding to specific political programs.

The United States has also had its share of political movements strongly associated with a regional base. One of the best known cases is the Populist movement, which in the 1880s and 1890s had three regional centers. Each was overwhelmingly rural and each was associated with a product whose price had fallen catastrophically; the mountain states were based mainly upon silver; the South was based chiefly upon cotton; and the four trans-Mississippi states of Kansas, Nebraska, and the two Dakotas were based principally upon wheat.[3]

Among these three strands of populism, the trans-Mississippi movement has been the focus of much attention, largely because of the electoral successes of this movement during the 1890s. In the 1892 presidential election James Weaver, the Populist party candidate, obtained a popular vote of 48.96 percent in North Dakota, 48.44 percent in Kansas, 41.0 percent in Nebraska, and 37.58 percent in South Dakota.[4] The mode-of-production model may help explain the phenomenal regional success of the Populist party. After 1865, small cash-crop wheat farming became the predominant form of cultivation in Nebraska, Kansas, and North and South Dakota.[5] Wheat farming entails considerable risks, principally because it depends on the weather, the international market, and the chance of disease.[6] Moreover, much like small wheat farmers of the 1970s and 1980s, the small wheat producers of the 1870s and 1880s could not resist the avalanche of credit offered them in times of bumper crops, high prices, and rising land values. With borrowed funds these wheat farmers enlarged their holdings and purchased the latest and best machinery. Hicks observes that the federal census figures of 1890 ranked Kansas, Nebraska, and North and South Dakota at the top of the list of states in the amount of mortgage debt per capita.[7]

With a downturn in the wheat economy in the 1890s, the roof fell in on the small wheat farmers. Those who were over-extended, subject to the vagaries of the export market, and dependent on a single cash crop suffered severely. These farmers sought a political forum to redress their plight. Their answer came in the Populist party platform of 1892. It called for the federal government to repossess unused lands it had given to the railroads and demanded a graduated income tax and an expanded currency and credit structure.[8] For the trans-Mississippi small wheat growers these proposals promised a remedy to their economic problems.

In particular, the small wheat growers saw the railroads as their enemy. The government had turned over substantial amounts of land to the railroads at virtually no cost. The railroads eventually placed much of this land on the market, at a price, however, that was three to ten times higher than they had originally paid. To make matters worse, the railroads instituted a punitive credit system.[9] But the disdain of small wheat growers for the railroads went beyond this land issue. The railroads consistently discriminated against the small farmers by offering to the large wheat growers lower transportation costs, rebates, and preferential treatment.[10] In addition, the land-grant railroads and large landowning corporations had continually avoided paying taxes on their holdings, and the bulk of taxation in Kansas, Nebraska, and the two Dakotas fell disproportionately on the shoulders of the small wheat farmers. The trans-Mississippi small wheat farmers, therefore, favored progressive income taxation. For them, progressive income taxation would shift the tax burden to the rich.[11] Faced with a critical debt burden, small wheat growers favored easy credit and expansion of the currency that would cause the value of the dollar to fall and would consequently require fewer sales of wheat for them to pay back the same dollar amount of debt.[12] It comes as no surprise that these trans-Mississippi small wheat farmers climbed on the pro-silver bandwagon. In the minds of these pro-silver advocates, the demonetization of silver was an attempt to enrich the creditor class at the expense of the debtor class.[13]

But why didn't the Populist movement catch on in other U.S. agricultural regions? Here again the mode-of-production model may provide a clue. The Populist party failed to attract a sizable proportion of the farming population in the midwestern states of Iowa, Illinois, and Wisconsin. These farmers specialized in dairying and growing corn as feed for hogs, both more stable than growing wheat since neither was as dependent upon exports, the world market, and the weather as growing wheat.[14] Because of their mode of production these farmers were not particularly affected by the agricultural crisis of the 1890s. Thus the agricultural program of the Populist party did not reflect the material interests of midwestern farmers.

The mode-of-production model may also help untangle the issue of popular support for fascist parties in Western Europe during the 1920s and 1930s. It is well known that popular support for fascist parties varied by region, and the best known case of such regional variation occurred in Germany. In the four Reichstag elections between September 1930 and March 1933 the NSDAP (Nazi Party) averaged 44 percent of the popular vote in Schleswig-Holstein but only 20.6 percent of the popular vote in Cologne-Aachen.[15] At first glance it might appear that the Nazi success in Schleswig-Holstein and failure in Cologne-Aachen were the results of the former being rural and Protestant and the latter being urban and Catholic. The predictive strength of the religious and urbanization thesis is attenuated, however, when it is applied to other areas in Germany. The thesis cannot explain why the districts of Liegnitz and Breslau, Catholic and urban, and the district of the Palatinate, Catholic and rural, voted strongly Nazi.[16]

The mode-of-production model may provide some clues to the regional variation in Nazi popular support. Consider the Nazis' greatest electoral success in the province of Schleswig-Holstein, where they gained 51.3 percent of the popular vote in the election of July 1932. I would argue that the farmers of Schleswig-Holstein voted for the NSDAP because the party's agrarian program reflected their material interests. The typical farmers of Schleswig-Holstein were small owner-cultivators (*Kleinbauern*) engaged in the highly speculative activities of dairy farming and hog fattening.[17] These farmers were regularly subject to falling agricultural prices, and a highly fluctuating world market.[18] Between 1926 and 1932 many of the *Kleinbauern* of Schleswig-Holstein defaulted on their loans and lost their farms. The Nazis addressed the needs of these farmers better than other German political parties; their agrarian program called for security of tenure, protection of German farmers from the vagaries of the world market, institution of guaranteed prices for the full range of agricultural products, lower taxes and interest rates, and severe action against usury.[19] In short, the small independent farmers of Schleswig-Holstein found in the Nazi agrarian program the promise of improved economic welfare. Future research should demonstrate the applicability of the mode-of-production model to voting in other German regions where the Nazis obtained only minimal support.

Moreover, the regional mode-of-production theory may explain more fully the causes of rural voting patterns in Third World nations. A case that warrants attention is India. In the 1967 Indian national elections the Indian Communist party obtained 32.1 percent of the popular vote in the province of Kerala and 24.6 percent of the popular vote in the province of West Bengal. By contrast, it received only 4.5 percent of the popular vote in the province of Uttar Pradesh and 2.2 percent in the province of Rajasthan.[20] A highly commercial mode of production in Kerala and West Bengal and a more subsistence-oriented mode of production in Uttar Pradesh and Rajasthan explain this regional variation in voting. For example, agriculture in West Bengal is organized around huge capitalist plantations employing large numbers of landless wage laborers. In advocating land redistribution and higher wages, the Indian Communist party's program should have appealed directly to the material interests of the West Bengal peasantry. By contrast, the Indian Communist party's call for land redistribution and higher wages should have stirred less interest among the less commercial landowning peasants of the provinces of Uttar Pradesh and Rajasthan.[21]

REVOLUTIONARY SOCIAL UPHEAVAL

The mode-of-production theory may have substantial validity also for cases of regional variation in revolutionary social upheaval. The model may have particular relevance to European rebellions of the sixteenth and seventeenth centuries, which have engendered one of the longest debates in social history. Were they essentially spontaneous outbreaks and expressions of class conflict,[22] or were they instigated by nobility and officials who made common cause with peasants against royal fiscality and centralism?[23] The issue of the meaning of revolts will remain unresolved as long as each side continues to refer only to the historical cases that support its position. The historical record indicates that both class-conflict rebellions and class-collaboration rebellions occurred. Once this variation is recognized, a more fruitful question is, how can we explain it?

The debate over the meaning of rebellion generally ignores the systematic relation between particular forms of collective action and particular types of regions. Each rebellion corresponded to a particular region. Those with commercial modes of production were likely to have class conflict whereas those with subsistence modes of production were likely to have class collaboration. Consequently, the mode-of-production model predicts that class-conflict rebellions were more likely to occur in commercial regions such as southeastern and midland England, northeastern and Mediterranean France, and central and eastern Spain because the commercial modes of production of these regions made for antagonistic interests and interclass independence of cultivators and landlords. By contrast, the model predicts that class-cooperative rebellions were more likely to happen in subsistence regions such as northern and western England, western and southwestern France, and northern and western Spain because the subsistence modes of production of these regions made for cooperative interests and mutual dependence among cultivators and landlords.[24] The literature pertaining to the major social upheavals supports the mode-of-production theory's predictions about the form of rebellion.[25]

The model should help explain other instances of regional variation in revolutionary social upheaval. In each of the following examples of revolutionary upheaval, regions possessing commercial modes of production tended to be characterized by antagonistic class relations. Furthermore, cultivators within these regions often supported attempts to undermine the authority of the landlord classes. Regions possessing subsistence modes of production tended to be characterized by cooperative class relations, and cultivators within these regions frequently resisted attempts to emasculate the authority of the landlord class.

During the French Revolution, the cultivators of the commercialized Northeast favored the antiseigneurial program of the French radicals whereas the cultivators of the subsistence West joined with their landlords in the Revolution's two most famous counterrevolutionary movements, the Vendée and the Chouannerie.[26] The Russian antilandlord agrarian riots of 1905–1917 found fertile soil in the more commercialized central black-earth provinces although these riots stirred only minor interest in the less commercialized northern provinces.[27] Finally, during the Spanish civil war (1936–1939) the coalition of the right, which spoke for the church and landlord class, obtained substantial support from the cultivators of the subsistence regions of Old Castile and Galicia whereas the Popular Front, which extolled the virtues of social democracy and land redistribution, received its hardiest support from the commercial regions of Andalusia, Catalonia, and Valencia.[28]

URBAN VOTING PATTERNS

Although the present study has concentrated on rural political behavior, the model should also be useful in explaining why some cities tend to be more politically conservative than others. Cities are generally more leftist than rural areas, as scholars studying political behavior in India, the United States, or France will acknowledge. In France, for example, the principal urban centers, with their large industrial work force and concentrated population, have historically been the backbone of the political Left. Yet in contrast to northeastern and western cities, the major cities of the Mediterranean region stand out frequently as bastions of political conservatism.[29] As early as the French

Revolution, cities such as Montpellier, Nîmes, and Toulouse opposed the prorevolutionary forces of Lower Languedoc.[30] The
major impetus for the "white terror" of 1815 came from such
cities as Toulouse, Montpellier, Nîmes, and Avignon.[31] Between
the Restoration of 1815 and the advent of the Second Republic
in 1848, much of the support for the Legitimists came from
Mediterranean cities.[32] The results of the legislative elections of
1848 and 1849 demonstrated little change in Mediterranean
urban voting.[33] Urban political conservatism in the Mediterranean did not end with the Second Republic. As late as 1914 the
principal conservative forces were situated in the large cities
and not in the countryside.[34] For instance, in the election of 1914,
four out of the five politically conservative deputies elected from
Provence came from the highly urban arrondissements of Aix,
Toulon, and Marseille.[35] Even the late-nineteenth- and early-
twentieth-century reactionary movement, the *Action française*,
found its electoral support in Mediterranean cities and not in
the countryside.[36] Thus it would appear that Mediterranean
cities have consistently served as the loci for political conservatism. But why should these cities be more conservative than
the surrounding countryside? I suggest that the region's mode
of production is largely responsible.

Unlike northern and western cities, Mediterranean cities do
not have a concentrated working-class population. These Mediterranean cities are, instead, centers of commerce and administration, and they serve principally as the residence of major
landowners who live comfortably from revenues generated by
their estates.[37] Throughout the nineteenth century, members of
the upper bourgeoisie and nobility gained great wealth through
their ownership of vast lands. Together the upper bourgeoisie
and nobility of the Mediterranean cities formed the backbone
of royalist support during the first half of the nineteenth century.[38] Through their dominance as absentee landowners and
in some cases as commercial employers the upper bourgeoisie
and nobility were successful in affecting the voting behavior of
the urban lower classes. As in the western countryside, the resi-
dent social elites, through their control over vital resources,
were able to affect the perception of interests of the lower classes.
Complementing the substantial noble and bourgeois influence

in Mediterranean cities was the considerable presence of the church. The clergy found the urban populace much more receptive to their proselytizing than the rural cultivators and, through their presence and considerable resources, were able to influence the perception of interests of the urban lower classes.

In short, the distinctive mode of production of the Mediterranean, which included a resource-controlling nobility, bourgeoisie, and church and lacked a concentrated working class, has shaped the political behavior of the Mediterranean cities, namely, right-wing voting patterns. By contrast, the western and northeastern modes, which had a concentrated working class and lacked an urban-residing landlord class, have contributed significantly to the left-wing voting patterns of western and northeastern cities.

POLITICAL FORECASTING

Heretofore the mode-of-production model has been utilized to explain past political behavior. The model's greatest potential may lie, however, in its ability to explain present and to predict future patterns of political behavior, from electoral outcomes to regional variation within revolutionary social upheaval. Consider the examples of voting in the state of Utah and the growth of communist insurgency in the Philippines.

The model would predict that the population of Utah, with its reliance on defense-related jobs and its preponderance of Mormons (who receive substantial social and economic benefits from tithing), should continue to support the conservative wing of the Republican party as long as that wing forcefully advocates a strong military and lower federal taxes.

The model would also predict that the strongest rural support for the Marxist NPA (New Peoples' Army) should come from the southern Philippine island of Mindanao.[39] Mindanao includes one-third of the total land area in the Philippines and less than one-fourth of the total Philippine population and yet accounts for half the coconut exports and all banana and pineapple exports in the Philippines.[40] A large share of arable land on Mindanao is held either by large multinational fruit companies like Del Monte, Castle and Cooke, and United Fruits or by wealthy Philippine absentee landlords.[41] The capital-intensive demands of the fruit-exporting industry have led in some cases to the accumulation of large debts by small farmers and in other cases to the eviction (sometimes forcible) of small farmers. For example, in 1979 in the district of Davao del Norte, the Del Monte company, with the assistance of the Philippine government, evicted two hundred small farmers to make way for the intensive cultivation of bananas.[42]

The economic situation for small tenant farmers and landless agricultural laborers in Mindanao is miserable. Landlords are known to set rents at between 50 and 80 percent of the harvested crop and to charge exorbitant interest rates on loans to peasants. Wages paid to agricultural laborers on the large estates are extremely low although profits made by these estates are quite high.[43] The various governments of the Philippines have paid only lip service to land reform, especially for areas dominated by fruit and sugar production, for example, Mindanao.

Thus I would predict that the small tenant cultivators and landless agricultural laborers of Mindanao should find considerable promise in the NPA's revolutionary guide to land reform. The program calls for the free distribution of land to tillers who have no land or insufficient land, the reduction of rent to no more than 10 percent of the market value of the harvest, the elimination of usury, and the betterment of wages and living conditions for farm workers on landed estates.[44]

By learning the regional variations in modes of production, scholars will be better equipped to predict the constellation of interests of a given population and the consequent likelihood of its support for a particular political party or social movement. In this fashion the mode-of-production model may hold considerable relevance for the study of future social change in both the developed and the developing nations.

FINAL THOUGHTS

My goal has been to demonstrate the utility of the mode-of-production model as an explanation of the persistence of French political regionalism. I have argued that voters are rational actors whose voting reflects their interests as determined by their positions in a particular mode of production; this argument has led me to criticize both normative and structural explanations of political behavior. To recapitulate: normative explanations are inherently difficult to measure, and are therefore difficult to test and refute because they emphasize the determinant role of values; they strain logic in supposing that the votes of individuals reflect nonrational factors such as tradition rather than self-interest; and they employ a questionable assumption in supposing that compliance can be presumed from the fact that individuals are subject to particular norms. By concentrating on macrostructures, structural explanations reveal how individuals come to share circumstances; however, by ignoring the extent to which the motivations of individuals can shape their behavior and thereby provide them independent discretion in making choices, structural explanations cannot explain how individuals will react to their circumstances.

To test the explanatory power of the mode-of-production model for French voting patterns I analyzed data for the national legislative elections of 1849, 1914, and 1981. Data analysis shows that mode of production is indeed a significant predictor of French peasant voting. But the data also suggest that the variation in voting patterns can be attributed to other factors. They indicate in particular that religious values and region influence the preferences of voters. Yet I would suggest that the relation between voting and religiosity may have to do less with social values than with material interests and that religious values may be less an explanation of political behavior than the other side of the same coin. That is, religiosity and political behavior are actually the effects of a common cause. As an acceptable explanation region must remain suspect until its proponents specify what it means. I propose that the substantial correlation between region and mode of production that has been observed (see Table 14) may reveal that "regional effect" is another term for the regional mode of production.

How might I improve my theory and thereby explain political regionalism more completely? One approach worth pursuing is to examine the role of party organization. My readers may have noticed that I have ignored party organization as an influence on voting preferences and have probably limited the explanatory value of my model. In future research I plan to show that including party organization in my explanation of political behavior should strengthen the predictive capacity of my theory and at the same time allow me to incorporate in my analysis a factor that is quite compatible with my rational-choice assumption of behavior: I shall argue that the extent to which political parties establish local and regional organizations should influence the voting choices of individuals. If my assumption is valid, if voters are rational actors who vote for the party whose programs most closely reflect their perception of self-interest, then the ability of a political party to make its positions known to voters becomes even more important. For rational individuals, voting depends on an awareness of the political programs of each competing party. Otherwise, individuals may be unaware of political parties whose programs better reflect their self-interest.

Party organization may shape voting preferences in another important way. Rational individuals may be reluctant to waste votes on a party with little promise. If a party can convince voters that their votes for it would be useful, voters will be more likely to select that party as long as their interests coincided with its program. The ability of a party to convince voters of its chances for success may hinge on its local or regional presence, which is a function of its organizational capacity.

What then do we conclude about the place of the regional mode-of-production theory within the pantheon of treatments of political behavior that includes such standard approaches as class, religion, and ethnicity? The regional mode of production perspective should enrich the study of political behavior in at least two important respects. First, focus on the regional dimension of a society's political experience sharpens our analytical understanding of that experience. Students of political behavior usually take the modern state to be the basic entity within which social reality occurs. But in his study of the rise of the modern economic order, Immanuel Wallerstein argued that by changing the analytical focus from individual states to the international division of labor (world system) we would gain a more exact understanding of the social reality. In a similar fashion, I would argue that by employing the region as the analytical unit we would gain a more realistic picture of a society's political experience. For instance, a regional examination of the French Revolution would clearly show that responses to it diverged dramatically by region: although in 1789 northeastern farmers enthusiastically welcomed the radicals' antiseigneurial and anticlerical programs and western farmers greeted them with considerable approbation, Mediterranean farmers supported them only tepidly. That a regional approach can increase our knowledge of the French Revolution suggests that it may contribute equally to a fuller understanding of other great revolutions such as the Russian, Chinese, and Iranian. Ultimately, the application of the regional mode-of-production model to the study of revolution may shed light on the social causes of revolutionary collective action.

Second, acceptance of the model would lead us to reexamine widely held but misleading notions regarding the nonrationality of political behavior. Consider, for instance, the concept of "false consciousness," frequently employed to explain such supposedly nonrational behaviors as workers' refusing to join unions, dispossessed Third World peasants' ignoring calls to participate in communist-led insurgencies, and lower-class individuals' voting for conservative political parties. Not surprisingly, such thinking has led many students of the French political experience to observe, incorrectly, that the Vendéen counterrevolutionary peasants of 1793 and the conservative-voting western French tenants and sharecroppers would have acted differently if only they had possessed a true consciousness. Many likewise contend that "false consciousness" explains why the crisis-ridden farmers of Schleswig-Holstein voted overwhelmingly for Hitler's Nazi party in the election of July 1932 and why in the 1980s many South African blacks support the proapartheid white regime. I propose that if we were to examine thoroughly the motivations of the individuals engaged in these activities, we would find that these behaviors are rational. If this study can inspire others to challenge what is so frequently characterized as nonrational political behavior, then it will have gone a long way to fulfilling its purpose.

Notes

INTRODUCTION

1. This definition of political regionalism approximates closely that found in R. Alford, *Party and Society* (Chicago: Rand McNally, 1963).

2. V. O. Key, Jr., *Politics, Parties, and Pressure Groups,* 5th ed. (New York: Thomas Y. Crowell, 1964); S. M. Lipset, *Agrarian Socialism* (Garden City, N.Y.: Doubleday Anchor, 1968); C. Baxter, *District Voting Trends in India; A Research Tool* (New York: Columbia University Press, 1969); A. L. Stinchcombe, *Economic Sociology* (New York: Academic Press, 1983); E. Wolf, *Peasant Wars of the Twentieth Century* (New York: Harper & Row, 1969); C. C. Cumberland, *Mexican Revolution, Genesis Under Madero* (Austin: University of Texas Press, 1952); S. G. Payne, *Politics and Society in Twentieth-Century Spain* (New York: New Viewpoints, 1976).

3. F. Goguel, *Géographie des élections françaises de 1870 à 1951* (Paris: Armand Colin, 1951); J. Bouillon, "Les Démocrates-socialistes aux élections de 1849," *Revue française de science politique* 6, no. 1 (January–March 1956); P. Barral, *Les Agrairiens français de Méline à Pisani* (Paris: Presses de la Fondation nationale des sciences politiques, 1968); P. Converse and R. Pierce, *Political Representation in France* (Cambridge, Mass.: Harvard University Press, 1986).

CHAPTER 1

1. For heuristic purposes the following summary of the literature pertaining to French political regionalism reduces complex arguments to their most simplistic form.

2. See especially T. Parsons, *Sociological Theory and Modern Society* (New York: The Free Press, 1967) and P. E. Converse, "The Concept of a Normal Vote," in *Elections and the Political Order,* ed. A. Campbell et al. (New York: John Wiley, 1966), pp. 9–39.

3. A. Campbell et al., *The American Voter* (New York: John Wiley & Sons, Inc., 1960), p. 152.

4. It should be noted that Gouault, Derivry and Dogan, and Klatzmann mention other factors that may be responsible for French political preferences (J. Gouault, *Comment la France est devenue républicaine* [Paris: Armand Colin, 1954]; D. Derivry and M. Dogan, "Unité d'ana-

lyse et espace de référence en écologie politique: Le Canton et le département français," *Revue française de science politique* 21, no. 3 [June 1971]: 517–70; J. Klatzmann, "Géographie électorale de l'agriculture française," in *Les Paysans et la politique dans la France contemporaine*, ed. J. Fauvet and H. Mendras [Paris: Armand Colin, 1958], pp. 36–68).

5. Y. M. Bercé, *Croquants et Nu-Pieds* (Paris: Gallimard/Julliard, 1974), pp. 228–31.

6. Ibid., p. 229.

7. F. Goguel, *Géographie des élections françaises de 1870 à 1951* (Paris: Armand Colin, 1951), pp. 103–5.

8. P. Bois, *Paysans de l'Ouest* (Le Mans: M. Vilaire, 1960). For a brief summary of the causes of the counterrevolutionary insurrections throughout western France, see P. Bois, "Aperçu sur les causes des insurrections de l'Ouest à l'époque révolutionnaire," in *Vendée Chouannerie*, ed. J.-C. Martin (Nantes: Reflets du passé, 1981), pp. 121–26.

9. Ibid., pp. 672–74.

10. In the 1967 edition of *The Vendée*, Tilly revised his earlier thinking about the effect of urbanization on the Vendéen counterrevolution. In an earlier edition (Tilly, 1962), like Bois, he argued that the rural areas were the most supportive of the counterrevolution; C. Tilly, *The Vendée*, 3d ed. (New York: John Wiley, 1967).

11. Ibid., p. 156.

12. P. L'Agrée employs a similar argument to explain the political divergence between the conservative and republican zones of the western department of Ille-et-Vilaine. For Ille-et-Vilaine, the cleavage ensued from the period of the sixteenth-century Catholic Leagues. L'Agrée claims that the Protestant areas attacked by the Catholic Leagues became strongholds of moderate republicanism; those areas in which the Catholic Leagues drew support became bastions of conservative strength. Like Bois, Tilly, Hunt, Le Goff and Sutherland, L'Agrée sees the legacy of this sixteenth-century struggle as continuing to affect the political behavior of Ille-et-Vilaine (P. L'Agrée, "La Structure pérenne, événement et histoire en Bretagne orientale, XVIe–XXe siècles," *Revue d'histoire moderne et contemporaine* 23 [July–September 1976]: 394–407). Additionally, in a massive work on the counterrevolution in Anjou, Claude Petitfrère offers evidence supporting Bois's and Tilly's commercialization thesis. Moreover, Petitfrère confirms Bois's point concerning the pivotal role of the sale of church property in crystallizing peasant resentment toward the revolution. In regard to the persistence of the Right-Left cleavage in the West, Petitfrère, like Bois and Tilly, evokes the legacy argument: "L'insurrection vendéenne fut pour les habitants du Maine-et-Loire,

comme pour leurs voisins bretons et poitevens, la grande déchirure dont le traumatisme allait se répercuter jusqú'à nos jours, déterminant les choix politiques pour un siècle et davantage" (C. Petitfrère, *Blancs et bleus d'Anjou [1789–1793]* [Lille: Atelier de reproduction des thèses, Université de Lille 3, 1974]).

13. P. Vigier, *La Seconde République dans la région alpine: etude politique et sociale*, 2 vols. (Paris: Presses universitaires de France, 1963); E. Le Roy Ladurie, *Histoire du Languedoc*, Que sais-je? 953 (Paris: Presses universitaires de France, 1967); M. Agulhon, "La Provence républicaine à l'ère industrielle (1870–1940): La Vie politique de 1870 à 1940," in *Histoire de la Provence*, ed. E. Baratier (Toulouse: Privat, 1969), pp. 512–33; B. Moore, Jr., *Social Origins of Dictatorship and Democracy* (Boston: Beacon Press, 1966), pp. 102–3.

14. Tilly, *Vendée*, p. 157.

15. T.J.A. Le Goff and D.M.G. Sutherland, "The Social Origins of Counter-Revolution in Western France," *Past and Present* 99 (1983): 65–87.

16. Ibid., p. 87.

17. L. Hunt, *Politics, Culture, and Class in the French Revolution* (Berkeley: University of California Press, 1984).

18. Ibid., pp. 132–33.

19. Ibid.

20. At first glance, it might appear that the religiosity explanation of French political regionalism should be considered a structural explanation because it posits a relation between church membership (a structure) and voting behavior. I have decided to consider it a normative explanation, however, because the principal causal relation is between a set of values and voting behavior.

21. Gouault, *Comment la France;* Derivry and Dogan, "Unité d'analyse"; Klatzmann, "Géographie électorale." Unlike other normative explanations of French voting persistence, however, the religiosity thesis does not account for the structures or events that cause the initial cultural cleavage.

22. R. Collins, *Conflict Sociology* (New York: Academic Press, 1975), p. 6; M. Hechter, introduction to *The Microfoundations of Macrosociology*, ed. M. Hechter (Philadelphia: Temple University Press, 1983), pp. 4–5. Some criticisms that have recently been leveled against normative explanations may be unjust. Both Collins and Hechter criticize normative explanations for not explaining variation in behavior. However, a careful reading of both Parsons and Merton reveals that they attempted to explain variation in behavior by stressing that the mechanisms of socialization and social control account for deviant behavior.

Hence, the issue is not whether normativists provide an explanation of behavior but whether their explanation is a satisfactory one.

23. J. Paige, *Agrarian Revolution* (New York: Free Press, 1975).

24. Hechter, *The Microfoundations,* p. 5.

25. In my survey of structural explanations of French political behavior I have selected only a few studies that I believe best represent the literature. There are undoubtedly other important explanations that I have excluded. I might mention one of these that has recently received some attention. Hervé Le Bras and Emmanuel Todd argue that variation in the type of family structure is the principal cause of differences in French political behavior. Right-wing voting associates highly with simple, or nuclear, family structure and left-wing voting corresponds highly with a hybrid type of complex, or extended, family structure (H. Le Bras and E. Todd, *L'Invention de la France* [Paris: Pluriel, 1981]). But as Jones points out, this argument has empirical failings. In Brittany, the Basque country, and the southern massif Central—all regions in which the patriarchal extended family flourishes—the peasantry votes Right, not Left (P. M. Jones, *Politics and Rural Society* [Cambridge: Cambridge University Press, 1985], p. 250).

26. A. Siegfried, *Tableau politique de la France de l'Ouest sous la Troisième République* (Paris: Armand Colin, 1913), pp. 383–84.

27. Ibid., p. 409.

28. Ibid., pp. 416–17.

29. Bois, *Paysans de l'Ouest,* p. 21.

30. See M. Hechter, *Principles of Group Solidarity* (Berkeley: University of California Press, 1987).

31. The model that I shall present in chapter 2 draws heavily upon Siegfried's pioneering study. I plan to reformulate and recast his analysis. Among other things, I shall try to remedy the major flaws of his model by enlarging his sample, by employing more rigorous research methods, and by accounting for voting compliance.

32. L. A. Loubere, *Radicalism in Mediterranean France, 1848–1914* (Albany: State University of New York Press, 1974); T. Judt, *Socialism in Provence, 1871–1914* (Cambridge: Cambridge University Press, 1979).

33. Loubere, pp. 5, 8.

34. Ibid., p. 8.

35. Judt, *Socialism in Provence,* p. 136. Ironically, when it comes to explaining the persistence of the attachment of Mediterranean French cultivators to the socialist Left, Judt turns to the role of tradition. Judt writes: "That the new relationship established in the Var between the much diminished rural communities and the socialist movement be-

came, in its turn, a tradition, in time as much a 'structural' feature of the region's social and political life as anti-clericalism had been in an earlier period. The conjunctural circumstances which had brought the relationship into being once past, voting for the socialists formed part of the 'historical' character of Provençal life, long after the SFIO had ceased to perform any obvious function of the local population, and had indeed lost much of its revolutionary character and impetus" (p. 237).

36. J. E. Farquharson, *The Plough and the Swastika: The NSDAP and Agriculture in Germany, 1928—45* (London: Sage, 1976); T. A. Tilton, *Nazism, Neo-Nazism, and the Peasantry* (Bloomington: Indiana University Press, 1975).

37. R. Laurent, "Les Quatre Ages du vignoble du Bas-Languedoc et du Roussillon," in *Economie et société en Languedoc-Roussillon de 1789 à nos jours,* ed. Centre d'histoire contemporaine du Languedoc Mediterranéen et du Roussillon (Montpellier: Centre national de la recherche scientifique, 1978), p. 20.

38. Ibid.

39. G. Walter, *Histoire des paysans de France* (Paris: Flammarion, 1963), p. 426.

40. Both Loubere and Judt adhere to the commonly held French view that the French Mediterranean region was characterized by a virulent royalism until 1848 and then, after 1848, performed a *volte-face.* Also see Vigier, *La Seconde République;* S. Vila, "Les Milieux populaires et la République dans l'Hérault, 1815—1852" (thèse, troisième cycle, University of Paris, 1966); M. Agulhon, *The Republic in the Village* (Cambridge: Cambridge University Press, 1982; originally published as *La République au village* [Paris: Plon, 1970]). Since these scholars relegate the Mediterranean to the royalist camp between 1815 and 1848, they tend to explain the region's turnabout by exogenous cataclysmic events. The contention that the French Mediterranean was truly royalist between 1815 and 1848, however, is based on tenuous evidence. For example, the "white terror" of 1814—1815 is not proof of the Mediterranean's political conservatism, because it was directed against specific programs and groups and was not widespread, occurring predominantly in the major urban centers of Toulouse, Montpellier, Nîmes, Avignon, and Marseille (D. Higgs, *Ultra Royalism in Toulouse: From Its Origins to the Revolution of 1830* [Baltimore: Johns Hopkins University Press, 1973]; J. J. Oéscheslin, *Le Mouvement ultra-royaliste sous la Restauration* [Paris: R. Pichon & R. Durand-Auzias, 1960]; D. P. Resnick, *The White Terror and the Political Reaction After Waterloo* [Cambridge, Mass.: Harvard University Press, 1966]; G. Four-

nier, "Aspects économiques et sociaux de la Révolution dans quelques communes du Languedoc, de 1789 à l'an III," in *Economie et société en Languedoc-Roussillon de 1789 à nos jours,* pp. 169–89). The election of Carlist deputies to the National Assembly between 1815 and 1848 is also an inadequate indicator of the region's political proclivities since the eligible electorate (*liste du jury*) consisted primarily of the major property holders, a class that shares to a great extent the interests of the political Right. Lastly, Loubere's and Judt's implicit assumption that depressed wine-producing areas lend themselves more readily to the promulgation of radical political ideology than do non-wine-producing areas is also suspect. For instance, there was great variation in the reaction of France's depressed wine-producing regions to the 1851 coup d'état of Louis Bonaparte. Relatively few wine producers from the Burgundy and Bordeaux vineyards participated in the revolts; yet a sizable proportion of wine producers from Lower Languedoc joined the agitation against Bonaparte (T. W. Margadant, *French Peasants in Revolt* [Princeton: Princeton University Press, 1979], p. 83). Furthermore, the principal wine-producing area of western France, the Saumur region of Maine-et-Loire, has consistently supported the political Right in every major election since 1849. The reason for this support is obvious when we compare Mediterranean France and Maine-et-Loire with respect to the form of land tenure, size of farm, and type of wine produced. The typical Mediterranean vintner is a small owner-cultivator of a mediocre quality of wine (*vin ordinaire*); the Saumur vintner is a medium-scale tenant-cultivator of a select high-quality wine (Muscadet).

41. H. Espieux, *Histoire de l'Occitanie* (Nîmes: Barnier, 1970); J. Vedel, "Une Réduction historique à l'unité," in *Le Sud et le nord,* ed. R. Lafont (Toulouse: Domaine Occitan, 1971).

CHAPTER 2

1. A. Downs, *An Economic Theory of Democracy* (New York: Harper & Row, 1957); B. Barry, *Sociologists, Economists, and Democracy* (Chicago: University of Chicago Press, 1978), p. 53. See also, M. J. Shapiro, "Rational Political Man: A Synthesis of Economic & Social-Psychological Perspectives," *American Political Science Review* 63 (1969): 1106–19; D. E. Repass, "Issue Salience and Party Choice," *American Political Science Review* 65 (1971): 389–400; J. E. Jackson, "Issues, Party Choices, and Presidential Votes," *American Journal of Political Science* 19, no. 2 (May 1975): 161–86; N. H. Nie et al., *The Changing American Voter* (Cambridge, Mass.: Harvard University Press, 1976).

2. For a more detailed examination of Downs's theory of voting see R. Hardin, *Collective Action* (Baltimore: Johns Hopkins University Press, 1982).

3. Ibid., pp. 11–12.

4. See Barry, *Sociologists, Economists, and Democracy,* p. 101; R. L. Curry and L. L. Wade, *A Theory of Political Exchange* (Englewood Cliffs: Prentice-Hall, 1968), p. 39.

5. H. F. Weisberg and M. P. Fiorina, "Candidate Preference Under Uncertainty: An Expanded View of Rational Voting," in *The Electorate Reconsidered,* ed. J. C. Pierce and J. L. Sullivan (Beverly Hills: Sage Publications, 1980): pp. 237–56.

6. In a recent study of political regionalism, R. F. Bensel (*Sectionalism and American Political Development, 1880–1980* [Madison: University of Wisconsin Press, 1984]) acknowledges the compatibility of a macrolevel theory and rational-choice theories in considering economic interests as the primary motivator of voting. However, Bensel ignores rational-choice assumptions as a possible link between structure and individual behavior.

7. R. Aya, "Review of Barry Hindess and Paul Q. Hirst: *Pre-Capitalist Modes of Production,*" *Theory and Society* 3 (1976): 623–29.

8. L. Althusser and E. Balibar, *Reading Capital* (London: New Left Books, 1970); B. Hindess and P. Q. Hirst, *Pre-Capitalist Modes of Production* (London: Routledge & Kegan Paul); M. Godelier, *Horizon, trajets marxistes en anthropologie,* 2 vols. (Paris: Maspero, 1977); E. Terray, "Classes and Class Consciousness in the Abron Kingdom of Gyaman," in *Marxist Analyses and Social Anthropology,* ed. Maurice Bloch (London: Malaby Press, 1975), pp. 85–136.

9. K. Marx, *A Contribution to the Critique of Political Economy* (Moscow: Progress Publishers, 1970), pp. 20–21.

10. My definition of mode of production differs from the one employed by G. A. Cohen (*Karl Marx's Theory of History: A Defence* [Princeton: Princeton University Press, 1978]). Whereas Cohen distinguishes between the economic structure, material mode of production, and social mode of production, I combine them. In this fashion, my definition of mode of production encompasses a society's entire set of production relations (economic structure), a society's material process of production (material mode), and a society's mode of exploitation and form of producer's surplus (social mode).

11. The concept of mode of production is useful only in ideal-typical analysis. None of these modes of production has existed in a pure state. All historical societies are social formations and thus involve a combination of several modes of production. Within any social forma-

tion, however, one mode of production is dominant and the others are subordinate. The dominant mode of production within each social formation circumscribes the composition and functioning of the subordinate modes of production. Consequently, the principal class relations of any social formation are determined by its dominant mode of production.

12. This argument suggests, among other things, that the degree of a group's religiosity may be not only the result of an ideological attachment but the product of a material tie.

13. For another example of this argument in the French political literature, see M. Agulhon, *The Republic in the Village* (Cambridge: Cambridge University Press, 1982). For non-French applications of this see J. C. Scott, "Patron-Client Politics and Political Change in Southeast Asia," in *Friends, Followers, and Factions,* ed. S. W. Schmidt et al. (Berkeley: University of California Press, 1977), p. 125.

14. S. Rokkan, "Mass Suffrage, Secret Voting, and Political Participation," in *Political Sociology,* ed. L. A. Coser (New York: Harper Torchbooks, 1966), p. 115. Nevertheless, landlord intimidation of voters continued well after the introduction of the secret ballot in the nineteenth century. Only in 1861 did the French government begin to dispatch legally certified ballot boxes to communes (P. M. Jones, *Politics and Rural Society* [Cambridge: Cambridge University Press, 1985], p. 225). Also, by the electoral law of December 1878, the ballot distribution occurred outside the voting station, ostensibly to limit interference by local notables. However, being obliged to complete their choice before entering the voting station and lacking the relative privacy of the voting station, the peasants were subject to even more external pressure. Not until 1913 did the government ensure the protection of the secret ballot by introducing the voting booth (Ibid.). Methods of intimidation varied in subtlety. During the nineteenth and early twentieth centuries it was common in some locales for landlords to march their tenants to the polls on election day with explicit instructions given under the threat of eviction (T. Judt, "The Origins of Rural Socialism in Europe: Economic Change and the Provençal Peasantry, 1870–1914," *Social History* 1 [January 1976]: 51). Similarly, rural notables in the department of Ille-et-Vilaine threatened their tenants with expulsion or with *écoles sans Dieu* to make sure they opposed the lay legislation (R. Gildéa, "L'Enseignement en Bretagne au XIXe siècle: L'Ille-et-Vilaine [1800–1914]," *Annales de Bretagne et des pays de l'Ouest* 84, no. 3 [1977]: 462). In the town of Guilivenic (Finistère), during the 1885 election, the church rector stationed himself at the door of the voting booth shredding republican votes (L. Ogès, "La

Vie politique en Basse-Bretagne sous la IIIᵉ République," *Le Télé-gramme de Brest,* August 1959, p. 4). Also in 1885, in the towns of Crozon and Camaret (Finistère), the church served as the voting center, with the choir distributing the ballots (Ibid.). Still others employed various forms of bribery, ranging from providing a free meal to the promise of employment.

15. My decision to include northeastern France in the analysis is based on methodological concerns, namely, to increase the validity of my theory and to provide a fuller range of variation on my two major factors: mode of production and voting.

CHAPTER 3

1. Marc Bloch, *Feudal Society* (Chicago: University of Chicago Press, 1961); G. Duby, *Rural Economy and Country Life in the Medieval West* (London: Collins, 1968); G. Fourquin, *Lordship and Feudalism in the Middle Ages* (London: George Allen & Unwinn, 1976).

2. C. T. Smith, *An Historical Geography of Western Europe Before 1800* (New York: Praeger, 1967).

3. P. Vinogradoff, *The Growth of the Manor* (London: George Allen & Unwinn, 1911); H. L. Gray, *English Field Systems* (Cambridge, Mass.: Harvard University Press, 1915); G. C. Homans, "The Explanation of English Regional Differences," *Past and Present* 42 (February 1969): 19–34.

4. J. Thirsk, "Debates: The Origin of the Common Fields," *Past and Present* 33 (January 1966): 142–47; R. C. Hoffman, "Medieval Origins of the Common Fields," in *European Peasants and Their Markets,* ed. W. N. Parker and E. L. Jones (Princeton: Princeton University Press, 1975), pp. 23–71; Smith, *An Historical Geography;* J. Blum, "The European Village as Community: Origins and Functions," *Agricultural History* 45, no. 3 (July 1971): 157–78.

5. P. Anderson, *Lineages of the Absolutist State* (London: New Left Books, 1974).

6. A.R.H. Baker, "Field Systems of Southeast England," in *Studies of Field Systems in the British Isles,* ed. A.R.H. Baker and R. Butlin (Cambridge: Cambridge University Press, 1973), pp. 377–429; Thirsk, "Debates"; A. Mayhew, *Rural Settlement and Farming in Germany* (London: Batsford, 1973), pp. 23–28; B. H. Slicher van Bath, *The Agrarian History of Western Europe, A.D. 500–1850* (London: Arnold, 1963), p. 53; Marc Bloch, *French Rural History* (London: Routledge & Kegan Paul, 1966), pp. 58–59; R. Dion, *Essai sur la formation du paysage rural français* (Tours: Arrault, 1934), pp. 29–30.

7. E. Kerridge, "Review Article: British Field Systems," *Agricultural History Review* 24, no. 1 (1976): 48–50.

8. Dion, *Essai sur la formation,* p. 7.

9. J. Blum, *The End of the Old Order in Rural Europe* (Princeton: Princeton University Press, 1978); A. L. Stinchcombe, *Economic Sociology* (New York: Academic Press, 1983); P. Goubert, "Les Cadres de la vie rurale," in *Histoire économique et social de la France,* ed. F. Braudel and E. Labrousse, vol. 2 (Paris: Presses universitaires de France, 1970), pp. 105–7.

10. H. Sée, *Histoire économique de la France (le moyen âge et l'ancien régime)* (Paris: Armand Colin, 1948), p. 197; M. Morineau, "Y a-t-il eu une révolution agricole en France au XVIIIᵉ siècle?" *Revue historique* 239 (April–June 1968): 304; J. Jacquart, "French Agriculture in the Seventeenth Century," in *Essays in European Economic History (1500–1800),* ed. P. Earle (Oxford: Clarendon Press, 1974), p. 171; Blum, *The End of the Old Order,* p. 144.

11. A. Demangeon, *La Picardie et les régions voisines* (Paris: Armand Colin, 1925); E. Juillard, *La Vie rurale dans la plaine de Basse-Alsace* (Strasbourg: Editions F.-X. Le Roux, 1953); L. White, Jr., *Medieval Technology and Social Change* (Oxford: Clarendon Press, 1962); J. H. Clapham, *Economic Development of France and Germany, 1815–1914* (Cambridge: Cambridge University Press, 1963); P. Goubert, "The French Peasantry of the Seventeenth Century: A Regional Example," in *Crises in Europe, 1560–1660,* ed. T. Aston (New York: Basic Books, 1965); D. Herlihy, "Ecological Conditions and Demographic Change," in *One Thousand Years: Western Europe in the Middle Ages,* ed. R. L. Demolen (Boston: Houghton Mifflin, 1974); Blum, *The End of the Old Order;* Stinchcombe, *Economic Sociology.* In fact, the Northeast stood out for its high proportion of *terre labourable* (cultivated surface). By 1851 no more than 19 percent of total agricultural surface went uncultivated whereas in the Mediterranean the proportion of permanent fallow averaged 39 percent. The Alsatian department of Bas-Rhin in the Northeast, in particular, had a meager 6.7 percent of its agricultural surface left uncultivated (G. Desert and R. Specklin, "L'Essor de la paysannerie 1789–1852," in *Histoire de la France rurale,* ed. E. Juillard, vol. 3 [Paris: Seuil, 1976], pp. 134–35).

12. H. Sée, *Les Classes rurales en Bretagne du XVIᵉ siècle à la Révolution* (Paris: V. Giord & E. Baière, 1906), pp. 18, 262; Dion, *Essai sur la formation,* pp. 60–62; J. Imbert and H. Legoherel, *Histoire économique des origines à 1789* (Paris: Presses universitaires de France, 1965), pp. 335–36.

13. J. Sion, *Les Paysans de la Normandie orientale* (Paris: Armand

Colin, 1909); Bloch, *French Rural History;* Blum, *The End of the Old Order.*

14. However, it should be noted that the consolidation of strips and commons did not occur at the same pace throughout northeastern France. The pace was certainly brisk in Flanders, Artois, Picardy, Bray, Vexin, Beauce, and Brie. In Burgundy and Lorraine, consolidation progressed more slowly because there was less incentive to terminate the practice of *vaine pâture* (the communal grazing of livestock) (Demangeon, *La Picardie;* Dion, *Essai sur la formation;* Sée, *Histoire économique;* Clapham, *Economic Development*).

15. *Koppelwirtschaft,* or convertible husbandry, was the regular rotation of grain and grass on the enclosed fields. Convertible husbandry produced excellent yields because the fields were richly fertilized by animal droppings during the years in which they served as pasture (Blum, *The End of the Old Order,* p. 129).

16. Ibid., p. 262.

17. P. Goubert, *La Vie quotidienne des paysans français au XVIIe siècle* (Paris: Hachette, 1982), p. 53; Demangeon, *La Picardie,* p. 347.

18. J. Loutchisky, "Régimes agraires et populations agricoles dans les environs de Paris à la veille de la Révolution," *Revue d'histoire moderne,* 7 (1933); P. de Saint-Jacob, *Les Paysans de la Bourgogne du nord au dernier siècle de l'ancien régime* (Paris: Société des belles lettres, 1960); Sée, *Histoire économique;* Juillard, *La Vie rurale;* Imbert and Legoherel, *Histoire économique des origines.*

19. Loutchisky, "Régimes agraires", p. 42.

20. Sée, *Histoire économique,* p. 179.

21. Ibid.

22. A. Davies, "The Origins of the French Peasant Revolution of 1789," *History* 49, no. 165 (February 1964): 26–27.

23. Sée, *Les Classes rurales,* p. 18; Bloch, *French Rural History.*

24. Georges Lefebvre, *Les Paysans du Nord pendant la Révolution Française* (Paris: Armand Colin, 1972); Juillard, *La Vie rurale,* p. 239.

25. A. Demangeon, *France économique et humaine* pt. 2, vol. 6 in *Géographie universelle,* ed. P. Vidal de la Blache and L. Gallois (Paris: Armand Colin, 1946), p. 151; B. H. Slicher van Bath, "Eighteenth-Century Agriculture on the Continent of Europe: Evolution or Revolution?," *Agricultural History* 43, no. 1 (January 1969); Juillard, *La Vie rurale;* Blum, *The End of the Old Order.*

26. A. Soboul, *Paysans, Sans-Culottes, et Jacobins* (Paris: Librairie Clavreuil, 1966); Lefebvre, *Les Paysans du Nord.*

27. P. Goubert, *The Ancien Régime French Society, 1600–1750* (London: Weidenfeld & Nicolson, 1973), pp. 113–15.

28. See Soboul's study of the village of Puiseux in Soboul, *Paysans, Sans-Culottes*. Soboul claims that little changed between 1789 and 1822. In Puiseux, 167 farmers out of 212 owned less than one hectare and 28 out of 212 owned only one to five hectares in 1822.

29. Smith, *An Historical Geography*, pp. 269–70; Goubert, *La Vie quotidienne*, pp. 19–26; Demangeon, *France économique*, pp. 186–88.

30. H. Fairhurst, "Types of Settlement in Spain," *Scottish Geographical Magazine* 51 (1935): 283–96; J. Thirsk, "The Common Fields," *Past and Present* 19 (December 1964).

31. Demangeon, *France économique*, pp. 186–88; Smith, *An Historical Geography*, pp. 269–71.

32. Dion, *Essai sur la formation*.

33. H. Kamen, *The Iron Century* (New York: Praeger, 1972), p. 208; Goubert, "The French Peasantry"; Soboul, *Paysans, Sans-Culottes*.

34. Demangeon, *La Picardie*, p. 337.

35. R. Forster, "Obstacles to Agricultural Growth in Eighteenth-Century France," *American Historical Review* 75, no. 6 (October 1970): 59; Stinchcombe, *Economic Sociology*, p. 153.

36. G. Lizerand, *Le Régime rural de l'ancienne France* (Paris: Presses universitaires de France, 1942).

37. Demangeon, *La Picardie*, p. 226; Stinchcombe, *Economic Sociology*, p. 99; Juillard, *La Vie rurale*, pp. 199–200.

38. Demangeon, *France économique*, pp. 151, 154.

39. P. Flatres, "Les Structures rurales de la frange atlantique de l'Europe," *Annales de L'Est, mémoire* 21 (1959); Smith, *An Historical Geography;* Blum, "European Village."

40. A. Bouton, *Le Maine: Histoire économique et sociale* (Le Mans: Imprimerie Monnoyer, 1962), pp. 240–41.

41. Demangeon, *France économique*, p. 227; Y. Poupinot, *La Bretagne contemporaine* (Paris: Kervreiz, 1954), pp. 23–24; G. Le Guen, "D'une révolution manquée à une révolution possible," in *Histoire de la Bretagne*, ed. J. Delumeau (Toulouse: Privat, 1969), pp. 509–10; J. Ousset, "L'Agriculture du Languedoc-Roussillon (1956–1971)," in *Economie et société en Languedoc-Roussillon de 1789 à nos jours*, ed. Centre d'histoire contemporaine du Languedoc méditerranéen et du Roussillon (Montpellier: Centre national de la recherche scientifique, 1978), p. 116.

42. Le Guen, "D'une révolution manquée," pp. 509–10; J. Meyer, "De la Révolution politique aux débuts du monde industriel (1789–1880)," in *Histoire de la Bretagne*, ed. J. Delumeau (Toulouse: Privat, 1969), p. 420.

43. R. Musset, *La Bretagne* (Paris: Armand Colin, 1948), p. 84;

Poupinot, *La Bretagne contemporaine,* pp. 23–24; H. Mendras, "Diversite des sociétés rurales françaises," in *Les Paysans et la politique dans la France contemporaine,* ed. J. Fauvet and H. Mendras (Paris: Armand Colin, 1958), pp. 33–34; S. Berger, *Peasants against Politics* (Cambridge, Mass.: Harvard University Press, 1972), p. 31; Y. Guin, *Histoire de la Bretagne* (Paris: Maspero, 1977), p. 137.

44. Blum, *The End of the Old Order,* p. 102.

45. Bloch, *French Rural History,* pp. 148–49; Forster, "Obstacles," p. 1064; Le Goff and Sutherland, "Social Origins," pp. 66–67.

46. R. H. Andrews, *Les Paysans des Mauges au XVIIIe siècle* (Tours: Arrault, 1935); Bloch, *French Rural History;* Forster, "Obstacles."

47. Andrews, *Les Paysans des Mauges,* p. 33.

48. Sée, *Les Classes rurales,* p. 4.

49. A. Soboul, *Problèmes paysans de la Révolution, 1789–1848* (Paris: Maspero, 1976), pp. 268–69.

50. A. Rebillon, *Histoire de Bretagne* (Paris: Armand Colin, 1957), p. 196; P. Masson, *Les Bouches-du-Rhône* (Marseille: Archives départementales des Bouches-du-Rhône, 1935), pp. 5–6.

51. L. Dubreuil, *Histoire des insurrections de l'Ouest* (Paris: Editions Rieder, 1929), p. 331.

52. R. Musset, *Le Bas-Maine: Étude géographique* (Paris: Armand Colin, 1917), pp. 389–90; Berger, *Peasants Against Politics,* pp. 27–28.

53. A. Kussmaul, *Servants in Husbandry in Early Modern England* (Cambridge: Cambridge University Press, 1981).

54. Ibid.; Blum, *The End of the Old Order.*

55. Rebillon, *Histoire de Bretagne,* pp. 199–200; P. Flatres, *La Région de l'Ouest* (Paris: Presses universitaires de France, 1964), p. 29; Le Goff and Sutherland, "Social Origins," p. 66.

56. Because *domaine congéable* entails remuneration for improvements and ownership of the edifice, many argue that it is a less dependent form of land tenure than sharecropping and tenancy (C. Vallaux, *La Basse-Bretagne: Etude de géographie humaine* [Paris: Editions Cornely, 1905]; J. Laurent, *Un Monde rural en Bretagne au XVe siècle: La Quévaise* [Paris: Service d'éditions et de vente des productions de l'éducation nationale, 1972]; L. Dubreuil, *Le Domaine congéable en Basse-Bretagne* [Rennes: Imprimerie Oberthur, 1915]; Guin, *Histoire de la Bretagne*). *Domaine congéable* produced numerous conflicts of interest between peasant and landlord, however, since the landlord was both obliged to reimburse the peasant for improvements and allowed to increase rents (Y. Brekilien, *Des Paysans bretons (au XIXe siécle)* [Paris: Hachette, 1966], pp. 34–35; Sée, *Histoire économique,* pp. 179–80).

57. Le Goff and Sutherland, "Social Origins," p. 67; Flatres, "Struc-

tures rurales," pp. 118–19; C. Servolin and Y. Tavernier, "La France: Réforme de structures ou politique des prix?," in *Terre, paysans, et politique*, ed. H. Mendras and Y. Tavernier (Paris: Futuribles, 1969), p. 158; Berger, *Peasants Against Politics*, p. 27; P. Bois, "Un Demi-Siècle d'incertitudes, 1815–1852," in *Histoire des pays de la Loire*, ed. F. Lebrun (Toulouse: Privat, 1972), pp. 369–70; B. Moore, Jr., *Social Origins of Dictatorship and Democracy* (Boston: Beacon Press, 1966), pp. 96–97.

58. Rebillon, *Histoire de Bretagne*, p. 157; Le Guen, "D'une révolution manquée," p. 478.

59. H. de Balzac, *Les Chouans* (Paris: Livres de poche, 1961), p. 39.

60. L. Merle, *La Métairie et l'évolution agraire de la Gatine poitevine de la fin du moyen âge à la Révolution* (Paris: Service d'éditions et de vente des productions de l'éducation nationale, 1958), p. 203.

61. Vallaux, *La Basse-Bretagne*, p. 124; Musset, *Le Bas-Maine*, pp. 422, 425; Flatres, "Structures rurales," p. 195.

62. Bois, "Un Demi-Siècle," p. 316.

63. Bloch, *French Rural History*, p. 57.

64. H. Roger, *Le Finistère* (Montpellier: Roumégous et Dehan, Imprimeurs, 1919), p. 14.

65. Goubert, *La Vie quotidienne*, p. 32; Demangeon, *France économique*, pp. 108–11; Duby, *Rural Economy*, pp. 84–85; Bouton, *Le Maine*, pp. 329–30.

66. H. Nabholz, "Medieval Agrarian Society in Transition," in *The Cambridge Economic History*, ed. J. H. Clapham and E. Power, vol. 1 (Cambridge: Cambridge University Press, 1941), pp. 494–95.

67. Ibid., p. 14; T. W. Margadant, *French Peasants in Revolt* (Princeton: Princeton University Press, 1979), p. 56.

68. A. J. Tudesq, *Les Grands notables en France (1840–1849): Etude historique d'une psychologie sociale* (Paris: Presses universitaires de France, 1964), p. 249; L. Ogès, "La Vie politique en Basse-Bretagne sous la IIIᵉ République," *Le Télégramme de Brest*, August 1959, p. 3; Y. Garlan and C. Nieres, *Les Révoltes bretonnes de 1675: Papier Timbré et Bonnets Rouges* (Paris: Editions sociales, 1975), p. 198; Guin, *Histoire de la Bretagne*, p. 83.

69. Ibid., p. 25.

70. Bois, "Un Demi-Siècle," pp. 327–28.

71. Guin, *Histoire de la Bretagne*, p. 25; L.-P. Le Maître, *Les Sillons de Beuzec* (Quimper: Bargain, 1975), p. 220.

72. Although data on the number of nobles maintaining rural residence during the eighteenth, nineteenth, and twentieth centuries are incomplete, it is known that the number in the West is greater than in all other regions of France (Musset, *La Bretagne*, p. 71; Le Guen,

"D'une révolution mánquée," pp. 482–83; J. Meyer, *La Noblesse bretonne au XVIIIe siècle* [Paris: Imprimerie nationale, 1966], p. 6; P. Barral, *Les Agrairiens français de Méline à Pisani* [Paris: Presses de la Fondation nationale des sciences politiques, 1968], p. 55; Andrews, *Les Paysans des Mauges*, p. 43; Goubert, *La Vie quotidienne*, p. 229).

73. Rebillon, *Histoire de Bretagne*, p. 42.

74. In the eighteenth century, the West had the highest proportion of noble property in all of France (J. de La Monneraye, *Le Régime féodal et les classes rurales dans le Maine au XVIIIe siècle* [Paris: Recueil Sirey, 1922], p. 44; Sée, *Histoire économique*).

75. Tudesq, *Les Grands notables*, p. 139; Musset, *Le Bas-Maine*, p. 326; Guin, *Histoire de la Bretagne*, pp. 97–98, 108; P. Bois, *Paysans de l'Ouest* (Le Mans: M. Vilaire, 1960), pp. 675–76.

76. Ibid.

77. A. Guillemin, "Patrimoine foncier et pouvoir nobiliaire: La Noblesse de la manche sous la monarchie de juillet," *Etudes rurales* (July–December 1976): 121.

78. Tudesq, *Les Grands notables*, p. 135.

79. Guillemin, "Patrimoine foncier," p. 121.

80. A. Siegfried, "Influence du régime de la propriété foncière sur la formation de l'opinion politique," in *Sociologie politique*, ed. P. Birnbaum and F. Chazel, vol. 2 (Paris: Armand Colin, 1971), p. 30.

81. Musset, *Le Bas-Maine*, p. 378.

82. Ibid.

83. Le Guen, "D'une révolution manquée," p. 466.

84. M. Anderson, *Conservative Politics in France* (London: George Allen & Unwinn, 1974), p. 100; A. Meynier, *Atlas et géographie de la Bretagne* (Paris: Flammarion, 1976), p. 71; Guin, *Histoire de la Bretagne*, p. 25; Rebillon, *Histoire de Bretagne*, pp. 203–4; C. Tilly, *The Vendée*, 3d. ed. (New York: John Wiley, 1967), p. 104; Moore, *Social Origins*, pp. 98–99.

85. Barral, *Les Agrairiens*, p. 55; Guillemin, "Patrimoine foncier," pp. 130–32; Bois, "Un Demi-Siècle," pp. 327–29; Le Guen, "D'une révolution manquée," p. 483; Sée, *Les Classes rurales*, p. 118; J. Gouault, *Comment la France est devenue républicaine* (Paris: Armand Colin, 1954), pp. 86–87.

86. Barral, *Les Agrairiens*, p. 55; J. Meyer, "Une Mutation manquée: De la Révolution politique aux débuts du monde industriel (1789–1880)," in *Histoire de la Bretagne*, ed. J. Delumeau (Toulouse: Privat, 1969), pp. 389–90; Dubreuil, *Histoire des insurrections*, pp. 330–31; Le Maître, *Les Sillons*, p. 191.

87. Guin, *Histoire de la Bretagne*, pp. 172–74; Barral, *Les Agrairiens*, p. 55.

88. Guin, *Histoire de la Bretagne*, pp. 166–67; Le Maître, *Les Sillons*, p. 192; Meyer, "De la Révolution politique."

89. Musset, *Le Bas-Maine*, p. 373.

90. J. Meyer, "Le Siècle de l'intendance (1688–1789), in *Histoire de la Bretagne*, ed. J. Delumeau (Toulouse: Privat, 1969), pp. 303–4; Sée, *Les Classes rurales*, p. 128.

91. A. Siegfried, *Tableau politique de la France de l'Ouest sous la Troisième République* (Paris: Armand Colin, 1913), p. 406.

92. Guillemin, "Patrimoine foncier," p. 123.

93. Tudesq, *Les Grands notables*, p. 123.

94. Demangeon, *France économique*, p. 216.

95. Ibid.

96. Musset, *La Bretagne*, p. 99.

97. Ibid., p. 92; Demangeon, *France économique*, pp. 144–47.

98. Ibid., pp. 27–28.

99. Smith, *An Historical Geography*, pp. 244–45.

100. Bloch, *French Rural History; R. Forster, *The Nobility of Toulouse in the Eighteenth Century: A Social and Economic Study* (Baltimore: Johns Hopkins University Press, 1960), pp. 41–42; Goubert, *La Vie quotidienne*, pp. 33–38; Herlihy, "Ecological Conditions," p. 17.

101. Smith, *An Historical Geography*, p. 256.

102. Goubert, "Les Cadres de la vie rurale," pp. 111–13; Forster, *The Nobility*, p. 66; G. Frêche, *Toulouse et la région Midi-Pyrénées au siècle des lumières vers 1670–1789* (Paris: Cujas, 1974), p. 242; Vila, "Les Milieux populaires," pp. 39–40; R. Livet, *Habitat rural et structures agraires en Basse-Provence* (Aix-en-Provence: Editions Ophrys, 1962); R. L. Reynolds, *Europe Emerges* (Madison: University of Wisconsin Press, 1961), p. 393; R. DuGrand, *Villes et campagnes en Bas-Languedoc* (Paris: Presses universitaires de France, 1963), p. 385; E. Le Roy Ladurie, *Histoire du Languedoc*, Que sais-je? 953 (Paris: Presses universitaires de France, 1967), pp. 27–28.

103. T. Zeldin, *France 1848–1945: Ambition and Love* (Oxford: Oxford University Press, 1979), p. 164; J. Laurent, "Les Quatre Ages du vignoble du Bas-Languedoc et du Roussillon," in *Economie et société en Languedoc-Roussillon de 1789 à nos jours*, ed. Centre d'histoire contemporaine du Languedoc méditerranéen et du Roussillon (Montpellier: Centre national de la recherche scientifique, 1978), p. 12. With a rising demand for wine, the wine-producing area grew from 134,000 hectares in 1788 to 232,000 hectares in 1839, replacing wheat-growing areas (Le Roy Ladurie, *Histoire du Languedoc*, p. 110).

104. P. Vigier, *La Seconde République dans la région alpine: Etude politique et sociale,* vol. 1 (Paris: Presses universitaires de France, 1963), p. 62.

105. Blum, *The End of the Old Order,* p. 29; Goubert, *The Ancien Régime,* pp. 84−85; Sée, *Histoire économique,* p. 175; J. Loutchisky, *L'Etat des classes agricoles en France à la veille de la Révolution* (Paris: Librairie ancienne, 1911), pp. 20−21.

106. Livet, *Habitat rural,* p. 311.

107. P. Vilar, *La Catalogne dans l'Espagne moderne* (Paris: Flammarion, 1977), p. 173; A. R. Lewis, *The Development of Southern French and Catalan Society, 718−1050* (Austin: University of Texas Press, 1965), pp. 402−3; Goubert, *La Vie quotidienne,* pp. 45−46.

108. Fourquin, *Lordship and Feudalism,* pp. 73, 140.

109. Ibid., p. 73; F. L. Ganshof, *Feudalism* (London: Longmans, 1964), p. 119.

110. Livet, *Habitat rural,* p. 343; Lewis, *The Development of Southern French,* pp. 402−3; Fourquin, *Lordship and Feudalism,* pp. 74−75; David Nicholas, "Patterns of Social Mobility," in *One Thousand Years: Western Europe in the Middle Ages,* ed. R. L. DeMolen (Boston: Houghton Mifflin, 1974), p. 54.

111. Smith, *An Historical Geography,* pp. 244−45.

112. G. C. Homans, "The Rural Sociology of Medieval England," *Past and Present* 4 (November 1953); Goubert, *The Ancien Régime,* p. 112.

113. Livet, *Habitat rural;* Goubert, *The Ancien Régime.*

114. P. George, *La Région du Bas-Rhône: Etude de géographie régionale* (Paris: Librairie J. B. Baillière, 1936), pp. 553−54; M. Agulhon, *La République au village* (Paris: Plon, 1970), p. 203; D. Fabre and J. Lacroix, *La Vie quotidienne des paysans du Languedoc au XIXe siècle* (Paris: Hachette, 1973), p. 247; N. Coulet and E. Stouff, "Les Institutions communales dans les villages de Provence au bas moyen âge, *Etudes rurales* (July−December 1976), pp. 69−72.

115. M. Dobb, *Studies in the Development of Capitalism* (London: Routledge & Kegan Paul, 1946), p. 51.

116. See I. Wallerstein, *The Modern World System* (New York: Academic Press, 1974); R. Brenner, "Agrarian Class Structure and Economic Development in Pre-Industrial Europe," *Past and Present* 70 (February 1976): 30−75.

117. Demangeon, *France économique,* pp. 149−50; G. Fournier, "Aspects économiques et sociaux de la Révolution dans quelques communes du Languedoc, de 1789 à l'an III," in *Economie et société en Languedoc-Roussillon de 1789 à nos jours,* ed. Centre d'histoire contem-

poraine du Languedoc méditerranéen et du Roussillon (Montpellier: Centre national de la recherche scientifique, 1978), p. 169; A. Soboul, *Les Campagnes montpelliéraines à la fin de l'Ancien Régime: Propriété et cultures d'Après les Compoix* (Paris: Presses universitaires de France, 1958), pp. 28–29; Livet, *Habitat rural;* M. Chevalier, *La Vie humaine dans les Pyrénées-ariégeoises* (Paris: Editions M. Th. Genin, 1956), p. 187.

118. Vigier, *La Seconde République,* vol. 1, pp. 42–43; George, *La Région du Bas-Rhône,* pp. 543–44.

119. J. Sion, *La France méditerranéenne* (Paris: Armand Colin, 1974), p. 124; Chevalier, *La Vie humaine,* pp. 182–86; P. Vigier, *Essai sur la répartition de la propriété foncière dans la région alpine* (Paris: Service d'éditions et de vente des productions de l'éducation nationale, 1963), pp. 129, 133–34; Vila, "Les Milieux populaires," p. 58; Livet, *Habitat rural,* p. 343.

120. *Préciput* followed from the Roman tradition of *patria potestas,* in that the wishes of the father with respect to inheritance were supreme. He alone determined who was to inherit the land and could will it to one of his children or divide it among many. Not uncommonly, daughters inherited under this system.

121. Fourquin, *Lordship and Feudalism,* p. 155; Livet, *Habitat rural,* pp. 350–51; Lewis, *The Development of Southern French,* p. 352; R. Aubenas, "La Famille dans l'ancienne Provence," *Annales d'histoire économique et sociale* 8 (November 1936): 526–30; E. Le Roy Ladurie, "Family Structure and Inheritance Customs in Sixteenth-Century France," in *Family and Inheritance,* ed. J. Goody, J. Thirsk, and E. P. Thompson (Cambridge: Cambridge University Press, 1976), pp. 61–62; W. L. Wakefield, *Heresy, Crusade, and Inquisition in Southern France, 1100–1250* (Berkeley: University of California Press, 1971), pp. 52–53.

122. Livet, *Habitat rural,* pp. 350–51; Sion, *La France méditerranéenne,* p. 124.

123. George, *La Région du Bas-Rhône,* pp. 431–32; Vigier, *Essai sur la répartition,* p. 126; Masson, *Les Bouches-du-Rhône,* p. 2. Medium-sized holdings, ten to fifty hectares, were rare in the Mediterranean except in the poorest locales (Livet, *Habitat rural,* pp. 339–42; Fabre and LaCroix, *La Vie quotidienne,* pp. 28–29; Vigier, *Essai sur la répartition,* p. 132; Chevalier, *La Vie humaine,* pp. 198–99). For the most part, the soil in these areas was so poor that small holdings were uneconomical (Demangeon, *France économique,* pp. 143–44).

124. George, *La Région du Bas-Rhône,* p. 545; Livet, *Habitat rural,* p. 426; Goubert, *La Vie quotidienne,* pp. 33–38.

125. M. Agulhon, *La Vie sociale en Provence intérieure au lendemain de la Révolution* (Paris: Société des études robespierristes, 1970), p. 59;

Smith, *An Historical Geography,* pp. 280–82; George, *La Région du Bas-Rhône,* pp. 550–53.

126. Musset, *La Bretagne,* pp. 422–25; Demangeon, *France économique,* pp. 205–6.

127. J. Merrington, "Town and Country in the Transition to Capitalism," *New Left Review* 93 (September–October 1975); Fourquin, *Lordship and Feudalism,* pp. 24–25; DuGrand, *Villes et campagnes,* pp. 143–45; Margadant, *French Peasants in Revolt,* pp. 86–87.

128. Agulhon, *La Vie sociale,* pp. 60–61.

129. George, *La Région du Bas-Rhône,* pp. 544–55; H. Boucau and J.L.H. Charles-Brun, *Le Vaucluse: Monographies régionales* (Paris: Librairie Grasset, 1938), pp. 29–30; Agulhon, *La Vie sociale,* p. 169.

130. Ibid., p. 168. Even the principal cities of the region are distinguished by their large active population (M. Vovelle, "La Provence et la Révolution," in *Histoire de la Provence,* ed. E. Baratier [Toulouse: Privat, 1969], p. 390).

131. R. Pillorget, *Les Mouvements insurrectionnels de Provence entre 1596 et 1715* (Paris: Editions A. Pedrone, 1975), p. 83.

132. Smith, *An Historical Geography,* pp. 310–11; A. B. Hibbert, "The Origins of the Medieval Town Patriciate," in *The Middle Ages,* ed. B. Tierney, vol. 2 (New York: Alfred A. Knopf, 1974), pp. 157–59; Masson, *Les Bouches-du-Rhône,* p. 474; Fourquin, *Lordship and Feudalism,* p. 213; Reynold, *Europe Emerges,* pp. 75–76; Nicholas, "Patterns of Social Mobility," p. 68.

133. Agulhon, *La Vie sociale,* p. 95; Wakefield, *Heresy, Crusade, and Inquisition,* p. 53.

134. Ibid., p. 55.

135. Vila, "Les Milieux populaires," pp. 142–44; Agulhon, *La Vie sociale.*

136. Vila, "Les Milieux populaires," p. 362; Agulhon, *La République,* pp. 464–65.

137. DuGrand, *Villes et campagnes,* pp. 129–31; Pillorget, *Les Mouvements insurrectionnels,* pp. 82–83; R. Baehrel, *Une Croissance: La Basse-Provence rurale (fin XVIe siècle—1789); essai d'économie historique statistique* (Paris: Service d'éditions et de vente des productions de l'education nationale, 1961), pp. 397–99.

138. Masson, *Les Bouches-du-Rhône,* p. 43; Vovelle, "La Provence," p. 393; DuGrand, *Villes et campagnes,* pp. 129–31; Loutchisky, *L'Etat des classes agricoles,* p. 58.

139. Soboul, *Les Campagnes,* p. 81.

140. Masson, *Les Bouches-du-Rhône,* p. 43; Agulhon, *La Vie sociale,* p. 90; Vila, "Les Milieux populaires," pp. 145–46. As one example, of

235 noble heads of families in Provence in 1789, only 33 lived in the countryside (Agulhon, *La Vie sociale*, p. 90).

141. Livet, *Habitat rural*, pp. 367, 416.

142. Le Roy Ladurie, *Histoire du Languedoc*, p. 121; DuGrand, *Villes et campagnes*, pp. 127–32; R. Moulinas, "La Composition et l'évolution du pays légal dans le Vaucluse, sous la Monarchie de juillet," in *Mémoire de l'Académie du Vaucluse*, ed. A. Autrand (Avignon: Imprimerie Rullière, 1957), pp. 78–81.

143. Vovelle, "La Provence," p. 390; Baehrel, *Une Croissance*, p. 397.

144. DuGrand, *Villes et campagnes*, pp. 149–50.

145. Vigier, *Essai sur la répartition*. Specifically, in 1848 of the 211 electors in Avignon paying more than two hundred francs in tax, 32 were noble; of the 13 electors in Carpentras paying a tax of one thousand francs or more, 10 were noble; and of the 20 electors in Orange paying more than one thousand francs, 17 were noble—ratios far exceeding the proportion of nobles within the general population (Vigier, *La Seconde République*, vol. 1, pp. 130–31; Moulinas, "La Composition," pp. 73–75).

146. Livet, *Habitat rural*, p. 347. Because of their preponderance in Mediterranean cities, these various social elites established powerful networks of conservative patronage. It thus comes as no surprise that through much of the ancien régime and the nineteenth century many of the Midi's principal cities backed the conservative politics of the social elites (see especially R. Aminzade, *Class, Politics, and Early Industrial Capitalism* [Albany: State University of New York Press, 1981]).

147. Frêche, *Toulouse et la région Midi-Pyrénées;* Forster, *The Nobility;* Baehrel, *Une Croissance*, p. 399; Soboul, *Les Campagnes*, pp. 28–29; Sée, *Histoire économique*, p. 174.

148. Frêche, *Toulouse et la région Midi-Pyrénées*, p. 140.

149. Agulhon, *La République*, pp. 211–12.

150. Ibid.; Vila, "Les Milieux populaires"; G. Galtier, *Etudes de géographie vinicole* (Montpellier: Edition Causse, Graille, & Castebriau, 1951), pp. 119, 125.

151. Agulhon, *La Vie sociale*, pp. 211–12; T. Judt, "The Development of Socialism in France: The Example of the Var," *Historical Journal* 18, no. 1 (1975): 66; Vila, "Les Milieux populaires"; Vigier, *La Seconde République*, vol. 2, pp. 185–86.

152. R. Vidal, "Les Royalistes et les légitimistes dans le Gard," (thèse, University of Paul Valéry, Montpellier, 1970), pp. 95–96, 100.

153. DuGrand, *Villes et campagnes*, p. 424; Agulhon, *La Vie sociale;* Coulet and Stouff, "Les Institutions communales"; George, *La Région*

du Bas-Rhône; Fabre and LaCroix, *La Vie quotidienne;* Sion, *La France méditerranéenne;* Wakefield, *Heresy, Crusade, and Inquisition.*

154. Coulet and Stouff, "Les Institutions communales," pp. 80–81; George, *La Région du Bas-Rhône,* p. 355.

155. DuGrand, *Villes et campagnes,* p. 424; Sion, *La France méditerranéenne,* p. 91; Fabre and LaCroix, *La Vie quotidienne,* p. 247.

156. George, *La Région du Bas-Rhône,* pp. 553–54.

157. Coulet and Stouff, "Les Institutions communales," pp. 69–70; Fabre and LaCroix, *La Vie quotidienne,* p. 247.

158. Fourquin, *Lordship and Feudalism,* p. 225; Wakefield, *Heresy, Crusade, and Inquisition,* pp. 62–63; George, *La Région du Bas-Rhône,* pp. 553–54; G. Fournier, "Sur l'administration municipale de quelques communautés languedociennes de 1750 à 1791," *Annales du Midi* 84, no. 109 (October-November 1972): 463–65. All males or heads of households between the ages of fourteen and sixty possessed the right to participate in local affairs. Moreover, attendance at meetings of *les assemblées générales des habitants* was mandatory. Besides supervising and coordinating the communal activities of the village, these assemblies met to discuss or approve agreements between the village community and the local seigneur and to elect village leaders (*procureurs* and *syndics*). These selected *procureurs* were usually the wealthiest members of the village; their duties entailed checking the arbitrary power of the seigneur and levying taxes for community funds (George, *La Région du Bas-Rhône,* p. 553; Coulet and Stouff, "Les Institutions communales," pp. 69–77; Fabre and LaCroix, *La Vie quotidienne,* p. 247).

159. Agulhon, *La Vie sociale.*

160. Ibid., pp. 203, 222, 223–24.

161. Fournier, "Sur l'administration," p. 481.

162. Moulinas, "La Composition," p. 77; Vigier, *La Seconde République,* vol. 1, p. 132.

163. Moulinas, "La Composition," pp. 75–77.

164. Musset, *La Bretagne,* p. 92; Siegfried, "Influence du régime," p. 25.

165. Demangeon, *France économique,* pp. 200–202.

166. Vila, "Les Milieux populaires," pp. 26–27; M.-F. Courtin and I. Pons, "Les Mouvements socialistes dans l'Hérault de 1871 à 1906" (maîtrise d'histoire contemporaine, University of Paul Valéry, Montpellier, 1971), p. 5.

167. G. Cholvy, "Religion et société au XIXᵉ Siècle: Le Diocèse de Montpellier" (thèse, premier cycle, University of Paris, 1972), p. 192.

168. Vila, "Les Milieux populaires"; Tudesq, *Les Grands notables,* pp. 155–56.

169. Cholvy, "Religion et société," p. 194.

170. Although this chapter has considered France's three principal modes of production, it should be noted that mixed modes did indeed exist. For example, in central France we find a subsistence economic activity associated with small-scale sharecropping and owner-cultivator land tenure, moderately compact villages, minimal town-countryside association, and a general absence of social elites (Loutchisky, *L'Etat des classes agricoles;* Sée, *Histoire économique;* Goubert, *The Ancien Régime;* Blum, *The End of the Old Order*).

CHAPTER 4

1. E. W. Fox, *History in Geographic Perspective* (New York: W. W. Norton, 1971), pp. 122, 132.

2. S. Berger, *Peasants Against Politics* (Cambridge, Mass.: Harvard University Press, 1972), pp. 52–53; Fox, *History in Geographic Perspective,* pp. 131–32.

3. D. I. Scargill, *Economic Geography of France* (New York: Macmillan, 1968), p. 34.

4. D. S. Landes, *The Unbound Prometheus* (Cambridge: Cambridge University Press, 1972), p. 454.

5. R. Aminzade, *Class, Politics, and Early Industrial Capitalism* (Albany: State University of New York Press, 1981), p. 43.

6. Ibid.

7. S. Shaber, "The Political Consequences of Regional Imbalances in Socio-Economic Development: Electoral Alignments and Socio-Economic Regionalism in Modern France" (Ph.D. dissertation, University of Pennsylvania, 1973).

8. C. P. Kindleberger, *Economic Growth in France and Britain* (Cambridge, Mass.: Harvard University Press, 1964), p. 259.

9. Enquêtes revenues 1975, (Tableau no. 13M), Institut national de la statistique et des études économiques.

10. Kindleberger, *Economic Growth,* p. 259.

11. Shaber, "The Political Consequences," pp. 36–37.

12. Scargill, *Economic Geography,* pp. 127–28; J. N. Tuppen, *France* (Boulder: Westview Press, 1980), pp. 100–101.

13. Scargill, *Economic Geography,* p. 129; Tuppen, *France,* p. 213.

14. J. Meyer, "Le Siècle de l'intendance (1688–1789)," in *Histoire de la Bretagne,* ed. J. Delumeau (Toulouse: Privat, 1969), pp. 324–25.

15. Ibid., pp. 325–26.

16. J. Meyer, "Une Mutation manquée: De la Révolution politique aux débuts du monde industriel (1789–1880)," in *Histoire de la Bretagne*, ed. J. Delumeau (Toulouse: Privat, 1969), p. 403.

17. H. Touchard, "Le Moyen Age breton (XIIe–XVIe siècles)," in *Histoire de la Bretagne*, ed. J. Delumeau (Toulouse: Privat, 1969), pp. 184–86, 200–202.

18. R. Musset, *La Bretagne* (Paris: Armand Colin, 1948), p. 120; P. E. Mayo, *The Roots of Identity* (London: Allen Lane, 1974), p. 19.

19. Meyer, "Mutation," p. 413; Y. Guin, *Histoire de la Bretagne* (Paris: Maspero, 1977), p. 113.

20. Meyer, "Mutation," pp. 411–12; G. Le Guen, "D'une révolution manquée à une révolution possible," in *Histoire de la Bretagne*, ed. J. Delumeau (Toulouse: Privat, 1969), pp. 471–72.

21. M. Th. Cloître, "Aspects de la vie politique dans le département du Finistère de 1848 à 1870," *Bulletin de la Société archéologigue du Finistère* 99, no. 2 (1972): 740–41.

22. Although the canals and railroads made Brittany more accessible to the rest of France, their location did not coincide with the flow of exchange in the region (Berger, *Peasants Against Politics*). Whereas the northeastern economy reaped substantial benefits from a developed transport network, the western economy suffered from its relative absence (P. Bois, "Un Demi-Siècle d'incertitudes, 1815–1852," in *Histoire des pays de la Loire*, ed. F. Lebrun [Toulouse: Privat, 1972], p. 369; Meyer, "Mutation," p. 408; C. Fohlen, "La France, 1700–1914," in *The Emergence of Industrial Societies* [The Fontana Economic History of Europe], ed. C. M. Cipolla [London: Collins, Fontana Books, 1973], p. 44).

23. Tuppen, *France*, p. 87.

24. A. Rebillon, *Histoire de Bretagne* (Paris: Armand Colin, 1957), pp. 162–63.

25. Musset, *La Bretagne*, p. 126.

26. Tuppen, *France*, pp. 104–5.

27. F. Crouzet, "Wars, Blockade, and Economic Change in Europe, 1792–1815," *Journal of Economic History* 24 (December 1964): 571.

28. J. Sion, *La France Méditerranéenne* (Paris: Armand Colin, 1974), p. 111; E. Le Roy Ladurie, *Histoire du Languedoc*, Que sais-je? 953 (Paris: Presses Universitaires de France, 1967), p. 54; P. Wolff, *Commerce et marchands de Toulouse (vers 1350–1450)* (Paris: Plon, 1954), p. 144.

29. P. Boissonnade, "La Crise de l'industrie languedocienne," *Annales du Midi* 21, no. 82 (April 1909): 174–76, 185; P. Vigier, *La Se-*

conde République dans la région alpine: Etude politique et sociale, vol. 1
(Paris: Presses universitaires de France, 1963), pp. 101–2.

30. R. DuGrand, *Villes et campagnes en Bas-Languedoc* (Paris: Presses
universitaires de France, 1963), p. 192; A. Cosson, "Industrie de la
soie et population ouvrière à Nîmes de 1815 à 1848," in *Economie
et société en Languedoc-Roussillon de 1789 à nos jours,* ed. Centre d'histoire contemporaine du Languedoc méditerranéen et du Roussillon
(Montpellier: Centre national de la recherche scientifique, 1978),
p. 192.

31. Cosson, "Industrie de la soie," p. 200.

32. Le Roy Ladurie, *Histoire du Languedoc,* p. 71; J. U. Nef, *Industry
and Government in France and England, 1540–1640* (Ithaca: Cornell
University Press, 1957), pp. 22–23; DuGrand, *Villes et campagnes,*
pp. 391–99; Boissonnade, "La Crise," pp. 170, 188; Wolff, *Commerce
et marchands,* pp. 622–23, 625–26.

33. Vigier, *La Seconde République,* vol. 1, pp. 95–100; DuGrand,
Villes et campagnes, p. 401; H. Espieux, *Histoire de l'Occitanie,* (Nîmes:
Barnier, 1970), pp. 151–53.

34. Le Roy Ladurie, *Histoire du Languedoc,* p. 115.

35. DuGrand, *Villes et campagnes,* p. 402.

36. Ibid., p. 391.

37. M.-F. Courtin and I. Pons, "Les Mouvements socialistes dans
l'Hérault de 1871 à 1906" (maîtrise d'histoire contemporaine, University of Paul Valéry, Montpellier, 1971), p. 24.

38. Vigier, *La Seconde République,* vol. 1, p. 95.

39. Cosson, "Industrie de la soie," p. 191.

40. L. A. Loubere, *Radicalism in Mediterranean France, 1848–1914*
(Albany: State University of New York Press, 1974), p. 85; DuGrand,
Villes et campagnes, p. 396.

41. Loubere, *Radicalism in Mediterranean France,* pp. 88–89.

42. R. Livet, *Habitat rural et structures agraires en Basse-Provence*
(Aix-en-Provence: Editions Ophrys, 1962), p. 101; DuGrand, *Villes et
campagnes,* pp. 389–90.

43. L. Pierrein, "La Provence républicaine à l'ère industrielle
(1870–1940): L'Economie de 1870 à 1940," in *Histoire de la Provence,*
ed. E. Baratier (Toulouse: Privat, 1969), p. 493; Sion, *La France méditerranéenne,* p. 115.

44. Pierrein, "La Provence républicaine," pp. 493–95.

45. J. F. Gravier, *Paris et le désert français* (Paris: Flammarion, 1965),
p. 10; Aminzade, *Class, Politics,* pp. 41–42; S. B. Clough, *France: A
History of National Economics, 1789–1939* (New York: Octagon Books,
1955), pp. 128–29; Loubere, *Radicalism in Mediterranean France,*

pp. 190, 194; M. Agulhon, *The Republic in the Village* (Cambridge: Cambridge University Press, 1982), p. 68.

46. Clough, *France: A History*, pp. 115, 128–29.

47. Aminzade, *Class, Politics*, pp. 41–42.

48. J. H. Clapham, *Economic Development of France and Germany, 1815–1914* (Cambridge: Cambridge University Press, 1963), p. 21; G. Fourquin, *Lordship and Feudalism in the Middle Ages* (London: George Allen & Unwinn, 1976), p. 212.

49. H. Sée, *Les Classes rurales en Bretagne du XVIᵉ siècle à la Révolution* (Paris: V. Giord & E. Baière, 1906), pp. 18, 226, 262; Clapham, *Economic Development*, pp. 16–17; R. Dion, *Essai sur la formation du paysage rural français* (Tours: Arrault, 1934), pp. 104–5.

50. C. T. Smith, *An Historical Geography of Western Europe Before 1800* (New York: Praeger, 1967), p. 266.

51. H. Sée, *Histoire économique de la France (les temps modernes, 1789–1914)* (Paris: Armand Colin, 1951), p. 90.

52. W. H. Newell, "The Agricultural Revolution in Nineteenth-Century France," *Journal of Economic History* 34 (December 1973): 714–15.

53. A. Demangeon, *La Picardie et les régions voisines* (Paris: Armand Colin, 1925), p. 226.

54. G. Desert and R. Specklin, "L'Ebranlement 1880–1914," in *Histoire de la France rurale*, ed. E. Juillard, vol. 3 (Paris: Seuil, 1976), p. 432.

55. G. Desert, "L'Ebranlement 1880–1914," in *Histoire de la France rurale*, ed. E. Juillard, vol. 3 (Paris: Seuil, 1976), p. 454.

56. J. Bastie, "Paris et l'Ile-de-France au temps d'une industrialisation et d'une urbanisation accélérées (1881–1920)," in *Histoire de l'Ile-de-France et de Paris*, ed. M. Mollat (Toulouse: Privat, 1971), p. 507.

57. G. Desert, "Les Campagnes à leur apogée," in *Histoire de la France rurale*, ed. E. Juillard, vol. 3 (Paris: Seuil, 1976), p. 225.

58. Desert and Specklin, "L'Ebranlement 1880–1914," pp. 442–44.

59. Demangeon, *La Picardie*, pp. 224–25; Sion, *Les Paysans*, pp. 504–5.

60. Desert and Specklin, "L'Ebranlement 1880–1914," p. 434.

61. M. Gervais, M. Jollivet, and Y. Tavernier, *La Fin de la France paysanne de 1914 à nos jours* vol. 4 of *Histoire de la France rurale*, dir. G. Duby and A. Wallon (Paris: Seuil, 1976), p. 193; A. Soboul, *Paysans, Sans-Culottes, et Jacobins* (Paris: Librairie Clavreuil, 1966), pp. 119–20; J. Bastie, "Paris et l'Ile-de-France au temps de la révolution des chemins de fer et des transformations agricoles (1836–1880)," in *Histoire de l'Ile-de-France et de Paris*, ed. M. Mollat (Toulouse: Privat, 1971),

pp. 463–64. In my own examination of the 1979–1980 Recensement général de l'agriculture (Agricultural census) for rural cantons in the northeastern departments of Seine-et-Marne and Meuse, I found that 52 percent of all farms were larger than fifty hectares. My finding is consistent with Demangeon's finding that the departments with the greatest proportion of farms larger than fifty hectares are situated in the northeastern departments of Aisne, Ardennes, Eure-et-Loire, Seine-et-Marne, and Aube (Demangeon, *France économique*, p. 154).

62. Demangeon, *La Picardie*, p. 347; E. Juillard, *La Vie rurale dans la plaine de Basse-Alsace* (Strasbourg: Editions F.-X. Le Roux, 1953), p. 423.

63. Bastie, "Transformations agricoles (1836–1880)," p. 465; Juillard, *La Vie rurale*, pp. 428–29.

64. Ibid.

65. Desert, "Les Campagnes," p. 225.

66. The Paris region, however, is one area where the number of agricultural laborers has not declined. Since 1900 the growth of huge farms has necessitated the employment of many full-time salaried workers (Gervais, Jollivet, and Tavernier, *La Fin de la France*, pp. 235–36). Although tenancy has remained the principal form of land tenure in the Northeast, owner cultivation is still important, especially in parts of eastern France and Flanders, where there appears to be a considerable number of small- and medium-sized farms involved in intensive cultivation. In this general way we can separate the North, where tenancy is predominant, from the East, where it is less so.

67. The following figures are given for the total number of individuals emigrating from Brittany: 8,000 for the period 1831–1851; 116,000 for the period 1852–1872; 126,000 for the period 1873–1891; and 206,000 for the period 1892–1911 (Le Guen, "D'une révolution manquée," p. 466).

68. Berger, *Peasants Against Politics*, p. 20.

69. Desert and Specklin, "L'Ebranlement 1880–1914," p. 433.

70. Demangeon, *France économique*, p. 227.

71. Le Guen does mention that the area along the Breton littoral, specializing in the cultivation of vegetables, is a notable exception to this general rule (Le Guen, "D'une révolution manquée," p. 478).

72. Bois, "Un Demi-Siècle," pp. 369–70.

73. Berger, *Peasants Against Politics*, p. 26.

74. Ibid., pp. 26–27.

75. Demangeon, *France économique*, p. 151.

76. Guin, *Histoire de la Bretagne*, p. 108.

77. Meyer, "Mutation," p. 424.

78. Le Guen, "D'une révolution manquée," pp. 482–83.
79. Ibid.
80. J. J. Monnier, "Géographie de l'opinion politique en Ille-et-Vilaine" (thèse, troisième cycle, University of Haute-Bretagne, Rennes, 1970), p. 33.
81. The dominance of nobles has also continued in the makeup of the *conseillers généraux*. For example: in the western department of Loire-Atlantique in 1956, fifteen of the forty-six *conseillers généraux* were noble (Monnier, "Géographie de l'opinion," p. 33).
82. J. Meyer, *La Noblesse bretonne au XVIIIe siècle* (Paris: Imprimerie nationale, 1966), pp. 135–42.
83. Le Guen, "D'une révolution manquée," p. 486; Berger, *Peasants Against Politics,* pp. 61–62, 72; A. Guillemen, "Patrimoine foncier et pouvoir nobiliaire: La Noblesse de la manche sous la monarchie de juillet," *Etudes rurales* (July–December 1976): 126–27; Guin, *Histoire de Bretagne,* pp. 112, 148–52; P. Barral, *Les Agrairiens français de Méline à Pisani* (Paris: Presses de la Fondation nationale des sciences politiques, 1968), p. 340; C. Servolin and Y. Tavernier, "La France: Réforme de structures ou politique des prix?" in *Terre, Paysans, et Politique,* ed. H. Mendras and Y. Tavernier (Paris: Futuribles, 1969), p. 169.
84. Berger, *Peasants Against Politics,* p. 61.
85. Ibid., p. 66.
86. Sée, *Les Classes rurales,* p. 129; Meyer, "Le Siècle," pp. 303–4; E. O. Golob, *The Meline Tariff: French Agriculture and Nationalist Economic Policy* (New York: Columbia University Press, 1944).
87. Since World War II, the authority of western social elites has survived in such associations as the Confédération nationale de la mutualité, de la coopération et du crédit agricole; Fédération nationale des syndicats d'exploitants agricoles; and the Assemblée permanente des présidents de chambre d'agriculture.
88. Rebillon, *Histoire de Bretagne,* pp. 203–4; A. Meynier, *Atlas et Géographie de la Bretagne* (Paris: Flammarion, 1976), p. 71; J. Meyer, "De la révolution politique aux débuts du monde industriel (1789–1880)," in *Histoire de la Bretagne,* ed. J. Delumeau (Toulouse: Privat, 1969), p. 438.
89. Meyer, "De la révolution politique," p. 438; R. Pierce, *French Politics and Political Institutions,* 2d ed. (New York: Harper & Row, 1973), p. 10.
90. Pierce, *French Politics,* p. 10.
91. Le Roy Ladurie, *Histoire du Languedoc,* p. 111; Livet, *Habitat rural,* pp. 99–100; Loubere, *Radicalism in Mediterranean France,* p. 18.

92. Le Roy Ladurie, *Histoire du Languedoc,* pp. 111–12; Laurent, "Les Quatre Ages," p. 14.

93. Loubere, *Radicalism in Mediterranean France,* p. 110.

94. Ibid., pp. 99–100.

95. G. Walter, *Histoire des paysans de France* (Paris: Flammarion, 1963), p. 426.

96. Le Roy Ladurie, *Histoire du Languedoc,* pp. 116–17.

97. Some localities, notably within the departments of Vaucluse and Pyrénées-Orientales, specialized in the intensive cultivation of fruits and vegetables. In 1970 the department of Pyrénées-Orientales had become the premier producer of apricots and the number two producer of peaches in France (G. Gavignaud, "Spécialisations maraîchères et fruitières en Roussillon et conjoncture viticole [XIXe–XXe siècles]," in *Economie et société en Languedoc-Roussillon de 1789 à nos jours,* ed. Centre d'histoire contemporaine du Languedoc méditerranéen et du Roussillon [Montpellier: Centre national de la recherche scientifique, 1978], p. 87).

98. J. H. Smith, "Work Routine and Social Structure in a French Village: Cruzy in the Nineteenth Century," *Journal of Interdisciplinary History* 5, no. 3 (1975): 365–66. Also see DuGrand, *Villes et campagnes,* p. 359; M. Chevalier, *La Vie humaine dans les Pyrénées-ariégeoises* (Paris: Editions M. Th. Genin, 1956), p. 764.

99. Demangeon, *France économique,* p. 154.

100. G. Cholvy, "Religion et société au XIXe siècle: Le Diocèse de Montpellier" (thèse, premier cycle, University of Paris, 1972), p. 442; DuGrand, *Villes et campagnes,* p. 359.

101. Loubere, *Radicalism in Mediterranean France,* p. 223.

102. Ibid., p. 188.

103. S. Vila, "Les Milieux populaires et la République dans l'Hérault, 1815–1852" (thèse, troisième cycle, University of Paris, 1966), p. 21.

104. Cholvy, "Religion et société," p. 442.

105. T. Judt, "The Origins of Rural Socialism in Europe: Economic Change and the Provençal Peasantry, 1870–1914," *Social History* (January 1976): 57.

106. Marc Bloch, *French Rural History* (London: Routledge & Kegan Paul, 1966); P. Goubert, *La Vie quotidienne des paysans français au XVIIe siècle* (Paris: Hachette, 1982); F. Furet and J. Ozouf, *Reading and Writing: Literacy in France From Calvin to Jules Ferry* (Cambridge: Cambridge University Press, 1982); H. Le Bras and E. Todd, *L'Invention de la France* (Paris: Pluriel, 1981); Barral, *Les Agrairiens;* Fox, *History in Geographic Perspective;* Le Roy Ladurie, "Family Structures and Inheritance Customs."

CHAPTER 5

1. I have not touched upon many divisive issues that less directly influenced the material interests of French cultivators, such as the 1893 Panama crisis or the 1936 Spanish civil war.

2. G. M. Foster, "Peasant Society and the Image of Limited Good," *American Anthropologist* 67 (April 1965): 293–315; E. C. Banfield, *The Moral Basis of a Backward Society* (New York: Free Press, 1967), pp. 83–101.

3. S. M. Lipset, *Agrarian Socialism* (Berkeley: University of California Press, 1950; Garden City, N.Y.: Doubleday, Anchor Books, 1968), pp. 25–26.

4. If the market-oriented farmer possesses a preponderant share of the market, however, he is less likely to oppose monopolistic practices and is thus unlikely to favor the Left.

5. "Tableau Agriculture," *Paysans* 73–74 (August–November 1968): 26–30.

6. T. Zeldin, *France 1848–1945: Ambition and Love* (Oxford: Oxford University Press, 1979), p. 151.

7. According to the 1892 census of agriculture, the mean size of an owner-cultivated plot was 4.37 hectares, compared to 11.71 hectares for a tenant's plot and 10.78 hectares for a sharecropper's. The ratios remained unchanged in the 1955 census of agriculture: the mean size for owner-cultivation was 16.9 hectares, compared to 35.6 hectares for tenancy and 32.2 hectares for sharecropping. Zeldin, *Ambition and Love*, p. 151; J. Fauvet, "Le Monde paysan et la politique," in *Les Paysans et la politique dans la France contemporaine*, ed. J. Fauvet and H. Mendras (Paris: Armand Colin, 1958), p. 10; P. Barral, *Les Agrairiens français de Méline à Pisani* (Paris: Presses de la Fondation nationale des sciences politiques, 1968), pp. 26, 303. For an explanation of why tenants and sharecroppers were likely to oppose land redistribution during the French Revolution see G. Lefebvre, "La Place de la Révolution dans l'histoire agraire de la France," *Annales d'histoire économique et sociale* 1 (1921): 517.

8. French sharecropping may differ from sharecropping practiced elsewhere. For example, French sharecroppers possess more sizable holdings than do sharecroppers in the American South.

9. P. Hoffman, "Sharecropping and Investment in Agriculture in Early Modern France," *Journal of Economic History* 42 (March 1982): 156–63. J. D. Powell, "Peasant Society and Clientelist Politics," *American Political Science Review* 64 (1970): 413; A. Weingrod, "Patrons, Patronage, and Political Parties," *Comparative Studies in Society and History* 10 (July 1968): 381.

10. Zeldin, *Ambition and Love*, p. 151.

11. See J. Paige, *Agrarian Revolution* (New York: Free Press, 1975).

12. For an excellent comparison of the differences between agricultural wage labor and agricultural servant labor in sixteenth- and seventeenth-century England see A. Kussmaul, *Servants in Husbandry in Early Modern England* (Cambridge: Cambridge University Press, 1981).

13. Powell, "Peasant Society and Clientelist Politics," p. 413; Weingrod, "Patrons, Patronage," p. 381.

14. S. Popkin, *The Rational Peasant* (Berkeley: University of California Press, 1979), p. 80.

15. J. C. Scott, "Patron-Client Politics and Political Change in Southeast Asia," in *Friends, Followers, and Factions*, ed. S. W. Schmidt et al. (Berkeley: University of California Press, 1977), p. 125.

CHAPTER 6

1. G. Dupeux, *Aspects de l'histoire sociale et politique du Loir-et-Cher, 1848–1914* (Paris: Mouton, 1962).

2. R. Rémond, *La Droite en France*, 3d ed. (Paris: Aubier, 1968).

3. F. Goguel, *Géographie des élections françaises de 1870 à 1951* (Paris: Armand Colin, 1951), p. 10; J. Guiffan, "Les Elections françaises de 1789 à nos jours," *Cahiers de l'histoire* 64 (March 1967): 64–65.

4. The member parties of the 1936 Popular Front were the Communist, S.F.I.O., Socialist Independent, Radical, *Ligue des droits de l'homme,* and *Comité de vigilance des intellectuels anti-fascistes;* Goguel, *Géographie des élections,* p. 10; A. Siegfried, *Tableau politique de la France de l'Ouest sous la Troisième République* (Paris: Armand Colin, 1913), p. xxv.

5. Rémond, *La Droite en France.*

6. L. Ogès, "La Vie politique en Basse-Bretagne sous la IIIᵉ République," *Le Télégramme de Brest,* August 1959, pp. 3–4; S. Berger, *Peasants Against Politics* (Cambridge, Mass.: Harvard University Press, 1972), p. 42; B. Hazo, *L'Idéologie politique paysanne sous la IIIᵉ République dans le nord-ouest de la Loire-Inférieure,* vol. 3 in *Formation sociale-politique de la France de l'Ouest,* ed. Centre de recherche politique (Nantes: Faculté de droit et des sciences politiques, 1975), pp. 25–27; Barral, *Les Agrairiens,* pp. 155–56; S. Vila, "Les Milieux populaires et la République dans l'Hérault, 1815–1852" (thèse, troisième cycle, University of Paris, 1966), p. 591; L. A. Loubere, *Radicalism in Mediterranean France 1848–1914* (Albany: State University of New York Press, 1974), pp. 35–36; Guiffan, "Les Elections françaises," pp. 35–

37; C. Servolin and Y. Tavernier, "La France: Réforme de structures ou politique des prix?," in *Terre, paysans, et politique,* ed. H. Mendras and Y. Tavernier (Paris: Futuribles, 1969), pp. 176–78; C. Mesliand, "Gauche et droite dans les campagnes provençales sous la IIIe République," *Etudes rurales* (July–December 1976): 212.

7. Judt, "The Origins of Rural Socialism," p. 64.

8. Vila, "Les Milieux populaires," pp. 366, 591; T. Margadant, *French Peasants in Revolt* (Princeton: Princeton University Press, 1979), p. 87.

9. R. Price, *The French Second Republic* (Ithaca: Cornell University Press, 1972), p. 202.

10. G. Walter, *Histoire des paysans de France* (Paris: Flammarion, 1963), p. 469.

11. P. Fabra, "La S.F.I.O.," in *Les Paysans et la politique dans la France contemporaine,* ed. J. Fauvet and H. Mendras (Paris: Armand Colin, 1958), p. 94.

12. Ibid., p. 95.

13. Barral, *Les Agrairiens,* p. 318.

14. Servolin and Tavernier, "La France," pp. 176–78.

15. V. Wright, "The Change in France," *Government and Opposition* 16 (Autumn 1981).

16. I. Murry, "How the Main Candidates See the Issues," *London Times,* 24 April 1981.

17. B. Criddle and D. Bell, "The 1981 French Elections: The Victory of the Left," *The World Today* 37 (July–August 1981). The Gaullists also oppose the enlargement of the European Common Market to include such predominantly agricultural countries as Greece, Spain, and Portugal. The Socialist party has been less vociferous than the Communist party in opposing the enlargement of the European Common Market.

18. Fabra, "La S.F.I.O.," p. 85; Barral, *Les Agrairiens,* p. 154; M. Dogan, "Political Cleavage and Social Stratification in France and Italy," in *Party Systems and Voter Alignments,* ed. S. M. Lipset and S. Rokkan (New York: Free Press, 1967), p. 179.

19. Fabra, "La S.F.I.O.," p. 85; Barral, *Les Agrairiens,* pp. 155–56, 317; G. Lefebvre, *Questions agraires au temps de la terreur* (La Roche-sur-Yon: Henri Poitier, 1954), p. 115.

20. Price, *The French Second Republic,* p. 202. Similar calls were echoed by Rollin's ideological successors. For instance, in 1897 Jean Juarès justified peasant smallholding by claiming "Entre la grande propriété et la petite propriété paysanne, il n'y a pas seulement une différence de degré mais en quelque sorte une différence de nature,

l'une étant une forme de capital, l'autre une forme de travail" (M. Gervais, M. Jollivet, and Y. Tavernier, *La Fin de la France paysanne de 1914 à nos jours* vol. 4 of *Histoire de la France rurale,* dir. G. Duby and A. Wallon [Paris: Seuil, 1976], pp. 404–5). And in 1921 the French Communist party made the defense of small property part of its agrarian program (Ibid.).

21. Servolin and Tavernier, "La France," pp. 176–78.

22. Walter, *Histoire des paysans,* pp. 476–77.

23. Servolin and Tavernier, "La France," pp. 176–78.

24. J. Keeler, "The New Politics of Agricultural Policymaking," *The French Socialist Experiment* (Philadelphia: Institute for the Study of Human Issues, 1984).

25. Walter, *Histoire des paysans,* p. 405.

26. Barral, *Les Agrairiens,* p. 26.

27. Ibid., p. 303.

28. E. Juillard, *La Vie rurale dans la plaine de Basse-Alsace* (Strasbourg: Editions F. -X. Le Roux, 1953), p. 225; A. Cobban, *The Social Interpretation of the French Revolution* (Cambridge: Cambridge University Press, 1964), pp. 111–12; Lefebvre, *Questions agraires,* pp. 129–32.

29. H. W. Erhman, "The French Peasant and Communism," *American Political Science Review* 46 (March 1962): 29.

30. C. Ezratty, "Les Communistes," in *Les Paysans et la politique dans la France contemporaine,* ed. J. Fauvet and H. Mendras (Paris: Armand Colin, 1958), p. 72; Fabra, "La S.F.I.O.," p. 85; Barral, *Les Agrairiens,* p. 317.

31. Ezratty, "Les Communistes," pp. 72–74.

32. Ibid., p. 73.

33. Vila, "Les Milieux populaires," p. 334.

34. A. -J. Tudesq, *Les Grands notables en France (1840–1849): Etude historique d'une psychologie sociale* (Paris: Presses universitaires de France, 1964), p. 1144.

35. Loubere, *Radicalism in Mediterranean France,* pp. 35–36; Vila, "Les Milieux populaires," p. 591; P. Vigier, *La Seconde République dans la région alpine: Etude politique et sociale,* vol. 2 (Paris: Presses universitaires de France, 1963), pp. 198–202; Guiffan, "Les Elections françaises," p. 35; Price, *The French Second Republic,* pp. 232–33.

36. Walter, *Histoire des paysans,* p. 445.

37. F. Goguel, *La Politique des partis sous la IIIe République,* 5th ed. (Paris: Seuil, 1957), p. 144.

38. Ibid., pp. 145–46. G. Lachapelle, *Elections législatives des 26 avril et 10 mai 1914: Résultats officiels* (Paris: G. Roustan, 1914).

39. Criddle and Bell, "The 1981 French Elections," p. 285; V. Lauber, *The Political Economy of France* (New York: Praeger, 1983), p. 115.

40. Criddle and Bell, "The 1981 French Elections"; Wright, "The Change in France"; Murry, "How the Main Candidates."

41. M. Agulhon, *La République au village* (Paris: Plon, 1970), pp. 471–72; T. Zeldin, *France 1848–1945: Ambition and Love* (Oxford: Oxford University Press, 1979), p. 141; A. Soboul, "La Question paysanne en 1848," *La Pensée* 20 (September–October 1948): 30–31.

42. Zeldin, *Ambition and Love*, p. 141.

43. E. Le Roy Ladurie, *Histoire du Languedoc*, Que sais-je? 953 (Paris: Presses universitaires de France, 1967), p. 123.

44. Lachapelle, *Elections législatives*.

45. M. Agulhon, "La Provence républicaine à l'ère industrielle (1870–1940): La Vie politique de 1870 à 1940," in *Histoire de la Provence*, ed. E. Barratier (Toulouse: Privat, 1969), pp. 531–32.

46. Gervais, Jollivet, and Tavernier, *La Fin de la France*, p. 404.

47. Barral, *Les Agrairiens*, p. 244; Servolin and Tavernier, "La France," pp. 176–78; *Courrier picard* (Somme) 15 June 1981; E. Cahm, *Politics and Society in Contemporary France (1789–1971)* (London: G. G. Harrap, 1972), p. 362.

48. Berger, *Peasants Against Politics*, p. 8; Hazo, "L'Idéologie politique," pp. 25–27.

49. Rémond, *La Droite en France*, p. 43.

50. The Orleanists were much more favorable to the Protestant church than was the extremely Catholic Bourbon branch.

51. R. Gildéa, "L'Enseignement en Bretagne au XIXᵉ siècle: L'Ile-et-Vilaine (1800–1914)," *Annales de Bretagne et des pays de l'Ouest* 84, no. 30 (1977): 458–60.

52. Vila, "Les Milieux populaires," p. 591; Guiffan, "Les Elections françaises," p. 35; Price, *The French Second Republic*, pp. 232–33.

53. Gildéa, "L'Enseignement en Bretagne," p. 473.

54. Loubere, *Radicalism in Mediterranean France*, pp. 115, 178–79; Y. Guin, *Histoire de la Bretagne* (Paris: Maspero, 1977), p. 155; Mesliand, "Gauche et droite," p. 62.

55. J. Desert, "Mentalités religieuses dans la France de l'Ouest aux XIXᵉ et XXᵉ siècles," *Cahiers des Annales de Normandie* 8 (1976): 142.

56. Berger, *Peasants Against Politics*, p. 51.

57. Ibid. In recent French history no other issue has had the effect of so clearly delineating the boundary between Left and Right as has the relationship between state and church. During the 1981 national election, for example, in a special article in the 23 June 1981 edition of *Le Provençal* (Hautes-Alpes), a prominent local Socialist characterized the Left's victory in the June Legislative elections as "une victoire pour la laïcité" (a victory for secular education). The author mentioned also that the Socialist victory ended twenty-three years of the

political Right's policy of eroding the secularization of education (C. Testanière, *Le Provençal* [Hautes-Alpes] 23 June 1981).

58. Rémond, *La Droite en France,* p. 42.

59. Berger, *Peasants Against Politics,* p. 66.

60. Rémond, *La Droite en France;* Vigier, *La Seconde République,* vol. 2, p. 202; Vila, "Les Milieux populaires," p. 150; Mesliand, "Gauche et droite," p. 212.

61. Barral, *Les Agrairiens,* p. 340.

62. Ibid., pp. 310–11.

63. Ibid., p. 277.

64. Ibid.

65. Vila, "Les Milieux populaires," p. 591.

66. In this way the structural formulations of Stinchcombe, Paige, and other scholars make more sense. Stinchcombe's and Paige's tenants and sharecroppers support revolutionary collective action because they are market-oriented smallholders whose surroundings are typified by intense town-countryside ties and population concentration, and by social elite absenteeism. Moreover, my theory supports Jenkins's (1983) findings that in 1917 the most radical Russian peasants were to be found in the black-earth region where, as tenants, they held insufficient land, resided in compact villages, and engaged in a market-oriented economic activity (C. Jenkins, "Why Do Peasants Rebel? Structural and Historical Theories of Modern Peasant Rebellions," *American Journal of Sociology* 88, no. 3 [November 1982]: 487–514).

67. K. Marx, *The Eighteenth Brumaire of Louis Bonaparte* (New York: International Publishers, 1963), p. 123.

68. A. L. Stinchcombe, "Agricultural Enterprise and Rural Class Relations," *American Journal of Sociology* 67 (September 1961): 165–76; J. Paige, *Agrarian Revolution* (New York: Free Press, 1975).

69. J. Linz, "Patterns of Land Tenure, Division of Labor, and Voting Behavior in Europe," *Comparative Politics* 8, no. 3 (April 1976): 386. Linz argues that for France, however, owner-cultivators are more likely to support the Left than are tenants and sharecroppers, as a consequence of historically unique factors (p. 385).

70. E. Wolf, *Peasant Wars of the Twentieth Century* (New York: Harper & Row, 1969).

71. Paige, *Agrarian Revolution,* p. 60.

72. It is interesting, Paige notes, that cotton sharecroppers are less prone to political radicalism than wet-rice sharecroppers. Paige explains the difference by the type of tenure, the interdependence of economic activity, and the extent to which landlords can effectively monitor workers (Ibid., pp. 63–65).

CHAPTER 7

1. L. Wylie, ed., *Chanzeaux: A Village in Anjou* (Cambridge, Mass.: Harvard University Press, 1966).

2. L. Wylie, *Village in the Vaucluse*, 3d ed. (Cambridge, Mass.: Harvard University Press, 1975).

3. A. de Tocqueville, *The Old Régime and the French Revolution* (Garden City, N.Y.: Doubleday, 1955); A. Davies, "The Origins of the French Peasant Revolution of 1789," *History* 49, no. 165 (February 1964): 24–41; H. Sée, *Histoire économique de la France (le moyen âge et l'ancien régime)* (Paris: Armand Colin, 1948); G. Lefebvre, *Les Paysans du Nord pendant la Révolution française* (Paris: Armand Colin, 1972); J. Loutchisky, "Régimes agraires et populations agricoles dans les environs de Paris à la veille de la Révolution," *Revue d'histoire moderne* 7 (1933); R. Forster, "Obstacles to Agricultural Growth in Eighteenth-Century France," *American Historical Review* 75, no. 6 (October 1970); P. Bois, *Paysans de l'Ouest* (Le Mans: M. Vilaire, 1960); C. Tilly, *The Vendée*, 3d ed. (New York: John Wiley, 1967). Also, for praiseworthy examples of quantitative studies of regional variation in political behavior during the French Revolution see L. Hunt, *Politics, Culture, and Class in the French Revolution* (Berkeley: University of California Press, 1984); and J. Markoff's excellent study of the basis of social conflict in 1789, in which he analyzed data at the *bailliages* level (J. Markoff, "The Social Geography of Rural Revolt at the Beginning of the French Revolution," *American Sociological Review* 50 [1985]: 761–81).

4. J. Bouillon, "Les Démocrates-socialistes aux élections de 1849," *Revue française de science politique* 6, no. 1 (January–March 1956); F. Goguel, *Géographie des élections françaises de 1870 à 1951* (Paris: Armand Colin, 1951); G. Dupeux, *Aspects de l'histoire sociale et politique du Loir-et-Cher, 1848–1914* (Paris: Mouton, 1962).

5. Bouillon notes, moreover, that the institution of the *scrutin de liste* (vote by list) made the 1849 election a choice between political opinions rather than personalities, since the list of candidates gravitated around common political programs.

6. F. Goguel, *La Politique des partis sous la IIIe République* (Paris: Seuil, 1957), p. 145; G. Lachapelle, *Elections législatives des 26 avril et 10 mai 1914: Résultats officiels* (Paris: G. Roustan, 1914), pp. 220–45.

7. It should be emphasized that these three elections are by no means anomalous. Throughout the nineteenth and twentieth centuries the parties or movements of the Right and Left have coalesced into two separate blocs, as in 1885, 1910, 1924, and 1936.

8. Although land value is an adequate measure of land productiv-

ity, it may reflect as well such other factors as farm size, quality of soil, population density, and crop type.

9. The 1929 agricultural census unfortunately combines into one measure the proportion of seasonal wage laborers and of permanent agricultural laborers. Because according to my model seasonal and permanent laborers are unlikely to share views on the key issues separating the Left and Right, I am not confident the measure is adequate.

10. Because data on population agglomeration for the departments of Ille-et-Vilaine and Meuse for the late nineteenth century were unavailable, I employed the 1921 measure in my analysis of the 1849 election. The utilization of the 1921 measure of population agglomeration for these two departments is generally appropriate since the proportion of population agglomeration has varied little during the nineteenth and twentieth centuries.

11. The proportion of electors who are noble is ascertained by locating those who have the word *de* preceding their name (*la particule nobiliaire*). The designation of nobility by the word *de* is not totally accurate, and designations of noble status varied regionally. Furthermore, certain individuals purchased titles and some simply placed the particule before their surnames. Whether noble by birth or usurpation, they held a common interest regarding the defense of noble privilege.

12. These religious data are taken from F. A. Isambert and J. P. Terrenoire, *Pratique religieuse des catholiques en France* (Paris: Presses de la Fondation des sciences politiques, 1980).

13. For an excellent discussion of problems and solutions regarding the use of quantitative techniques in longitudinal research see J. R. Hall, "Temporality, Social Action, and the Problem of Quantification in Historical Analysis," *Historical Methods* 17 (1984): 206–18.

14. Even when the assumption of randomness is violated, the standard procedure is to use standard tests of significance to provide guidelines concerning the existence of relationships (E. A. Hanushek and J. E. Jackson, *Statistical Methods for Social Scientists* [New York: Academic Press, 1977], especially chapter 2).

15. D. A. Belsley, E. Kuh, and R. E. Welsch, *Regression Diagnostics Identifying Influential Data and Sources of Collinearity* (New York: John Wiley, 1980).

16. W. S. Robinson, "Ecological Correlations and the Behavior of Individuals," *American Sociological Review* 15 (1950): 351–57. For the many subsequent discussions of the problems in historical research see W. P. Shively, "Ecological Inference: The Use of Aggregate Data to Study Individuals," *American Political Science Review* 63 (1969):

1183–96; E. T. Jones, "Ecological Inference and Electoral Analysis," *Journal of Interdisciplinary History* 2, no. 3 (1972): 249–62; A. J. Lichtman, "Correlation Regression and the Ecological Fallacy: A Critique," *Journal of Interdisciplinary History* 4, no. 3 (1974): 417–34; A. J. Lichtman and L. I. Langbein, "Ecological Regression Versus Homogeneous Units: A Specification Analysis," *Social Science History* 2 (1978): 172–93; M. Susser, *Causal Thinking in the Health Sciences: Concepts and Strategies of Epidemiology* (New York: Oxford University Press, 1973).

17. Jones, "Ecological Inference," p. 249.

18. The data on which Tables 11 through 29 are based come from French archival sources that are listed in the bibliography of archival sources.

19. Farms of more than fifty hectares are considered as large farms.

20. The strong relation between leftist voting and mode of production should not be interpreted as applicable solely to these three widely spaced elections. In an earlier study, I tested the mode of production model on voting for the French legislative elections of 1885 and 1978, and mode of production emerged as a strong and significant predictor (W. Brustein, "A Regional Mode-of-Production Analysis of French Political Behavior: The Cases of Western and Mediterranean France," *Politics and Society* 10 [Autumn 1981]: 355–98).

21. The relationship between mode of production and leftist voting remains positive and significant at the .000 level when I run the same regression across the 1849, 1914, and 1981 elections on only those 53 cases for which no data are missing.

22. In a separate test of the explanatory strengths of wine production and mode of production, I selected only those cases for which wine production constituted some part of the canton's economic activity. For 176 cases in 1849, 47 cases in 1914, and 122 cases in 1981, the mode of production emerges consistently as a stronger predictor of leftist voting in all three elections.

23. Brustein, "A Regional Mode-of-Production Analysis of French Political Behavior."

24. Converse and Pierce's recent analysis of the 1967, 1968, and 1969 French elections supports my finding that in western France religiosity predicts voting better than mode of production whereas in Mediterranean France mode of production predicts voting better than religiosity. Converse and Pierce arrive at their conclusion about the relative strengths of religiosity and class status from sample survey data (P. Converse and R. Pierce, *Political Representation in France* [Cambridge, Mass.: Harvard University Press, 1986], pp. 170–74).

25. I am not including the 1914 election in this test because its in-

clusion would reduce the sample size from 271 to 54 cantons.

26. Tilly, *The Vendée*, pp. 306–11.

27. Ibid., pp. 66–67.

28. Ibid., pp. 68–80.

29. T.J.A. Le Goff and D.M.G. Sutherland, "Social Origins of Counter-Revolution in Western France," *Past and Present* 99 (1983): 65–87.

30. Ibid., pp. 82–83.

31. T. Margadant, *French Peasants in Revolt* (Princeton: Princeton University Press, 1979), p. 175; T. Zeldin, *France 1848–1945: Politics and Anger* (Oxford: Oxford University Press, 1979), p. 3.

32. Margadant, *French Peasants in Revolt*, p. 136.

33. J. M. Merriman, *The Agony of the Republic* (New Haven: Yale University Press, 1978), pp. xxi–xxii.

34. Margadant, *French Peasants in Revolt*, pp. 34–35. By contrast, only 24 percent of those arrested in rebel communes of central and southwestern France were employed in agriculture.

35. Ibid., pp. 97–99.

36. L. A. Loubere, *Radicalism in Mediterranean France, 1848–1914* (Albany: State University of New York Press, 1974), pp. 72–74; Margadant, *French Peasants in Revolt*, p. 64; M. Agulhon, *The Republic in the Village* (Cambridge: Cambridge University Press, 1982), pp. 278–80; J. H. Smith, "Work Routine and Social Structure in a French Village: Cruzy in the Nineteenth Century," *Journal of Interdisciplinary History* 5, no. 3 (1975): 376.

37. Margadant, *French Peasants in Revolt*, p. 175.

38. Ibid., p. 175.

39. Ibid., pp. 240–41.

40. Ibid., pp. 97–99.

41. Ibid., p. 140.

42. Agulhon, *The Republic*, pp. 261–63.

43. Margadant, *French Peasants in Revolt*, p. 140.

44. J. M. Merriman, *The Agony of the Republic* (New Haven: Yale University Press, 1978), p. 184.

45. Dupeux, *Aspects de l'histoire*, pp. 373–74.

46. Ibid., pp. 113–16, 375.

47. S. Berger, *Peasants Against Politics* (Cambridge, Mass.: Harvard University Press, 1972), pp. 50–51.

48. Ibid.

49. Loubere, *Radicalism in Mediterranean France*, p. 185.

50. P. Barral, *Les Agrairiens français de Méline à Pisani* (Paris: Presses de la fondation nationale des sciences politiques, 1968), p. 146; Lou-

bere, *Radicalism in Mediterranean France,* pp. 187–88; J. H. Smith, "Work Routine," p. 379.

51. Ibid.

52. Ibid., p. 375.

53. Ibid.

54. Loubere, *Radicalism in Mediterranean France,* pp. 187–88; E. Shorter and C. Tilly, *Strikes in France, 1830–1968* (London: Cambridge University Press, 1974), pp. 249–50.

55. Loubere, *Radicalism in Mediterranean France,* p. 188.

56. Barral, *Les Agrairiens,* p. 146.

57. M. Agulhon, "La Provence républicaine à l'ère industrielle (1870–1940): La Vie politique de 1870 à 1940," in *Histoire de la Provence,* ed. E. Baratier (Toulouse: Privat, 1969), pp. 531–32.

58. J. H. Smith, "Work Routine," p. 379; Loubere, *Radicalism in Mediterranean France,* pp. 191–92.

59. B. Hazo, *L'Idéologie politique paysanne sous la IIIe République dans le nord-ouest de la Loire-Inférieure,* vol. 3 in *Formation sociale-politique de la France de l'Ouest,* ed. Centre de recherche politique (Nantes: Faculté de droit et des sciences politiques, 1975), p. 59.

60. Ibid., pp. 55–57.

61. Berger, *Peasants Against Politics,* p. 109.

62. C. K. Warner, *The Winegrowers of France and the Government since 1875* (New York: Columbia University Press, 1960), pp. 183–85.

63. Ibid., pp. 184–85.

64. P. Fabra, "La S.F.I.O.," in *Les Paysans et la politique dans la France contemporaine,* ed. J. Fauvet and H. Mendras (Paris: Armand Colin, 1958), pp. 94–95.

CHAPTER 8

1. M. Einaudi, "Political Change in France and Italy," *American Political Science Review* 40 (1946): 898–923; E. Caranti, "Il partito popolare nelle elezioni dell'altro dopoguerra," *Civitas, Rivista mensile di studi politici* 7 (September–October 1956): 48–64; G. Dore and E. Caranti, "Risultati elettorali dei socialisti dal 1895 al 1953," *Civitas, Rivista mensile di studi politici* 8 (August–September 1957): 135–48; S. Sadocchi, "Aree elettorali e forza dei partiti: 1968–1978," *Rivista italiana di scienza politica* 6, no. 3 (1976): 515–32; G. Brunetta, "Le Elezioni del 3 giugno 1979," *Aggiornamenti sociali* 30 (July–August 1979): 555–70.

2. M. Rossi-Doria, "The Land Tenure System and Class in Southern Italy," *American Historical Review* 64, no. 1 (October 1958): 46–53; V. Lutz, *Italy: A Study in Economic Development* (Oxford: Oxford Univer-

sity Press, 1962). Two major differences between western France and the southern Italian interior are that population agglomeration is extremely high and holdings are minuscule in southern Italy whereas in western France population dispersion is relatively high and holdings are medium-sized. The combination of poor soil and minuscule holdings, however, tends to reinforce the dependence of southern peasants on landlords.

3. J. D. Hicks, *The Populist Revolt* (Lincoln: University of Nebraska Press, 1961); M. R. Rogin, *The Intellectuals and McCarthy: The Radical Specter* (Cambridge, Mass.: MIT Press, 1967); R. Hofstadter, *The Age of Reform* (New York: Alfred A. Knopf, 1955).

4. Hicks, *The Populist Revolt,* p. 263.

5. Ibid., pp. 37–38.

6. Rogin, *The Intellectuals,* p. 107.

7. Hicks, *The Populist Revolt,* p. 23.

8. Ibid., pp. 427–44; Hofstadter, *The Age of Reform,* p. 108.

9. Hicks, *The Populist Revolt,* pp. 71–72.

10. Ibid., p. 67.

11. Ibid., p. 86.

12. Ibid., pp. 87–91.

13. Ibid., pp. 304–5.

14. Hofstadter, *The Age of Reform,* pp. 99–100; Rogin, *The Intellectuals.*

15. J. K. Pollock, "An Areal Study of the German Electorate, 1930–1933," *American Political Science Review* 38, (1944): 90.

16. J. Noakes, *The Nazi Party in Lower Saxony, 1921–1933* (London: Oxford University Press, 1971), pp. 81–82.

17. R. Heberle, *Social Movements* (New York: Appleton-Century-Crofts, 1951), p. 228; C. Loomis and P. Beegle, "The Spread of Nazism in Rural Areas," *American Sociological Review* 11 (1946): 725–27.

18. M. R. Lepsius, "From Fragmented Party Democracy to Government by Emergency Decree and Nationalist Socialist Takeover: Germany," in *The Breakdown of Democratic Regimes,* ed. J. J. Linz and A. Stepan (Baltimore: Johns Hopkins University Press, 1978), pp. 53–54; Loomis and Beegle, "The Spread of Nazism," pp. 725–27.

19. J. E. Farquharson, *The Plough and the Swastika: The NSDAP and Agriculture in Germany, 1928–45* (London: Sage, 1976), pp. 63–68, 249–50.

20. C. Baxter, *District Voting Trends in India; A Research Tool* (New York: Columbia University Press, 1969).

21. Similarly, in the 1962 Brazilian congressional elections the more right-wing Social Democratic party and the National Demo-

cratic party drew sizable support from the predominantly latifundia Northeast while the more left-wing Social Progressivist party and the Brazilian Labor party drew considerable support from the more commercialized and freeholding Southeast (G.A.D. Soares, "The Politics of Uneven Development: The Case of Brazil," in *Party Systems and Voter Alignments: Cross-National Perspectives,* ed. S. M. Lipset and S. Rokkan [New York: Free Press, 1967]).

22. B. Porchnev, *Les Soulèvements populaires en France de 1623 à 1648* (Paris: Service d'éditions et de vente des productions de l'éducation nationale, 1963); R. H. Tawney, *The Agrarian Problem in the Sixteenth Century* (London: Longmans, 1912), pp. 237–310.

23. R. Mousnier, "The Fronde," in *Preconditions of Revolution in Early Modern Europe,* ed. R. Forster and J. Greene (Baltimore: Johns Hopkins University Press, 1970), pp. 131–60; E. Kerridge, *Agrarian Problems in the Sixteenth Century and After* (London: George Allen & Unwinn, 1969), p. 93.

24. W. Brustein, "Class Conflict and Class Collaboration in Regional Rebellions, 1500 to 1700," *Theory and Society* 14 (1985): 445–68.

25. C. S. L. Davies, "Les Révoltes populaires en Angleterre (1500– 1700)," *Annales: Economies, sociétés, civilisations* 24 (1969): 26–40; P. Zagorin, *Rebels and Rulers, 1500–1660,* 2 vols. (Cambridge: Cambridge University Press, 1982); J. Perez, *La Révolution des Comunidades de Castille, 1520–1521* (Bordeaux: Institut d'études ibériques et ibéro-américaines de l'Université de Bordeaux, 1970); H. Kamen, *The Iron Century* (New York: Praeger, 1972); D. Bernard, "French Society and Popular Uprisings under Louis XIV," in *State and Society in Seventeenth-Century France,* ed. R. F. Kierstad (New York: New Viewpoints, 1975), pp. 157–79; C. Jago, "The Crisis of the Aristocracy in Seventeenth-Century Castile," *Past and Present* 84 (August 1979): 60–90.

26. A. de Tocqueville, *The Old Régime and the French Revolution* (Garden City, N.Y.: Doubleday, 1955); A. Davies, "The Origins of the French Peasant Revolution of 1789," *History* 49, no. 165 (February 1964); G. Lefebvre, *Les Paysans du Nord pendant la Révolution française* (Paris: Armand Colin, 1972); P. Bois, *Paysans de l'Ouest* (Le Mans: M. Vilaire, 1960); C. Tilly, *The Vendée,* 3d ed. (New York: John Wiley, 1967).

27. C. Jenkins, "Why Do Peasants Rebel? Structural and Historical Theories of Modern Peasant Rebellions," *American Journal of Sociology* 88, no. 3 (November 1982): 487–514; K. R. Cox and G. J. Demko, "Peasant Riot Propensity and Agrarian Structure in the Russian Revolution of 1905" (Department of Geography, Ohio State University, 1968, mimeographed).

228 Notes to Pages 180–181

28. G. Jackson, *The Spanish Republic and the Civil War, 1931–1939* (Princeton: Princeton University Press, 1965); Payne, *Politics and Society*. The commercial-versus-subsistence dichotomy may also be appropriate for the Mexican revolution of 1911–1917. It may explain to some extent why the provinces of Mexico, Morelos, and Pueblo supported the radical peasant revolution of Villa and Zapata whereas the provinces of Colima, Sinaloa, Nayarit, Tamaulipas, and Veracruz supported the constitutionalists of Carranza and Obregon (E. Wolf, *Peasant Wars of the Twentieth Century* [New York: Harper & Row, 1969]; C. C. Cumberland, *Mexican Revolution, Genesis Under Madero* [Austin: University of Texas Press, 1952]).

29. Not surprisingly, Shorter and Tilly observed that in the Mediterranean between 1915 and 1935 agricultural strikes constituted this region's principal contribution to the national aggregates. With the exception of Marseille, cities in the Mediterranean had few strikes (Shorter and Tilly, *Strikes in France*, pp. 249–50).

30. G. Cholvy, "Bitterois et narbonnais: Mutations économiques et évolutions des mentalités à l'époque contemporaine," in *Economie et société en Languedoc-Roussillon de 1789 à nos jours,* ed. Centre d'histoire contemporaine du Languedoc méditerranéen et du Roussillon (Montpellier: Centre national de la recherche scientifique, 1978), pp. 438–39; A. J. Tudesq, *Les Grands notables en France (1840–1849): Etude historique d'une psychologie sociale* (Paris: Presses universitaires de France, 1964), p. 146.

31. D. Higgs, *Ultra Royalism in Toulouse: From Its Origins to the Revolution of 1830* (Baltimore: Johns Hopkins University Press, 1973), p. 74; D. P. Resnick, *The White Terror and the Political Reaction after Waterloo* (Cambridge, Mass.: Harvard University Press, 1966), p. 2; J. J. Oéscheslin, *Le Mouvement ultra-royaliste sous la Restauration* (Paris: R. Pichon & R. Durand-Auzias, 1960), pp. 62–63; Tudesq, *Les Grands notables,* p. 146.

32. Ibid., p. 253.

33. M. Agulhon, "La Provence républicaine à l'ère industrielle (1870–1940): La Vie politique de 1870 à 1940," in *Histoire de la Provence,* ed. E. Baratier (Toulouse: Privat, 1969), p. 471; L. A. Loubere, *Radicalism in Mediterranean France, 1848–1914* (Albany: State University of New York Press, 1974), p. 54; P. Vigier, *La Seconde République dans la région alpine: Etude politique et sociale,* vol. 2 (Paris: Presses universitaires de France, 1963), p. 212; H. Chauvet, *Histoire du parti républicain dans les Pyrénées-Orientales* (Perpignan: Imprimerie de l'indépendant, 1906), pp. 71–72.

34. Agulhon, "La Provence républicaine," p. 515.

35. Ibid.

36. Ibid., p. 524.

37. Le Roy Ladurie refers to Montpellier as "une ville de rentiers du sol" (a city of absentee landlords). DuGrand, comparing the urban and rural social structures of Lower Languedoc, describes the countryside as dominated by either small property or latifundia employing agricultural labor and the cities as consisting of few industrialists but a great many absentee landowners (Le Roy Ladurie, *Histoire du Languedoc,* p. 126; DuGrand, *Villes et campagnes,* pp. 76–77, 161–62).

38. G. Cholvy, "Religion et société au XIXe siècle: Le Diocèse de Montpellier" (thèse, premier cycle, University of Paris, 1972), p. 192; Tudesq, *Les Grands notables,* pp. 153–54. Also, whereas the *chambrées populaires* (cafés) were used by artisans, liberal professions, and workers to disseminate a radical ideology during the election campaigns of 1848–1849, the nobles and upper bourgeoisie successfully employed the cafés during the nineteenth century to gain the support of the urban populace (R. Vidal, "Les Royalistes et les légitimistes dans le Gard," [thèse, University of Paul Valéry, Montpellier, 1970], p. 95).

39. R. H. Munro, "The New Khmer Rouge," *Commentary* 80, no. 6 (December 1985): 19–38; Permanent Peoples' Tribunal Session on the Philippines, *Philippines: Repression and Resistance* (London: Komite ng Sambayanang, Pilipino, 1981).

40. Ibid., p. 239.

41. Anti-Slavery Society, *The Philippines: Authoritarian Government, Multinationals and Ancestral Lands* (London: Anti-Slavery Society, 1983), pp. 56–59.

42. Permanent Peoples' Tribunal Session of the Philippines, *Philippines: Repression and Resistance,* p. 243.

43. Ibid., p. 240; Anti-Slavery Society, *The Philippines,* p. 140.

44. Permanent Peoples' Tribunal Session of the Philippines, *Philippines: Repression and Resistance,* pp. 50–51, 204.

Bibliography of Archival Sources

ARCHIVAL SOURCES FOR 1849 ELECTION

National Archives

F¹¹ 2697–2712; C 1469–1574

Departmental Archives

Tarn (A.D. V1 M²14, 19, 20; *Annuaire du Tarn* 1848)
Haute-Garonne (A.D. 25 U17; 1872 Census)
Ariège (A.D. 10M 1)
Mayenne (A.D. 7M 68; 6M 43; 3M 64; 7M 19)
Sarthe (A.D. W 5172; M Supp. 350, 357)
Maine-et-Loire (A.D. 3M 82; ex M 11, 12)
Gard (A.D. 3M 45; 6M 121)
Alpes de Haute-Provence [Basses-Alpes] (A.D. 9J 39; 10 bis M 33; 12M 22)
Vienne (A.D. 3M 318; 8M 2, 15)
Deux-Sèvres (A.D. 7M 4/5; 3M 2/3)
Finistère (A.D. 6M 53; 3M 22, 23; 1U; 6M 37–41, 76)
Loire-Atlantique [Loire-Inférieure] (A.D. 1M 78; 1M 1705)
Côtes-du-Nord (A.D. 3M; 6M 7)
Orne (A.D. M 321–23; *Annuaire Orne* 1847; M 1694)
Calvados (A.D. 10M 370; M 5377)
Pyrénées-Orientales (A.D. U 313; MNC 2182–83, 2460, 3065/2, 3086)
Aude (A.D. *Annuaire Aude* 1844; 11M 29–34; 11M 12–14)
Hérault (A.D. 9M 42; 114M 3, 16; 134M 12–14)
Vaucluse (A.D. 6M 20, 24–29, 278–79)
Vendée (A.D. 1U; 6M 17; *Annuaire Vendée* 1848)
Morbihan (A.D. 3M 72, 82, 90, 96; 6M 10, 22)
Ille-et-Vilaine (A.D. 3M 55; 6 Per. 3086; 23Ma 73–114; 32Ma 3–4)
Somme (A.D. M 107, 474; *Listes électorales et du jury* 1843–1844)
Meuse (A.D. *Annuaire Meuse* 1848; *Dénombrement de la population* 1921)
Seine-et-Marne (A.D. 3M 111; *Dénombrement de la population* 1886)

ARCHIVAL SOURCES FOR THE 1914 ELECTION

National Archives

C 7242–51

Departmental Archives

Pyrénées-Orientales (A.D. MNC 2182–83, 2460)
Aude (A.D. 11M 29–35, 52; 13M 298, 308–11)
Hérault (A.D. 9M 386; 113M 42; 114M 13, 23, 32; 134M 32, 72)
Vaucluse (A.D. 6M 33, 34, 393)
Vendée (A.D. 6M 23, 1134–59; 1926 *Almanach-Annuaire*)
Morbihan (A.D. 6M 10, 27, 1044)
Ille-et-Vilaine (A.D. 34 284–88; 32Ma 33, 37; 6 Per. 3086)

PRIMARY SOURCES FOR THE 1981 ELECTION

Ministry of Agriculture

1980 *Le Prix des terres agricoles*
1981 *Petites Régions agricoles*

Institut national de la statistique et des études économiques

Recensement général de la population de 1975
Recensement général de l'agriculture de 1979–1981

Regional Press

Somme (*Courrier picard,* 15 June 1981)
Tarn (*La Dépêche du Midi,* 14 June 1981)
Haute-Garonne (*La Dépêche du Midi,* 14 June 1981)
Ariège (*La Dépêche Ariège,* 15 June 1981)
Pyrénées-Orientales (*L'Indépendant,* 15 June 1981)
Aude (*La Dépêche Aude,* 15 June 1981)
Mayenne (*L'Ouest France,* 15 June 1981)
Sarthe (*L'Ouest France,* 16 June 1981)
Maine-et-Loire (*Le Courrier de l'Ouest,* 15 June 1981)
Hérault (*Midi Libre,* 15 June 1981)
Gard (*Midi Libre,* 15 June 1981)
Vaucluse (*Le Provençal,* 15 June 1981)

Alpes de Haute-Provence [Basses-Alpes] (*Le Provençal*, 16 June 1981)
Vienne (*La Nouvelle République*, 15 June 1981)
Deux-Sèvres (*Le Courrier de l'Ouest*, 15 June 1981)
Vendée (*L'Ouest France*, 15 June 1981)
Morbihan (*L'Ouest France*, 15 June 1981)
Finistère (*L'Ouest France*, 15 June 1981)
Ille-et-Vilaine (*L'Ouest France*, 15 June 1981)
Loire-Atlantique [Loire-Inférieure] (*L'Ouest France*, 15 June 1981)
Côtes-du-Nord (*Le Télégramme*, 15 June 1981)
Orne (*Le Réveil normand*, 15 June 1981)
Manche (*La Presse de la Manche*, 15 June 1981)
Calvados (*L'Ouest France*, 15 June 1981)
Meuse (*L'Est républicain*, 15 June 1981)
Seine-et-Marne (*La République*, 15 June 1981)

Index

Page numbers in italics denote figures; page numbers followed by "t" denote tables.

Nobles (*continued*)
58–59; in Parlement, 52; peasant politics and, 20–21; Western France and, 48–49, 51–52. *See also* Elites
Normative theory, 10
Northeastern region: agriculture in, 38–39, 78; class composition, 35, 38–44, 65, 80; class-conflict rebellions and, 179; compact villages in, 41; comparative advantages of, 70, 79; economic activity in, 38–39, 67; 1851 Insurrection and, 166; energy resources of, 70; European Economic Community and, 69; factors of production in, 142; farm sizes and, 80; French Left and, 119; industrialization of, 66–69; land tenure in, 39–41; modes of production and, 35, 38–44, 79–81; national market and, 65; pattern of settlement in, 41–42, 80; population explosion and, 40; property rights in, 39–41, 80; technology and, 38–39; sharecroppers in, 77
Notables petits, 58–59

Open-field systems, 78
Opportunists of 1885, 105
Orleanism, 106, 113
Owner-cultivators, 40–41, 56; 1851 Insurrection and, 165–167; interests of, 98; mean plot size of, 215 n.7; religiosity of, 100–101; voting behavior and, 118, 144; in Western France, 53. *See also* Landowners
Ozouf, J., 89–90

Paige, Jeffery, 19, 118–119
Paris, bank centralization and, 67
Parlement, noble-domination of, 52
Party loyalty: patterns of, 9; voting behavior and, 158–160
Party of Movement, 105–106
Party of Order, 105–107; progressive taxation and, 110; Second Republic and, 126; social order and, 115
Party organization, voting behavior and, 184–185
Pastoral farms, 44, 46
Patriot party, 105
Patterns of settlement. *See* Settlement patterns
Peasant(s): agricultural specialization and, 88; Bonaparte and, 164–166, 171–172; cooperatives, 84; dependencies of, 20; 1851 Insurrection

and, 164–167; freeholds of, 55; landlord controls, 82, 84; landowners, 40, 45; leaseholding of, 40; literacy of, 62; reactionary, 21, 164. *See also* Labor force; Sharecroppers
Peasant Wars of the Twentieth Century (Wolf), 118
Petites Régions agricoles, 131
Petits bourgeois, deindustrialization and, 88
Philippines, voting behavior in, 182–183
Phylloxéra, wine production and, 21, 23, 85
Plagues, landlord concessions and, 56
Poinso-Chapuis decree (1948), 114
Political behavior: of cultivators, 25; economic crises and, 21–23; ethnic regionalism and, 23–25; longitudinal studies of, 135; mode of production model of, 3, 25, 123–173; normative explanations for, 9–19, 25; structural explanations for, 19–25. *See also* Voting patterns
Political debate, French predilection for, 105
Polyculture, 64, 81–82
Popular Front party, 106, 112
Population, concentrations of: in Mediterranean France, 142; modes of production and, 29; in Northeastern France, 41–42, 80; in rural areas, 80; social interaction and, 100; voting behavior and, 124–125, 143–144; in Western France, 142. *See also* Settlement patterns
Populist party (U.S.), 175–177
Portugal, wine competition with, 86
Poujadists, 106
Priests. *See* Clergy
Primary education, church's role in, 113–114
Private property, French Left vs. Right and, 108–109. *See also* Property rights
Le Prix des terres agricoles, 131
Progressive taxation: agricultural laborers and, 99; Left vs. Right and, 107, 110–111; owner-cultivators and, 98; sharecroppers and, 98; tenant farmers and, 97; wheat farmers and, 176
Proletariats: rural, 40; wine industry and, 86, 88. *See also* Peasant(s)
Property redistribution. *See* Land redistribution

Property rights: economic activity and, 43; measure of, 129; in Mediterranean France, 55–57, 86; in Northeastern France, 39–41, 80; perception of interests and, 96–99; political behavior and, 29–30, 146; in Western France, 45–46, 81

Protestant church, political parties and, 106–107

Pyat, Félix, 108

Rack rents, 40

Radical movements, 105, 126; labor organization and, 89; Radical-Socialists, 106, 116; rural democracy and, 116; wine production and, 150

Railway systems: agriculture and, 78, 176; national market and, 32, 66

Rassemblement pour la République, 108, 111

Rational-choice theories, voting behavior and, 26–28, 171–173

Reaper, introduction of, 78

Rebellions. *See specific issue*

Regionalism, political: ethnic, 23–25; group-level phenomena and, 24; inequalities, 69; land tenure patterns and, 14; material interests and, 15; religiosity and, 17–19; structural theses, 19–25. *See also specific regions*

Religiosity: material interests and, 184; measure of, 133; voting behavior and, 17–18, 145, 152, 154–158

Rents. *See* Land tenure

Republicans, 106; idea dissemination by, 62; landowners and, 14; *petits notables* and, 59; Republican-Constitutionalists, 105; rural democracy and, 116

Resistance party, 105

Restoration of 1815, 105, 181

Revolt of Midi (1907), 169–170

Revolutions, mode-of-production theory and, 179–180. *See also specific issue, revolution*

Richelieu, Cardinal, 10

Right, political. *See* French Right

Robinson, W. S., 135–136

Rollin, Ledru, 109

Roman Catholic Church: educational influences of, 63, 113–114, 156, 167; French Right and, 18; Left vs. Right in, 112–114; Mediterranean cities and, 182; peasant politics and, 20–21; political authority of, 63; property of, 12–15, 49, 59, 113; resource-

control by, 100, 156–157; state separation, 100–101, 167; voter interference by, 194 n.14; Western France and, 49. *See also* Clergy; Religiosity

Roman law, institutions derived from, 37, 55

Rothschild family, 66

Royalist party, 16

Rural communities: autonomy of, 63; emigration from, 81; Left vs. Right democracy and, 107, 115–116; town associations and, 100; village communalism, 56, 80, 84, 112; voting patterns in, 174–178. *See also specific region*

Russia: agrarian riots (1905–1917), 180; wheat competition with, 84

Seasonal migrants. *See* Labor force

Secondary education, church's role in, 113

Second Republic, 181; chaos in, 125; Right vs. Left and, 105

Secret ballots, 31, 194 n.14

Seigneurial dues, abolition of, 41

Settlement patterns: literacy and, 90; measure of, 131–132; in Mediterranean France, 57–64, 86, 88; in Northeastern France, 41–42, 80; perception of interests and, 99–100; resource control and, 30–31; in Western France, 46–48, 82

Sharecroppers: decline of, 81–82, 96; interests of, 97–98; in Italy, 174–175; land redistribution and, 98; mean plot size of, 215 n.7; in Mediterranean France, 56; in Northeastern France, 77; political behavior and, 20, 143; Right and, 172; in Western France, 45–46. *See also* Land tenure

Siegfried, André, 12, 19–21, 31, 172

Silk industry, decline of, 74

Slave trade, French ships and, 69

Smith, J. H., 86, 165, 170

Soboul, A., 59

Social class. *See* Class composition; Class conflict

Social elites. *See* Elites; Nobles

Social interaction, population concentrations and, 100

Socialism. *See* French Left

Socialist party, 107–108; European Economic Community and, 217 n.17; Mediterranean France and, 22–23; 1953 wine protest and, 170; 1981

Compositor: G&S Typesetting
Text: 11/13 Baskerville
Display: Baskerville
Printer: Halliday Lithographing
Binder: Halliday Lithographing